Preface to the Fourteenth Edition

ACCOUNTING is concerned, among other things, with the measurement of increases and decreases in real wealth arising from commercial and industrial activities, and in this new edition of McKechnie I have felt it necessary to draw attention in the introductory chapter to some of the problems exercising the minds of the members of the accounting profession and business men generally at the present time. In a period of unprecedented inflation, accountants are having to reconsider the objectives of financial statements.

In this new edition of McKechnie a fresh approach has been thought desirable. McKechnie believed that it was a basic priprinciple of good teaching to proceed from the known to the unknown. 'Everyone knows something about receiving and paying cash,' he wrote. The Cash Book was therefore dealt with in the first lesson. A teacher using this edition and who still favours the Cash Book approach can, if he so wishes, start at Chapter 6 and return to the earlier chapters at a later stage.

Writers of textbooks on book-keeping and accounting are open to criticism on three grounds: (1) that modern trends have been ignored; (2) that traditional methods have not been followed; or (3) that the book is designed merely to get students through examinations and has little relevance to what generally happens in practice. As to the last of these criticisms, I have felt it desirable to introduce a simple method for dealing with VAT (one single rate), although in many exercises VAT has been ignored to allow concentrated attention on other aspects of book-keeping.

The present volume is intended for students preparing for the following examinations:

R.S.A.—Elementary and Intermediate.

O.N.D. and O.N.C. (First Year).

G.C.E. 'O' Level and S.C.E. 'O' Grade examinations.

Volume II will cover the second year of the O.N.D. and O.N.C., G.C.E. 'A' Level and S.C.E. 'H' Grade examinations.

Another change in the present volume has been to omit sections on Business Terms and Abbreviations. Explanations of the most important of these will be found in the relevant places in the text.

L. G. PEPPER

London, WC1
25th March, 1974

Acknowledgements

I AM grateful to the various General Certificate of Education Examining Boards, the Royal Society of Arts, the London Chamber of Commerce, the Association of Certified and Corporate Accountants and the Chartered Institute of Secretaries, for granting me permission to reproduce examination questions from past papers. Both the answers given in the text and those at the back of the book are my own and the various examining bodies are in no way responsible for any errors, either in calculation or construction, which may have been made.

L.G.P.

2—

RATIONAL BOOK-KEEPING AND ACCOUNTING

Part 1

by John McKechnie

Fourteenth edition fully revised by
L. G. PEPPER,
LL.B., B.Sc.(Econ.), A.C.I.S., Barrister at Law,
Polytechnic of Central London

CASSELL · London

CASSELL & COLLIER MACMILLAN PUBLISHERS LTD
35 Red Lion Square, London WC1R 4SG
Sydney, Toronto, Auckland, Johannesburg

First published as *Rational Book-keeping for Commercial Students* 1924
Seventh edition (fully revised) 1936
Tenth edition (with revisions) 1961
Twelfth edition (fully revised) 1966
Thirteenth edition (revised) 1969
Fourteenth edition (fully revised) as
Rational Book-keeping and Accounting 1974

I.S.B.N. 0 304 29286 9

Printed by Tinling (1973) Limited,
Prescot, Merseyside
(a member of the Oxley Printing Group Ltd)

Contents

Page

Chapter 1
Introduction 1

Chapter 2
The resources of the business unit, their origin and deployment 8

Chapter 3
Balance Sheets and position statements 13

Chapter 4
Recording transactions in the ledger 22

Chapter 5
Ledger accounts for recording gains and losses—the Trading and Profit & Loss Accounts 33

Chapter 6
The Cash Book — Value Added Tax 45

Chapter 7
Credit buying—purchases—purchases returns 61

Chapter 8
Credit selling—sales returns 72

Chapter 9
Cash discounts—petty cash book 82

Chapter 10
The journal 99

Chapter 11
Tabular or columnar book-keeping 120

Chapter 12
Banking– bank reconciliation statements 133

Chapter 13
Reserves and provisions—bad debts 145

Chapter 14
Provision for depreciation 157

Chapter 15
Other provisions and adjustments 170

Chapter 16
Partnership accounts 179

Chapter 17
Total or control accounts and sectional balancing 207

Chapter 18
Correction of errors—suspense accounts 224

Chapter 19
Manufacturing Accounts 231

Chapter 20
Some practical matters—P.A.Y.E., Graduated Pensions contributions and National Insurance 242

Chapter 21
Receipts & Payments Accounts—Income & Expenditure Accounts 246

Chapter 22
Incomplete records 254

Chapter 23
Consignment accounts—joint ventures 267

Chapter 24
Introduction to company accounts 277

Chapter 25
Interpretation of accounts 293

Answers to exercises 306

1
Introduction

BOOK-KEEPING AS A SYSTEMATIC WAY OF RECORDING TRANSACTIONS

When you bought this book you handed over a sum of money to the seller and received this book in exchange, or, if you had an account with the bookseller, you obtained the book in exchange for an implied promise to pay at a later date. Transfers of value of this kind are called *transactions*, and book-keeping is concerned with the systematic recording of transactions in monetary terms. Had you bought this book on credit, another transaction would have occurred when you subsequently paid for it. In all advanced economic societies, distinguished from others by intensive specialization and an elaborate system of markets, transactions are so numerous as to give rise to very sophisticated methods of book-keeping.

ACCOUNTING

Accounting goes beyond the mere recording of transactions; it is concerned with systems, with the analysis and interpretation of the data which the book-keeper has entered in the books of account of the business. Book-keeping is largely a clerical operation, whereas accounting calls for considerable knowledge, experience and analytical skill.

DOUBLE-ENTRY BOOK-KEEPING

The book-keeping system which most businesses employ is called double-entry book-keeping. This does not mean that under this system transactions are entered in the books twice but that both aspects of an exchange transaction, the giving of one thing in exchange for another, are recorded. Thus, when you bought this book you might have recorded (1) the payment of money; and (2) the value of the book received in exchange. As we shall see later, as an asset, such as a machine, wears out we record the diminution in the value of the machine and the corresponding fall in money terms of the proprietor's interest or equity in the business.

THE NEED FOR BOOK-KEEPING AND ACCOUNTING

The high standard of living which we in the western countries enjoy, as compared with less prosperous countries, is largely due to our more efficient use of resources. Instead of each of us seeking to satisfy his own wants for goods and services directly, we specialize and exchange our specialized products and services for those of other persons similarly specializing. In this way far more goods and services are produced per head of the population than would otherwise be the case.

Specialization and exchange on so large a scale call for all kinds of ancillary services such as banking, transport, insurance, warehousing, and distribution. Accounting has been described as the language of business because accounting is the method by which financial information about business is communicated. The owner of the business will need to know whether, over a period of time, his income from the sale of his products exceeds what it cost him to produce them. Other people too may want information about his financial status—his bank from which he may seek a loan, his suppliers of goods from whom he may wish to buy goods on credit, would-be employees who are concerned about job security and prospects, and the Government who will wish to ensure that the business, within certain statutory limits, is properly conducted and that the share of profits to which the State is entitled in the form of taxes is duly paid.

The owner of a business will of course need to know something more than just whether revenue exceeds expenses. If it is a small business, the proprietor will probably be able to control operations with relatively little accounting information, but as the business expands and he becomes more remote from day-to-day happenings, he will be able to manage the business efficiently only if he regularly receives up-to-date information on all aspects of the enterprise. It will be the accountant's job to supply much of this information.

ECONOMIC UNITS

Transactions are not confined to business enterprises, and book-keeping and accounting techniques therefore have a wide application. An individual may wish to record how he earns and disposes of his income, a housewife may wish to record the receipt of housekeeping monies and how they are spent. Consider too all the non-profit making bodies which need to record, classify, summarize and interpret a whole host of transactions. The Government, local authorities, schools, clubs and churches are some such bodies. If we put individuals and all associations of persons who receive and dispose of money incomes into a single category called economic units, then book-keeping and accounting apply to all economic units—indeed to almost everybody.

The Business Unit

In this book we shall be principally interested in those economic units which exist to make profits. We shall find that book-keeping systems will vary from one type of business to another not only according to the particular activities carried on, but also according to the legal form of the undertaking—whether the business is owned by one person, or is owned by two or more persons acting in partnership; whether it is a separate legal entity as in the case of a joint stock company, or is an enterprise owned and operated by the State. There are many ways of classifying business units: we can, for example, classify them according to their activities, e.g., agricultural, industrial, or commercial; or according to their objectives—profits or public service; or according to size—small, medium, large and very large. For our purposes we shall adopt the legal form of classification and consider first of all the type of business unit which is owned by one person.

To the economist the business unit is the place where the entrepreneur brings together the factors of production—land, labour and capital—to produce the goods and services which people want and for which they have the means to pay. When we look at the resources of a business unit as shown in the firm's Balance Sheet, we shall see that labour is not mentioned. Workpeople are hired and not owned by the enterprise and the Balance Sheet records, on the assets side, only those things which the business owns. And yet a skilled labour force may in reality be one of the chief assets of the business. Oddly enough, although a servant is not owned by his employer, the law recognizes an employer's proprietory rights in his servants by giving an employer the right to sue strangers who injure his servants and so deprive him of the servant's services. But for the moment we must accept the fact that despite the importance of a firm's labour force, we shall not find it mentioned in the list of the firm's resources.

THE ORGANIZATION OF THE BUSINESS UNIT

To attain its objectives the business unit must be efficiently organized and managed. The larger the unit the easier it is for administrative specialization to take place. In a very small firm the owner may perform all the administrative functions personally, but in the larger units there will be specialists in each field of management—someone in charge of the production of goods, a buyer to purchase all the things the business needs, a person responsible for the sale of the firm's products, an accountant to supervise the financial record-keeping and to supply management with the information it must have to make forecasts, to organize, co-ordinate and control the activities of the business unit.

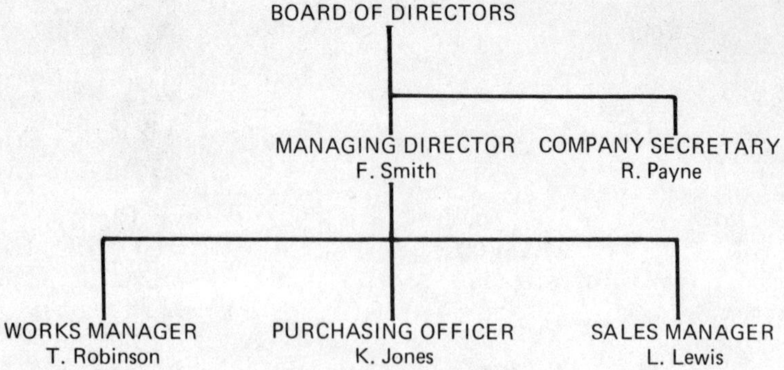

(Persons whose names appear on the same line may not necessarily be of the same status in the company)

Possible division of the principal administrative functions of a small manufacturing company

BUSINESS OPERATIONS AND THE ACCOUNTING FUNCTION

A business owns or hires property—premises, machinery, fixtures and fittings, motor transport, stocks of goods and so on—and with this property produces goods and services which it then sells at a profit. This profit is the reward for supplying consumers, directly or indirectly, with what they want. It is the book-keeping function to record the day-to-day transfer of values arising from the transactions which take place. This in turn involves the processing and classification of documents (invoices, credit notes, debit notes, vouchers, cheques etc.) which contain details of these transactions and which constitute the authority for the entries made in the books of account of the business. From the information so recorded the accountant is able to compare present with past performances, identify trends, highlight tendencies, determine when conditions are favourable for the purchase of goods or for the granting of credit, advise on possible expansions or contractions of business activities, and assist management generally to take those decisions which it must take if the business is to succeed.

Problems arising from the use of money

Money, as we have already noted, is indispensable to an economy based on specialization and exchange. Unfortunately money has the serious disadvantage of being an unstable measure of value. As everyone knows, the Pound today buys much less than it did ten years ago, and the businessman knows only too well that the machine which cost him

£5,000 five years ago will cost him much more when he comes to replace it even with an identical machine in three years time. Should the accountant record these assets in the Balance Sheet at cost (historical cost), or at a figure which more nearly represents the sum which the business would have to find now for a new machine (replacement cost)? These are questions which have to be faced if the accountant is to give a true and fair view of the state of the business.

Most firms meet this difficulty by building up reserves. Profits that might otherwise have been distributed to the owners are retained in the business.

If the business owns land and buildings, the money value of these will have risen steeply in the post-war years and if the Balance Sheet is to give a true and fair view of the business this property, which would ordinarily appear at historical cost, would have to be written up to give a figure corresponding with its current market value.

INFLATION ACCOUNTING

(1) *Price-Level Adjusted Accounts*

Many companies now 'stabilize' their accounts, i.e., they use the historical cost method of book-keeping but adjust these figures by means of a consumer index to take account of changes in the value of money. One company, British Printing Corporation, after converting the company's results to allow for inflation, cut pre-tax profits from £4·06 million to £3·52 million and earnings from 8·2p to 7·6p per share.

(2) *Replacement Accounting*

Another way of tackling the problem of inflation is to use a technique known as 'replacement' accounting. Under this method the basic historical cost approach is retained but current values are applied to stocks and depreciation of the company's fixed assets. The latter method has the advantage over stabilized accounts that it has a factual basis for most of the figures. We shall return to this subject in Book 2, but at the moment we wish you to be aware of some of the accounting problems arising from changes in the value of money.

ACCOUNTING PRINCIPLES

A memorandum prepared by the European Economic Community's Accountants Study Group made five points on accounting principles. Although these were largely made with joint-stock companies in mind, the principles are relevant to the accounts of all businesses.

(1) Company accounts should be required to show a 'true and fair' view rather than the 'accurate' view.
(2) Historic cost accounts need to be supplemented by price-level adjusted accounts, but the method of adjustment should not be restricted to replacement cost accounting.

(3) Four key accounting concepts should be observed:
  (a) prudence;
  (b) consistency;
  (c) the matching of costs with revenue;
  (d) the going-concern basis of valuation.

(4) Companies with material subsidiaries should produce consolidated accounts.

(5) The company's annual accounts are the responsibility of the directors.

(1) *Prudence*

This means not overstating gains. In choosing between which of two possible figures to take, the figure which gives the smaller profit is the one to be preferred. It is a long-established convention amongst accountants that whilst it is in order to anticipate losses it is imprudent to anticipate gains.

(2) *Consistency*

Proper comparisons of one year with another can only be made if the same method of treating like accounting data is observed. This does not mean that the method can never be changed, but if the method is changed, this should be made quite clear in the accounts or in the reports accompanying them.

(3) *Matching Costs with Revenue*

The costs occurring in the particular accounting period should be matched with the revenue earned in that period. Thus in a Trading Account the cost of the products are matched with the revenue from their sale. Expenses incurred in the course of producing goods must also be matched against the revenue produced from their sale.

(4) *The Going-Concern Basis of Valuation*

There is an assumption that the business will continue to operate in the future for an indefinite period of time. What the assets of the business would fetch if sold in the open market becomes a matter of importance only if the business is about to cease operations.

PROFIT AS THE MEASURE OF EFFICIENCY

How should the efficiency of a business be measured? The most commonly applied criterion is profitability. In comparing one firm with another of a similar kind we are inclined to say that the firm which makes the larger profit on the capital invested is the more efficient. It is now regarded as unrealistic to assume, as the old economists did, that all businessmen seek to maximize their profits. There are many one-man businesses which are, according to the late Dr.

Benham, making negative profits, that is, if their owners used their resources differently, including selling their labour to someone else, they could obtain greater returns than they do running their own businesses. The difference between what they actually earn and what they could earn is the price many are prepared to pay for independence. In the next chapter we begin our studies in book-keeping and accounting by looking at the resources at the disposal of a sole-trader, and the way in which these resources were financed.

EXERCISE 1.1

Make a list of the business undertakings in any area with which you are familiar and classify them according to whether you think they are (a) one man businesses; (b) partnerships; (c) joint-stock companies; (d) state or local authority undertakings; (e) co-operative societies; (f) any other type of organization.

EXERCISE 1.2

State as briefly as possible the services which wholesalers give to retailers.

EXERCISE 1.3

How do you suppose the different administrative functions are divided up in, say, a large London hotel? Give in some detail what you think the Chief Accountant's duties and responsibilities might be.

EXERCISE 1.4

What is meant by stabilizing accounts?

EXERCISE 1.5

Prepare two columns and list the transactions you have engaged in today, showing in the first column what you parted with and in the second what you received in exchange.

2

The Resources of the Business Unit, Their Origin and Deployment

A FIRM'S resources consist of all the things it possesses to produce the goods and services the business exists to supply. These resources may be provided partly by the owner of the business himself, partly by outsiders such as a bank by means of a loan, or by a supplier of goods on credit, and of course by the persons employed in the business, but as we have already seen, since the employees are not owned by the business they are excluded from the inventory of the firm's resources or assets.

The assets which are provided by the owner represent his capital and if these are the only assets,

CAPITAL = ASSETS

There is another way of looking at this. If we regard the business as separate from its owner, then, if a man deposits £3,000 in a special account at his bank, intending to open a small shop, this £3,000 represents the value of the assets which the business owns at this point in time and it also represents the sum which the business owes to the owner.

CAPITAL £3,000 = ASSETS £3,000 IN THE BANK

Let us suppose that the man's name is Carr and that he obtains a bank loan of £500; the equation will now read:

CAPITAL £3,000 + BANK LOAN £500 = ASSETS £3,500

The assets of the business are now £3,500 and the liabilities of £3,500 are made up of £3,000 owed to Mr. Carr and £500 owed to the bank. We can show this in the form of a Balance Sheet which is merely a statement showing what the business owns and what it owes at a moment in time.

BALANCE SHEET AS AT 1ST JANUARY 19—

Liabilities (things owed)		*Assets (things owned)*	
	£		£
Capital	3,000	Money at Bank	3,500
Bank Loan	500		
	£3,500		£3,500

Most Continental countries show the assets on the left and the liabilities on the right, viz.

BALANCE SHEET AS AT 1ST JANUARY 19—

Assets		*Liabilities*	
	£		£
Money at bank	3,500	Capital	3,000
		Bank loan	500
	£3,500		£3,500

Another way of giving the same information would be:

Assets:		
Money at bank		£3,500
Provided by:		
Mr Carr (Capital)	£3,000	
Bank loan	500	
		£3,500

There are certain things Mr. Carr will need to buy either for cash or on credit before he can start trading. Let us suppose that by the 5th January he has entered into the following transactions:

	£
Bought and paid cash for lease of shop	500
Bought shop fittings for cash	300
Bought stock-in-trade for cash	1,000
Bought stock-in-trade from L.X. Materials Ltd, on credit ...	1,500

We can draw up another Balance Sheet on 5th January 19— showing how the resources of Mr. Carr's business have now been deployed.

BALANCE SHEET AS AT 5TH JANUARY 19—

Assets	£	*Liabilities*	
Lease of shop	500	Capital (Mr Carr)	3,000
Shop fittings	300	Bank loan	500
Stock-in-trade	2,500	Trade creditor (L.X. Materials)	1,500
Cash at bank	1,700		
	£5,000		£5,000

or

	£	£
Assets:		
Lease of shop	500	
Shop fittings	300	
Stock-in-trade	2,500	
Cash at bank	1,700	£5,000
Financed by:		
Mr Carr (Capital)	3,000	
Bank loan	500	
Creditor (L.X. Materials)	1,500	£5,000

It should be noted that the accounting equation Assets = Liabilities always holds true and that we can draw up a new Balance Sheet after each transaction. For example, if a Balance Sheet had been compiled immediately following Mr. Carr's purchase of the lease, the Balance Sheet would have been as follows:

BALANCE SHEET AS AT 5TH JANUARY, 19—

Assets	£	*Liabilities*	£
Lease	500	Mr Carr (Capital)	3,000
Bank	3,000	Bank loan	500
	£3,500		£3,500

Capital represents the owner's interest or equity in the business or the net worth of the business and it will be seen that the purchases made by Mr. Carr did not affect Mr. Carr's equity. All that happened was that some cash was converted into another form of property. In the case of the goods bought on credit this was very similar to the bank loan—the resources have been increased by £1,500 and the liabilities of the business have gone up by the same amount.

It is customary in a Balance Sheet to divide assets into 'Fixed Assets', those assets which will normally be retained to earn profits such as buildings, machines, fixtures and fittings, vans etc., and 'Current Assets', things which will change their form within the next financial period, usually one year. Thus raw materials will be made into finished goods, stock converted into cash, debtors pay their debts, and cash be used to buy more goods.

We have referred earlier in this Chapter to the accounting equation Capital (a liability to the owner) + Other liabilities = Assets. Put another way, Assets − Outside liabilities = Capital. If the net assets increase in value (i.e., assets less liabilities other than capital), the owner's equity (the worth of the business to the owner) will rise in value too. Let us suppose that Mr. Carr hires a shop assistant and pays him £10 wages a week in advance. At the moment of engaging him and before the assistant starts work, Mr. Carr has merely exchanged one asset (£10 cash) for £10's worth of effort still to be given and at that point Mr. Carr's capital is unaffected. But at the end of the week when this asset (Labour) has been used up, Mr. Carr's capital will have been reduced by £10. At the same time, however, Mr. Carr's equity may have been increased by more than £10 by profits which the worker has helped to make; but this is something we must look at more closely in the later chapters.

We referred just now to Mr. Carr's employment of an assistant and compared the position at the beginning of the week when the worker had been paid £10 but had not started work with the situation at the end of the week when this asset or benefit had been used up. When money is paid out in this way, it is a *cost.* It is not an *expense* until the benefit represented by the thing purchased has been consumed, that is, used up. This distinction is important because in preparing Revenue and Expense Accounts we must include under expenses only those things which have been used up during the financial period under review. Let us suppose Mr. Carr decided to prepare a Profit and Loss Account half way through the week in which the assistant was employed. Then the *cost* of the assistant's services was £10 but the wage *expense* at the point in time when the account was prepared was only £5. And if a Balance Sheet had been prepared at the same time it would have shown an asset of £5 in respect of the assistant's unexpired services.

When goods and services, which are bought for use within the business, last for more than one accounting period the costs of such goods and services are apportioned between the different accounting periods. Sometimes, however, the costs are so small that the time and expense of making such an apportionment is not justified and the costs are all charged to the year in which they were incurred. For example, the cost of typewriter cleaning fluid is likely to be charged to the accounts in the year of purchase, even though the fluid might last for several years. This accounting convention is referred to as *materiality.* What may be material in the case of one business may be insignificant in the case of another.

ILLUSTRATION 2.1

A young man and a young woman, preparatory to their marriage, each save exactly £3,000. They marry on 10th January 19— and with their savings and some money borrowed from a building society buy a house. (a) Draw up an imaginary Balance Sheet as at 10th January 19—, in any of the ways described in this chapter, to show the assets they own and how these have been financed. (b) What is their net worth on 10th January?

(a) BALANCE SHEET AS AT 10TH JANUARY 19—

Assets	£	*Capital and Liabilities*		£
Freehold house	10,000	Husband	£3,000	
Furniture	1,500	Wife	3,000	
Other household equipment	200			6,000
Motor car	800	Building society loan		8,000
Bank	1,470			
Cash in hand	30			
	£14,000			£14,000

(b) Their joint net worth is £6,000.

ILLUSTRATION 2.2

The assets and liabilities of a business owned by James Scott on 10th February 19— are as follows: Cash at bank £580, Cash in hand £63, Debtors £1,800, Loan £2,000, Stock-in-trade £3,200, Freehold premises £10,000, Fixtures and fittings £2,000, Creditors £1,300.

(a) Calculate James Scott's equity.

(b) Draw up a Balance Sheet to show the financial position of the business on 10th February, 19—.

(a) Owner's equity = Assets less money owed to persons outside the business
= £17,643 − £3,300
= £14,343

(b) BALANCE SHEET AS AT 10TH FEBRUARY, 19—

	£			£
Capital	14,343	*Fixed Assets:*		
Loan	2,000	Freehold premises	£10,000	
Creditors	1,300	Fixtures and fittings	2,000	
				12,000
		Current Assets:		
		Stock	£3,200	
		Debtors	1,800	
		Cash at bank	580	
		Cash in hand	63	
				5,643
	£17,643			£17,643

3

Balance Sheets and Position Statements

In the last chapter we saw that a Balance Sheet is a statement showing the position of a business at a moment in time. It details the assets at the disposal of the business and tells us how these assets were financed. In most cases the finance will have been provided by the proprietor himself and will constitute the owner's equity. Other assets may have been financed by loans or by suppliers of goods on credit. A Balance Sheet will always balance, for the reason that the claims of the owner (his capital) plus the firm's liabilities will always equal the firm's assets, but it need not necessarily give a true and fair view of the position of the business at a moment in time. The figures might, for example, be historical cost figures bearing little relationship to present-day costs.

Some American accountants distinguish between Balance Sheets and Position Statements and reserve the latter term for Balance Sheets drawn up by accountants to give a true and fair picture of the financial position of the enterprise. In Great Britain there is a statutory requirement, in the case of joint-stock companies, that Balance Sheets *shall* give a true and fair view of the position of the companies to which they refer, and as we saw in Chapter 1, the EEC's Accountants Study Group recommend that company accounts should be required to show a 'true and fair' view rather than the 'accurate' view.

In this chapter we shall examine the way different transactions affect the Balance Sheet.

THE PURCHASE OF AN ASSET FOR CASH

When Mr. Carr started business he had £3,500 in his bank account, £3,000 of his own money and £500 lent to him by the bank. His Balance Sheet on 1st January was as shown on page 9 and after the purchase of the lease, as shown on page 10. His financial interest in the business was unaffected by this transaction; he merely exchanged £500 for another type of property. When he bought stock for cash his balance at the bank went down and the figure for stock went up by the same amount. Again the total of the assets remained the same.

THE PURCHASE OF AN ASSET ON CREDIT

On page 9 we showed the position of Mr. Carr's Balance Sheet before and after he had bought some stock for resale on credit. The value of the assets increased by £1,500 and the liabilities by the same amount and we said that this transaction was similar to a bank loan. By buying goods on credit Mr. Carr managed to increase the assets employed in the business, but the period of credit is likely to be short, probably no longer than one month. He will hope, however, to sell some of the goods before the time for payment arrives. When the supplier is paid, Mr. Carr's bank balance will be reduced by £1,500, and £1,500 will disappear from the liabilities side of the Balance Sheet, viz.,

BALANCE SHEET AS AT 5TH JANUARY, 19—

	£		£
Lease of shop	500	Capital	3,000
Shop fittings	300	Bank loan	500
Stock in trade	2,500	Creditor	1,500
Cash in bank	1,700		
	£5,000		£5,000

The position after payment of the creditor will be:

BALANCE SHEET AS AT ....

	£		£
Lease	500	Capital	3,000
Shop fittings	300	Bank loan	500
Stock in trade	2,500		
Cash at bank	200		
	£3,500		£3,500

SALE OF ASSETS FOR CASH AND ON CREDIT

When Mr. Carr starts trading, he will want to sell his stock at a price higher than that he paid for it. But for the moment let us assume he sells some stock at the price he paid for it. If he sells for cash, his cash will go up and his stock will go down by the same amount. Again he has exchanged one asset for another of the same value. Had he sold on credit, and again assume he sells at his buying price, his stock would go down and he would acquire a new asset, namely a debt owed to him, and this would be shown in his Balance Sheet under debtors on the asset side. When the debt is paid cash will increase and the total for debtors will go down by the amount of the debt.

EXERCISE 3.1

Mr P. Robinson, having decided to open a small café, deposits on 1st March 19— £2,000 with his banker. On 3rd March 19— he bought fixtures costing £100 and paid by cheque. On 6th March Mr P. Robinson won £1,000 on the football pools and paid this into the bank account of the business. On 7th March 19— Mr. P. Robinson bought supplies on credit from The Bakewell Tart Co., costing £75. Draw up a Balance Sheet showing the position of Mr Robinson's business on 7th March, 19—.

EXERCISE 3.2

Say how each of the following transactions will affect a Balance Sheet. We give an example to show what is required.

Example: Bought stock for cash.

Answer: On asset side of Balance Sheet stock figure increases and cash figure decreases by amount of the purchase.

(a) Bought stock on credit
(b) Paid creditor by cheque
(c) Sold stock on credit
(d) Bought a delivery van and paid by cheque
(e) A debtor returns some of the goods supplied to him and we give him a credit note for £10
(f) The proprietor draws some money from the business for his personal use
(g) Bank lends the business £1,000

(Assume for this exercise that goods were sold at cost price.)

You will recall that in the previous chapter it was said that assets were usually classified according to whether they were Fixed Assets, i.e., buildings, machinery, motor vans etc., which are retained in the business, and Current Assets, those assets which will change their form during the next financial period. From the latter must come the money to pay the short-term debts of the business. It is important, therefore, that they are adequate for this purpose. The liabilities which will become payable during the next financial period appear in the Balance Sheet as Current Liabilities and *the difference between Current Assets and Current Liabilities represents the firm's working capital.* Another way of expressing this is to say that Working Capital is the amount by which capital exceeds the value of the fixed assets. Current Assets are listed in order of illiquidity, that is, those assets furthest removed from cash are listed first, viz.

Current Assets	£
Stock-in-trade (goods still to be sold and so more illiquid than debtors)	1,000
Sundry debtors (goods sold and cash likely to be received within a few weeks)	2,500
Cash at bank (very liquid)	150
Cash in hand (most liquid of all)	30
	£3,680

If the firm's current liabilities are as follows:

Current Liabilities		
Trade Creditors	£1,250	
Accrued charges (consisting of money owed for wages and rent)	50	
		1,300
		£2,380

total Current Liabilities amount to £1,300 and working capital equals £2,380.

How much working capital a business needs depends upon the kind of activity being carried on, but bankers, called upon to advance loans, will normally expect current assets to be twice as great as current liabilities. Working capital is important, because if a business has insufficient working capital, it may not be able to pay creditors when accounts become due, or be able to acquire those things essential for carrying on the business. A more detailed analysis of Balance Sheets and final accounts is undertaken in Chapter 25.

ILLUSTRATION 3.1

(a) Give explanations of the following terms: (i) Fixed Assets (ii) Current Assets (iii) Current Liabilities (iv) Working Capital.
(b) Below is a summary of a Balance Sheet of a trader as at 31 December, 1970:

BALANCE SHEET AS AT 31 DECEMBER, 1970

	£		£	£
Capital Account 1.1.70	6,000	Premises	6,000	
Add net profits	1,400	*Less* depreciation	2,000	
				4,000
	7,400	Furniture & Fittings	1,000	
Less drawings	1,600	*Less* depreciation	400	
				600
	5,800	Motor van		700
Bank Overdraft	400	Trade debtors		325
Trade creditors	215	Stock		740
		Cash in hand		50
	£6,415			£6,415

(i) Give the amount of the trader's current assets
(ii) Give the amount of the trader's fixed assets
(iii) Give the amount of the trader's current liabilities
(iv) What is the amount of the working capital?
(v) Why is the capital balance on 31 December, 1970 less than it was on 1 January, 1970?
(vi) No depreciation had yet been provided for the motor van. If this was done at 10 per cent, what would his net profit have been?

A.E.B. G.C.E. 'O' Level 1971

Answer

(a) See text
(b) (The Balance Sheet which follows is not essential to the answer.)

BALANCE SHEET AS AT 31 DECEMBER 1970

Fixed Assets:	£	£	£
Premises	6,000		
Less depreciation	2,000		
		4,000	
Fixtures and fittings	1,000		
Less depreciation	400		
		600	
Motor van		700	
			5,300

Current Assets:			
Stock	740		
Trade debtors	325		
Cash in hand	50		
		1,115	
Less *Current liabilities:*			
Bank overdraft	400		
Trade creditors	215		
		615	
Net current assets			500
			£5,800
Financed by			
Capital 1 January, 1970	6,000		
Add profits for 1970	1,400		
	7,400		
Less drawings	1,600		
			5,800
			£5,800

(i) Trader's current assets = £1,115
(ii) Trader's fixed assets = 5,300
(iii) Trader's current liabilities = 615
(iv) Amount of working capital = net current assets = £500.
(The working capital is the amount by which Capital [£5,800] exceeds the fixed assets [£5,300].)
(v) The owner has taken out of the business for his personal use £200 in excess of the profits for 1970, which means that he has withdrawn during the year £200 of his capital.
(vi) Depreciation is an expense and represents the amount by which an asset has declined in value or, put another way, the estimated part of the fixed asset which has been used up. If depreciation had been provided for the motor van, the net profit would have been £1,400 less 10% of £700 which equals £1,330, and so the proprietor has in effect withdrawn £270 of his capital. (Provision for depreciation should be made in all cases where the value of the asset has diminished. If provision is not made, then there may be no funds available to replace the asset when it wears out. We return to the subject of depreciation in Chapter 14.)

ILLUSTRATION 3.2

BALANCE SHEET OF B. BETA AS AT 31 MAY, 1971

Liabilities	£	*Assets*	£
Capital	10,000	Premises	8,000
Mortgage on Premises (repayable 1985)	2,000	Equipment	1,600
		Stock	2,600
Bank Overdraft	160	Debtors	580
Creditors	640	Cash	20
	£12,800		£12,800

(a) State the amount of B. Beta's (i) Fixed Assets, (ii) Current Assets, (iii) short-term liabilities, (iv) long-term liabilities, (v) working capital.
(b) On 1 June, 1971 B. Beta sells one-tenth of his stock for £300 (payment by cheque); he receives cheques for £250 from his debtors and pays £220 to his creditors. Show how you would calculate the amount of his working capital at the end of the day.
(c) How far is it true that an absence of working capital denotes insolvency?

W.J.E.C. 'O' Level 1971

Answer

This time using the conventional British format, the Balance Sheet can be rewritten as follows:

BALANCE SHEET OF B. BETA AS AT 31 MAY, 1971

	£	£		£	£
Capital		10,000	*Fixed Assets*		
Mortgage of premises		2,000	Premises	8,000	
			Equipment	1,600	
					9,600
Current Liabilities			*Current Assets*		
Bank overdraft	160		Stock	2,600	
Creditors	640		Debtors	580	
		800	Cash	20	
					3,200
		£12,800			£12,800

(a) (i) Fixed Assets = £9,600
(ii) Current Assets = £3,200
(iii) Short-term liabilities = £800
(iv) Long-term liabilities = £2,000 (Mortgage)
(v) Working capital = £3,000 − £800 = £2,400
(Capital £12,000 − £9,600)

(b) *Current Assets*

Stock £2,600 *less* £260 (sold)		=	£2,340
Debtors £580 *less* £250 (paid)		=	330
Cash at Bank			
Sale of stock	£300		
Add paid by debtors	250		
	550		
Less amount paid to creditors	220		
	330		
Less Bank overdraft now extinguished	160		
		=	170
Cash in hand		=	20
			£2,860
Less *Current Liabilities*			
Creditors £640 *less* £220 (paid)		=	420
Working Capital			£2,440

A new Balance Sheet in narrative form can be drawn up as follows showing that Mr Beta's capital has increased by £40, the amount of profit from the sale of stock, viz.:

BALANCE SHEET AS AT 1 JUNE, 1971

		£
Fixed Assets		9,600
Net Current Assets...		2,440
		£12,040
Financed by:		
Capital	£10,000	
Add profit	40	
		10,040
Long-term liability (Mortgage)		2,000
		£12,040

The effect of profits and losses on a firm's Balance sheet

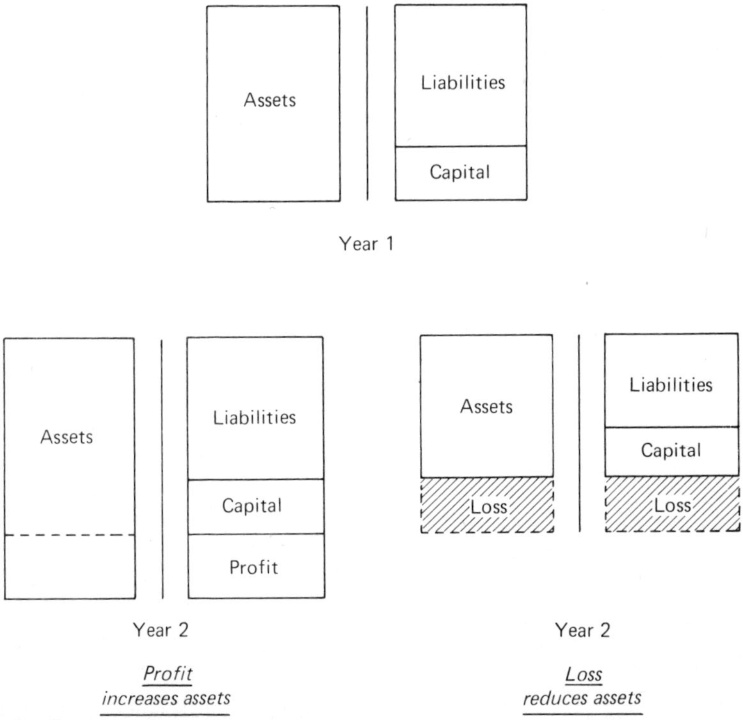

(c) In the absence of working capital a businessman would have no available resources with which to carry on the business, and if he has obtained goods on credit he might have to sell his Fixed Assets in order to pay for them. Although not strictly insolvent, his business would almost certainly fail.

Points to notice

The total net assets have increased by the amount of the gross profit, the difference between what the stock cost to buy and the proceeds from its sale (see diagram on p. 19).

Over a longer period of time some administrative and selling expenses would have been incurred and these would have reduced the gross profit. Gross profit less administrative and selling expenses = Net profit. The owner's capital would then have increased by the amount of the net profit only, thus equalling the amount by which the net assets have increased.

EXERCISE 3.3

The Balance Sheet of J. Smith on 1 February 19— was as follows:

BALANCE SHEET AS AT 1 FEBRUARY 19—

Fixed Assets:	£	£	*Long-Term Liabilities*	£
Premises	4,000		Capital	5,000
Fixtures	200		Loan	300
		4,200		
Current Assets:			*Current Liabilities:*	
Stock	750		Creditors	30
Debtors	40			
Bank	310			
Cash	30			
		1,130		
		£5,330		£5,330

(a) On 2 February, 19— Mr Smith pays off the loan by cheque. Draw up a new Balance Sheet to show the position at this date.

(b) On 3 February, 19— Mr Smith: (i) bought £600 of stock from Wholesale Supplies Co., Ltd, on credit; (ii) sold stock which cost £100 for £130, which sum he immediately banked; (iii) paid £3 cash to have the goods in (ii) delivered to his customer (this cost is not recoverable from the customer). Draw up his Balance Sheet, with assets on the left and capital and liabilities on the right, to show the position after these transactions.

EXERCISE 3.4

BALANCE SHEET OF T. BATE AS AT 10TH MARCH 19—

	£	£		£
Fixed Assets:				
Leasehold Premises	6,000		Capital	16,000
Plant & Machinery	3,200			
Fixtures & Fittings	670			
Motor Van	500			
		10,370		
Current Assets:			*Current Liabilities:*	
Stock	5,200		Creditors	2,570
Debtors	1,300		Accrued charges	40
Cash at Bank	1,700			
Cash in hand	40			
		8,240		
		£18,610		£18,610

Draw up this Balance Sheet in narrative or vertical form to show clearly Mr Bate's working capital.

EXERCISE 3.5

Mr Goddard runs a small manufacturing business which he has registered under the Business Names Registration Acts as Weldon Enterprises. On 31 March, 19— his assets and liabilities were as follows: Freehold premises £40,000; Plant and Machinery £11,000; Fixtures & Fittings £5,000; Motor Vehicles £2,000; Creditors £700; Building Society (Mortgage on premises) £30,000; Stock of raw materials £1,000; Cash at Bank £800; Cash in hand £30.

(a) Draw up a Balance Sheet as at 31 March, 19— showing clearly: (i) Mr Goddard's equity; (ii) Mr Goddard's working capital.

EXERCISE 3.6

The following are the balance sheets of L. Parkinson as at 31 December, 1969 and 1970:

BALANCE SHEETS AS AT 31 DECEMBER, 1969 AND 1970

	1969	1970		1969	1970
	£	£		£	£
Capital at commencement of each year	5,150	5,900	Fixed assets at cost	5,080	6,200
Add profit for year	1,700	2,000			
	6,850	7,900			
Less drawings	950	1,400			
	5,900	6,500			
Bank overdraft	400	1,350	Stock	1,200	1,400
Creditors	1,000	1,400	Debtors	1,020	1,650
	£7,300	£9,250		£7,300	£9,250

L. Parkinson is puzzled. His net profit has increased in 1970 by £300 over the 1969 figure and yet his bank overdraft has increased over the same period from £400 to £1,350. You are his accountant. Prepare a statement showing why this has occurred.

Candidates should ignore depreciation.

G.C.E. 'O' Level

4

Recording Transactions in the Ledger — Capital, Liabilities And Asset Accounts

The Dual Aspect of Transactions

In the previous chapter we saw how each transaction affected the Balance Sheet in two ways. When a lease was bought costing £500 a new asset was acquired and the bank balance was reduced by the same amount. Similarly when a loan was obtained the bank balance went up by the amount of the loan and the claims of the lender were acknowledged by an entry for the same amount on the liabilities side of the Balance Sheet. In this chapter we shall look at the way these two aspects of a transaction are recorded in the ledger.

KEEPING PERSONAL AND BUSINESS TRANSACTIONS SEPARATE

In book-keeping, the business and the owner of the business are treated as distinct and separate entities. When the owner of a one-man business draws money out of the business for his personal needs (called drawings), he reduces the amount of cash available to the business. As far as the business is concerned, there are two ways of looking at this, either that the owner has become a debtor of the business for the sum taken out or that he has withdrawn capital equal to this sum. Similarly when he takes items of stock for his personal use the stocks of goods at the disposal of the business are reduced. Keeping personal and business transactions separate becomes more difficult when the building occupied serves both as business premises and living accommodation. How should the gas and electricity consumed, for example, be apportioned, say, between the shop and the owner's flat above the shop?

Although for book-keeping purposes it is necessary to regard the business of a sole trader as separate from its owner, English law does not in fact look upon a one-man business as a separate legal entity. Mr Carr could not, in his personal capacity, sue the business and he may have to draw on his private possessions to pay its debts.

In order to decide whether a business is efficiently managed and is showing a satisfactory return on the capital invested in it, it is nevertheless necessary to keep the transactions of the business separate from those of the owner or owners, whether in law the enterprise exists as a distinct legal entity or not.

The Ledger

The ledger is the book of account in which the dual aspect of each transaction is recorded. In practice the ledger may be contained in several books or, if a mechanized system of book-keeping is employed, on cards. For convenience in handling the ledger and in order to allow more than one person to work on it at the same time the ledger is usually subdivided.

But why have a ledger at all? It would be possible, as we have seen, to draw up a new Balance Sheet after each transaction. Apart from the sheer impracticability of doing this, the results would not be of much use to the owner of the business. The Balance Sheets would not give him the kind of information needed for the efficient control of the business. From a comparison of Balance Sheets produced at intervals of time an estimate of the profits of the business can be made but the Balance Sheets will not tell him, for example, who owes him money and how much, nor the names of his creditors and the extent of his indebtedness to each, nor for that matter how the profits or losses were made. The ledger will give him this information. In each account the history of like transactions are recorded. Thus the Bank Account will show what money has been deposited at the bank and what sums have been withdrawn and for what purpose. Let us look again at Mr Carr's Balance Sheet on page 9.

BALANCE SHEET AS AT 1ST JANUARY, 19—

Assets:	£	*Liabilities:*	£
Money at bank	3,500	Capital	3,000
		Bank Loan	500
	£3,500		£3,500

In the ledger, three accounts will be opened to record these transactions.

(1) A Bank Account to record the money paid into Mr Carr's bank account—two entries.
(2) A Capital Account to record Mr Carr's equity.
(3) A Loan Account to record the claim of the lender—in this case the bank.

BANK ACCOUNT (C.B.1.)

Debit Side *Credit Side*

Date	Particulars	Fol.	Amount	Date	Particulars	Fol.	Amount
19—			£				
Jan. 1	Mr. Carr (Capital)	L.1	3,000				
Jan. 1	X Bank (Loan)	L.2	500				

Notice that the account has two sides; the left-hand side is called the *debit side* and the right-hand side the *credit side.* When entries are made to the debit side the account is said to be *debited,* and when entries are made to the right-hand (credit) side the account is said to be *credited.* In the column headed 'Fol.', short for 'folio', is entered the ledger page number containing the account in which the second, corresponding debit or credit entry is made. Money paid into the bank is entered on the debit side of this account and money withdrawn on the credit side. The two corresponding accounts in the ledger, the Capital Account and the Loan Account will contain the credit entries, viz.:

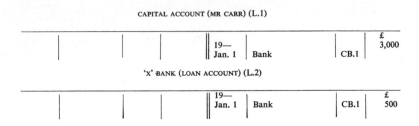

CAPITAL ACCOUNT (MR CARR) (L.1)

							£
				19—			3,000
				Jan. 1	Bank	CB.1	

'X' BANK (LOAN ACCOUNT) (L.2)

				19—			£
				Jan. 1	Bank	CB.1	500

The 'Particulars' columns are fairly self-explanatory and tell us not only something of the transactions which gave rise to the entries but also the names of the accounts in which the corresponding entries appear.

A Balance Sheet is not an account but merely a statement and it does not much matter on which side we show respectively the assets and liabilities. (We have chosen to adopt the Continental pattern and have shown the assets on the left; as the asset accounts in the ledger normally have debit balances and capital and liabilities have credit ones, there is much to commend the Continental method.) It is, however, essential to enter transactions on the correct side of each ledger account.

From what has already been said about the dual aspect of a transaction, it follows that for every debit entry in the ledger there must be a corresponding credit entry. Thus the Bank Account was debited with £3,000; Mr. Carr's Capital Account was credited with £3,000. The Bank Account was debited with £500; the Loan Account was credited with £500.

If you are in doubt about which account to debit and which account to credit, it might help to remember that as far as assets and liabilities are concerned the account which receives the benefit is debited and the account which yields the benefit is credited. Apply this to the entries above. When Mr Carr opened an account at the bank, which account received the benefit and which account yielded one? Clearly the Bank Account received the benefit and Mr. Carr's Capital Account yielded it. Consider the loan—again the Bank Account received the benefit and 'X' Bank yielded it.

Turn back now to page 9 and let us see how the transactions entered into by Mr Carr on the 5th January would have been recorded in the ledger.

BANK ACCOUNT (C.B.1)

19—			£	19—			£
Jan. 1	Capital	L.1	3,000	Jan. 5	Lease	L.3	500
,, 1	Bank loan	L.2	500	,, 5	Shop fittings	L.4	300
				,, 5	Goods	L.5	1,000

CAPITAL ACCOUNT (L.1)

				19—			£
				Jan. 1	Bank	C.B.1	3,000

'X' BANK LOAN ACCOUNT (L.2)

				19—			£
				Jan. 1	Bank	C.B.1	500

LEASE ACCOUNT (L.3)

19—			£				
Jan. 5	Bank	C.B.1	500				

SHOP FITTINGS ACCOUNT (L.4)

19—			£				
Jan. 5	Bank	C.B.1	300				

GOODS (STOCK IN TRADE) ACCOUNT (L.5)

19—			£				
Jan. 5	Bank	C.B.1	1,000				
,, 5	L.X. Materials	L.6	1,500				

No entry will appear in the Bank Account for the materials bought from L.X. Materials Ltd, because these were not paid for; the corresponding credit entry will appear in the account of L.X. Materials Ltd, viz.:

L.X. MATERIALS LTD (L.6)

				19—			£
				Jan. 5	Goods	L.5	1,500

An account in the name of a person or a business is called a *personal account* and a credit balance indicates a liability, money owed to the person or firm named in the account. A debit balance in a personal account means that the person named owes money to the firm. It is an asset.

When Mr Carr pays the account of L.X. Materials Ltd, the latter's account will be debited and the Bank Account credited. (Incidentally it will be the Bank Account which will be credited first and the entry in L.X. Materials Ltd account made from the Bank Account.) When L.X. Materials Ltd's Account is debited both sides of the account will show equal amounts and so the balance will be zero—nothing owing, nothing owed.

Balancing an Account

Refer to the Bank Account on page 25. It will be seen that £3,500 was paid into the bank and £1,800 was withdrawn from the bank, leaving a balance at the bank of £1,700.

To balance an account we add up both sides of the account and subtract the smaller from the larger total. We then add the resulting figure to the smaller side to make both sides equal, viz.:

BANK ACCOUNT

19—			£	19—			£
Jan. 1	Capital	L.1	3,000	Jan. 5	Lease	L.3	500
,, 1	Bank Loan	L.2	500	,, 5	Shop fittings	L.4	300
				,, 5	Stock in trade	L.5	1,000
				,, 5	Balance c/d		1,700
			£3,500				£3,500
Jan. 6	Balance b/d		1,700				

Next bring the sum which has been added to the smaller side down to the opposite side of the account. The abbreviations used here, c/d and b/d, stand for 'carried down' and 'brought down' respectively. If the balance had been carried over to a new page, the abbreviations would have been c/f and b/f—'carried forward' and 'brought forward'. The balance of £1,700 brought down tells us that Mr Carr has this sum left in his bank account. When an account is balanced in this way, usually at the end of a period of time, a week or a month, the entry carried down bears the commencing date of the new period.

Posting to the Ledger

So far, in speaking of the entries made to the ledger, nothing has been said about the documents which provide the information from which the entries are made. Debit entries in the bank account are made from paying-in slips which customers complete when paying money into their bank accounts. Credit entries are made from cheque counterfoils or cheque stubs as they are sometimes called.

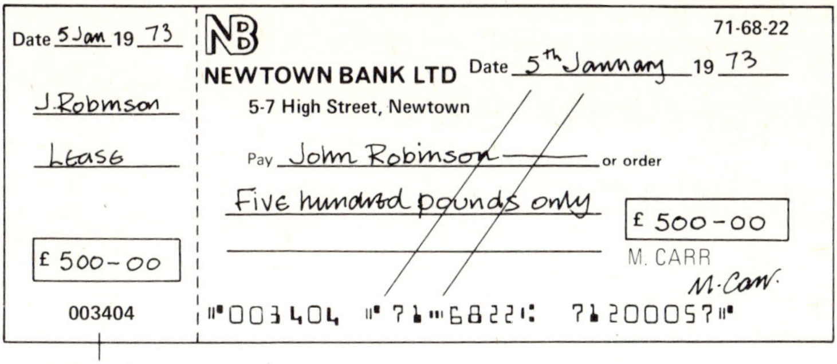
Date 5 Jan 19 73
J. Robinson
Lease
£ 500-00
003404

NB
NEWTOWN BANK LTD
5-7 High Street, Newtown
71-68-22
Date 5th January 19 73
Pay John Robinson — or order
Five hundred pounds only
£ 500-00
M. CARR
M. Carr
⑈003404⑈ 71⑆68221⑆ 71200057⑈

Counterfoil

In practice the entries are made to the bank account in the manner just described, and then the corresponding credit or debit entries in the ledger are made from the bank account.

When Mr Carr paid £3,000 into his bank account on 1st January he made out a paying-in slip, viz.:

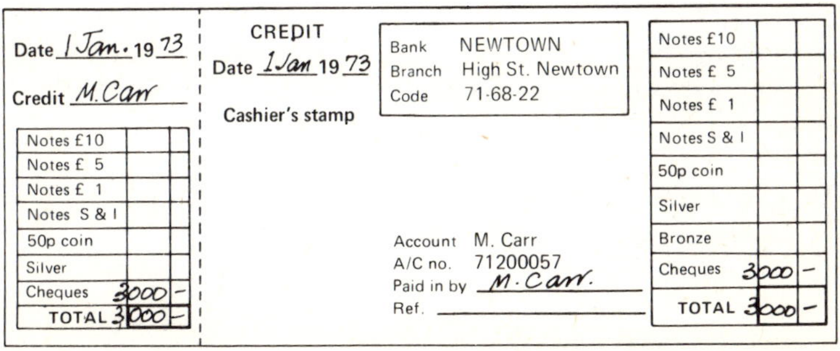
Date 1 Jan. 19 73
Credit M. Carr

Notes £10		
Notes £ 5		
Notes £ 1		
Notes S & I		
50p coin		
Silver		
Cheques	3000	–
TOTAL	3000	–

CREDIT
Date 1 Jan 19 73
Cashier's stamp

Bank NEWTOWN
Branch High St. Newtown
Code 71-68-22

Account M. Carr
A/C no. 71200057
Paid in by M. Carr.
Ref.

Notes £10		
Notes £ 5		
Notes £ 1		
Notes S & I		
50p coin		
Silver		
Bronze		
Cheques	3000	–
TOTAL	3000	–

and from his retained copy of this paying-in slip he made an entry in his bank account.

BANK ACCOUNT (PAGE 1)

19—			£				
Jan. 1	Capital	2	3,000				

This entry was then posted to Mr Carr's capital account.

CAPITAL ACCOUNT (PAGE 2)

				19— Jan. 1	Bank	1	£ 3,000

Note that there are two cross references in each account. In the 'Particulars column' in the Bank Account is the name of the other account and in the folio column is the page number in the ledger of this account. In the Capital Account the entry gives the name of the other account (Bank) and the ledger page on which this account appears (page 1). It is not usual to post the Cash Book after each entry but to do it periodically—daily, weekly, monthly etc., or at longer intervals of time.

The accounts we have so far considered have been accounts for assets and liabilities which appear in the Balance Sheet, and we have seen that assets usually have debit balances in the ledger, and Capital and liabilities accounts, credit balances. Let us suppose a businessman buys three machines each costing £600 and pays by cheque. The entries in his ledger accounts would be as follows.

BANK ACCOUNT

19— Jan. 1	Balance	b/d	£ 5,000	19— Jan. 16	Machinery		£ 1,800

MACHINERY ACCOUNT

19— Jan 16	Bank		£ 1,800				

If he were now to sell one of these machines to someone for what he paid for it, the entries to record this in the ledger would be as follows:

BANK ACCOUNT

19—			£	19—			£
Jan. 1	Balance	b/d	5,000	Jan. 16	Machinery		1,800
„ 18	Machinery		600				

MACHINERY ACCOUNT

19— Jan. 16	Bank		£ 1,800	19— Jan. 18	Bank		£ 600

A debit entry in an asset account increases the value of that asset and a credit entry reduces the value of the particular asset. When goods are bought on credit, the supplier's account is credited, viz.:

L.X. MATERIALS LTD

				19— Mar. 6	Goods		£ 1,500

Entries on the credit side of a personal account of this kind will increase the liability and entries on the debit side will reduce it. Thus when the account is paid the Bank Account is credited, reducing the asset, cash, and the L.X. Materials Ltd, account is debited, cancelling the liability.

FORMAT OF LEDGER ACCOUNTS UNDER A MECHANIZED BOOK-KEEPING SYSTEM

When you receive your monthly or quarterly bank statement, which is a copy of your bank account as it appears in the books of the bank, you will notice that it has three columns, a debit, a credit, and a balance column. If Mr Carr were to employ a similar mechanized system, his bank account would look like this:

Bank Account (Mr Carr's books)

19—		Debit	Credit	Balance
		£	£	£
Jan 1.	Capital	3,000		3,000 Dr
Jan 1.	Loan	500		3,500 Dr
Jan 5.	Lease		500	3,000 Dr
Jan 5.	Shop Fittings		300	2,700 Dr
Jan 5.	Stock-in-trade		1,000	1,700 Dr

Although the above would be the form of Mr Carr's bank account, the bank's record of Mr Carr's account would be the opposite of the above; Mr Carr is a creditor of the bank as long as he has money in his account and a debtor when he overdraws it.

Mr Carr's Bank Account in the books of his bank

19—	Ref.	Debit	Credit	Balance
		£	£	£
Jan 1.			3,500	3,500 Cr
Jan 5.	150	500		3,000 Cr
Jan 5.	151	300		2,700 Cr
Jan 5.	152	1,000		1,700 Cr

(The numbers 150, 151, 152 are the last three figures of the cheque numbers)

This bring us to a very important point. In keeping the accounts of a firm, the bookkeeper records the dual aspect of each transaction from the firm's point of view. Thus when Mr Carr bought goods on credit he debited his goods account (purchases) and credited the account of the supplier. The supplier on the other hand recorded this transaction from his point of view and debited Mr Carr's account and credited his goods (sales) account. Some students experience difficulty in understanding how a credit balance in a personal account can be a liability. This is probably because a person knows that if he has a credit balance at his bank he has money there. He is of course looking at his financial position from the bank's point of view which is understandable since the periodic statements he receives from his bank are copies of the account as it appears in the bank's ledger. Remember that from the firm's point of view a credit balance in a personal account represents a liability and a debit balance an asset.

T ACCOUNTS

Knowing which accounts to debit and which to credit and the significance of a particular ledger account balance demonstrate whether a student has a real grasp or not of his subject. To increase the amount of practice in these activities, use is often made of T accounts. These are accounts which merely show the balance figure and omit the other particulars. Thus a student might be asked to record in T account form how the purchase by cheque of a piece of machinery costing £1,000 would be recorded in the ledger. He would do so as follows;

Bank Account

	£1,000

Machinery Account

£1,000	

EXERCISE 4.1

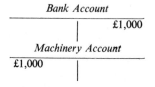

Mr Robinson is a sole trader. Open T accounts to show whether the accounts in Mr Robinson's ledger, recording the following, have debit or credit balances. *Example*—Mr Robinson owns a lease of his shop valued at £1,600.

Lease Account

£1,600	

1. Fixtures and Fittings are valued at £370
2. Stock at cost price is worth £1,200
3. Mr Robinson has a bank overdraft of £560
4. Mr Robinson owes John Louis & Co. £120 in respect of stock-in-trade supplied on credit
5. Mr Robinson has sold goods on credit to Mr M. Chivers for £200 which is still outstanding
6. Mr Robinson's equity is £2,700
7. Mr Robinson has £10 cash in his office cash box.

EXERCISE 4.2

Balance the following accounts in a similar manner to the model given, bringing down the new balances.

Plant and Machinery Account

	£		£
	3,600		200
	1,200	Balance c/d	5,300
	700		
	£5,500		£5,500
Balance b/d	5,300		

Bank Account

	£		£
	2,700		100
	5,300		850
	2,100		50
	700		

Fixtures and Fittings Account

	£		£
	700		
	850		
	1,400		

Purchases Account

	£		£
	11,000		100
	960		
	520		

Capital Account

	£		£
	600		17,000
			500
			70

Motor Vehicles Account

	£		£
	1,400		500
	600		
	1,200		

James Thistlewaite

	£		£
	50		1,800
			700

EXERCISE 4.3

From the following ledger account balances draw up a Balance Sheet as at 31 March 19—.

BANK ACCOUNT

19— Mar. 31	Balance	b/d	£ 2,500				

CAPITAL ACCOUNT

				19— Mar 31	Balance	b/d	£ 24,300

FREEHOLD PREMISES

19— Mar 31	Balance	b/d	£ 20,000				

FIXTURES & FITTINGS

19— Mar 31	Balance	b/d	£ 800				

STOCK IN TRADE

19— Mar 31	Balance	b/d	£ 1,700				

REGIONAL CHEMICAL CO. LTD

				19— Mar 31	Balance	b/d	£ 700

EXERCISE 4.4

The following Balance Sheet of A. Fox was drawn up on 31 March, 1972:

Liabilities:	£	£	*Assets*	£	£
Capital (1 Apr. 1971)	17,250		Buildings		10,000
Add Net Profit	1,960		Machinery		5,000
			Motor Van	1,200	
	£19,210		*Less* Depreciation	120	
Less Drawings	1,500				1,080
		17,710	Stock		2,150
Long-term Loan		2,000	Debtors		1,975
Loan Interest due		75	Cash at Bank		965
Creditors		1,385			
		£21,170			£21,170

You are required to state, showing your working:

(a) The total of Current Assets.
(b) Working Capital.
(c) The effect on the Balance Sheet if A. Fox decided (i) to write off a debt of £75 as irrecoverable and make a provision of 5 per cent for doubtful debts, and (ii) to provide for Wages due, amounting to £15.

G.C.E. 'O' Level

5

Ledger Accounts for Recording Gains and Losses—The Trading and Profit & Loss Accounts

So far we have considered those ledger accounts which are kept to record assets, liabilities and capital. These accounts are more or less permanent and their balances are carried down at the end of the financial period. They provide the information from which, when all the other accounts have been closed and the net profit calculated, the Balance Sheet is prepared. The net profits for the year will equal the amount by which the total value of the net assets has increased. We have seen that if stock which cost £500 is sold for £700 cash, the assets side of the Balance Sheet increases by £200 and that the owner's capital or equity increases by a similar sum. During the course of the trading year there will be expenses which will reduce this gross profit, and although it would be possible to produce a new Balance Sheet after each transaction, we know that this is impracticable and so certain temporary accounts are opened to record (a) the receipt of revenue; and (b) expenses and losses. From these temporary accounts net profit or net loss can be estimated.

They are temporary accounts because for the most part they represent goods or services which have been used up in the course of trading—for example, goods which have been sold, services (represented by wage payments) used up, telephone charges, advertising expenses, rates to local authorities, and these accounts are closed at the end of the financial year.

When wages are paid, the Bank Account is credited and Wages Account debited:

WAGES ACCOUNT

			£				
(Date)	Bank		700·00				

Each time wages are paid similar entries will be made and at the end of the financial year the Wages Account will tell us how much money has been paid out in wages. And similarly we can keep temporary, or *nominal* accounts as they are sometimes called, for all the other expenses incurred throughout the trading period. By closing these accounts at the end of the year and bringing them together in a Trading and Profit & Loss Account we can calculate the gross profit (the difference between what the goods cost us to buy and what we received from their sale), and when the expenses have been deducted from this figure, we shall be left with the net profit. This profit is already in the business in the form of an increase in the value of the net assets; the Trading and Profit & Loss Account merely shows us how this net profit for the year was made.

Remember that throughout the trading year, day after day, goods are being bought and sold, expenses paid, profits converted into more stock or into more debts or more fixed assets. At the end of the period we summarize all these transactions and so estimate our net profit.

TRADING AND PROFIT & LOSS ACCOUNT FOR THE YEAR ENDED 31 DEC 19—

	£	£
Sales		32,000
Cost of goods sold		26,000
Gross Profit		6,000
Expenses and Losses:		
Rent and rates	550	
Wages and salaries	3,500	
Telephone	15	
Carriage	20	
Commission paid to sales staff	70	
Bad debts	10	
Depreciation of fixtures & fittings	120	
		4,285
Net Profit		£1,715

This Trading and Profit & Loss Account might appear in the ledger in the following form.

TRADING AND PROFIT & LOSS ACCOUNT FOR THE YEAR ENDED 31 DEC. 19—

	£		£
Cost of goods sold	26,000	Sales	32,000
Gross Profit c/d	6,000		
	£32,000		£32,000
Rent & Rates	550	Gross Profit b/d	6,000
Wages & Salaries	3,500		
Telephone	15		
Carriage	20		
Commission to sales staff	70		
Bad debts	10		
Depreciation (F. & F.)	120		
Net Profit	1,715		
	£6,000		£6,000

Note that a Trading and Profit & Loss Account is a ledger account covering a period of time whereas a Balance Sheet is merely a statement showing, at a moment in time, what assets the business owns and how these have been financed.

When a Trading and Profit & Loss Account is prepared in the conventional form all the expenses are recorded on the debit side and all the gains on the credit side. If the total of the credit entries are greater than the debit entries we have made a profit; if the debit entries are greater than the credit ones then we have made a loss.

Classifying Accounts

There are three types of ledger account to which we have so far referred.

(1) *Personal Accounts*

Accounts of persons to whom we have supplied goods on credit or from whom we have bought goods on credit. Thus:

J. MCGRATH

19— Mar 3	Goods		£ 7,000				

This is the personal account of a customer to whom we have supplied goods on credit. It shows a balance of £7,000 due to us. It is an asset. J. McGrath is a debtor for the sum of £7,000.

M. CARR & CO. LTD

				19— Jan 10	Goods		£ 420

This is the personal account of a company which has supplied us with goods on credit. It is a liability. M. Carr & Co. Ltd is a creditor.

Debit balances on personal accounts = money owed to us = assets

Credit balances on personal accounts = money owed by us = liabilities

Debit balances appear in the Balance Sheet under current assets and credit balances on the liabilities side usually under current liabilities.

(2) *Real Accounts*

Accounts of tangible things owned by the business e.g., real property, plant and machinery, motor vans, stocks, money. They are usually debit balances and are of course assets. If the Bank Account has been overdrawn, it will have a credit balance and appear in the Balance Sheet under current liabilities.

(3) *Nominal or Temporary Accounts*

These represent either gains or losses. Gains may consist of money received from the sale of goods, discounts earned by paying suppliers of goods promptly, rents received from letting property and, when gains, are credit balances. A debit balance represents an expense or a loss. Notice that gross profit and net profit are both credit balances. Gross loss and net loss would be debit balances. Nominal accounts are closed at the end of the financial period by transfer to the Trading and Profit & Loss Account.

AN ALTERNATIVE CLASSIFICATION

In recent years the classification just described has come in for a good deal of criticism. Many teachers of book-keeping now prefer a simpler classification, a classification into 'capital' accounts and 'revenue' accounts. Accounts relating to business assets and the financing of these assets are capital accounts; all other accounts are revenue accounts and like the nominal accounts referred to above, they provide the information from which profits and losses can be calculated. Whether a businessman is manufacturing goods for sale or simply providing a service, he will himself be using goods and services, and one of the principal differences between capital and revenue accounts is that the former in each case represent services which will be used up more slowly than the rest. A machine may go on rendering services to the business for many years, whereas an insurance premium may provide insurance cover for one year only.

Closing Adjustments

We shall see later that if a service has been bought and has not been used up, the value of the unexpired part will appear in the Balance Sheet as an asset, and similarly, if we have used up a service which has not been paid for, this will appear in the Balance Sheet as a liability. It is one of the tasks of the Accountant to make adjustments of this kind at the end of the financial period so that all expenses relating to the trading period in question are properly charged against the profits and all revenue earned within that period properly credited.

There is one adjustment which we will deal with in more detail here. It concerns unsold stock at the end of the trading period. No trader is likely to finish his financial year with all his stock disposed of unless of course he sells up everything with the object of winding up the business. To work out what the gross profit is, the Accountant must calculate first the cost of the goods that have actually been sold—this is an example of matching costs with revenue referred to in the first chapter.

STOCK-IN-TRADE

The one-man retailer may buy goods for re-sale either for cash or on credit. When he buys and pays by cheque he credits his Bank Account and debits a Purchases Account, viz.:

BANK ACCOUNT

				19—			£
				Feb 1	Purchases		700

PURCHASES ACCOUNT

19—			£				
Feb 1	Bank		700				

If he buys on credit, he credits the suppliers account and debits his Purchases Account. Assume that on April 1 goods are bought on credit from Wren Trading Co. for £80:

WREN TRADING CO.

				19—			£
				Apr 1	Purchases		80

PURCHASES ACCOUNT

19—			£				
Feb 1	Bank		700				
Apr 1	Wren Trading		80				

Let us suppose that at the end of the year the Purchases Account has a debit balance of £9,800, viz.:

PURCHASES ACCOUNT

19—			£	19—			£
Dec 31	Balance	b/d	9,800	Dec 31	Trading Account		9,800

A method commonly employed is to close the Purchases Account by transferring the whole of the balance to the Trading Account, even though some of the goods have not been sold and are still in stock.

TRADING ACCOUNT FOR THE YEAR ENDED 31ST DEC. ......

Purchases	£9,800	

These purchases have been recorded at cost price and the next step is to take stock by listing the goods remaining unsold, again at cost price. A Stock Account is then opened in the ledger to record this. Assume the unsold stock was valued at £1,800:

STOCK ACCOUNT

19—			£				
Dec 31	Trading Account		1,800				

The corresponding credit is posted to the Trading Account, having the effect of reducing the amount charged to the Trading Account by the amount of the stock unsold.

TRADING ACCOUNT FOR THE YEAR ENDED 31ST DEC. ......

Purchases	£9,800	Stock at close	£1,800

And so the amount which has actually been debited to the Trading Account is the cost of the goods that have been sold, namely £8,000 worth.

Instead of showing the £1,800 on the credit side of the Trading Account, we could have deducted it from the £9,800 on the debit side, viz.:

TRADING ACCOUNT FOR THE YEAR ENDED 31ST DEC. ......

Purchases	£9,800	
Less Stock at close	1,800	
Cost of goods sold	£8,000	

One can always transpose an item from one side of an account to the other, by showing the item as a deduction from the side to which it has been transposed, without changing the balance in any way. This was made clear in an earlier chapter when it was explained that debit entries in an asset account increased the value of that particular asset and entries on the credit side reduced its value.

A CONTINUING STOCK ACCOUNT

One of the great disadvantages of the method described above is that before financial accounts and a Balance Sheet can be prepared a firm has to go to the expense of taking stock. Since this is usually done after business hours or at week-ends, the costs in overtime payments can be considerable. By opening a Purchases and Stock Account in place of a Purchases Account and by debiting it with goods bought, and crediting it with sales at cost price, the balance on this account will give the estimated value of unsold stock at any time.

Using the figures employed above, but remembering that postings to these accounts would be made at regular intervals, we show below the way the accounts would appear in the ledger.

PURCHASES AND STOCK ACCOUNT

	£		£
Balance b/d	9,800	Sales at cost	8,000
		Balance c/d	1,800
	£9,800		£9,800
Balance b/d	1,800		

COST OF GOODS SOLD ACCOUNT

Stock Account	£8,000	Trading Account	£8,000

A physical stock-taking would take place at least once a year and the results ought, of course, to agree with the balance on the Purchases and Stock Account. If there is a disparity of some consequence a thorough investigation would be called for.

This system is possible only if the sales can be reliably reduced to cost price. In department stores, where a standard mark-up is employed, this is not too difficult, although at sales times and when the selling price of goods is marked down the necessary adjustments have to be made in the Stock Account and Sales at Cost Account. We shall return to this subject again and study it in greater detail under the heading of costing. For the moment it is well to recognize that there are many ways of dealing with transactions in the books of account of the business and the firm will choose those ways which suit its purposes best.

THE SALES ACCOUNT

When goods are sold for cash, the Bank Account is debited with the money received and the Sales Account is credited, viz.:

BANK ACCOUNT

19—			£				
Feb 2	Sales		1,700				

SALES ACCOUNT

				19—			£
				Feb 2	Bank		1,700

The Sales Account is a revenue account and because it always has a credit balance this balance represents gains made by the business. The day's sales, or if posted weekly the week's sales, will be entered on the credit side of the Sales Account, and at the end of the financial year this account will tell us the total sum earned from the firm's trading activities. Like the Purchases Account, the Sales Account is closed and transferred to the Trading Account.

ILLUSTRATION 5.1

On 31st December, 19— the following balances appeared in the ledger:

Purchases Account	£12,000
Sales Account	16,000

If all the purchases had been sold, then

TRADING ACCOUNT FOR THE YEAR ENDED 31ST DECEMBER, 19—

	£		£
Purchases	12,000	Sales	16,000
Gross profit c/d	4,000		
	£16,000		£16,000
		Gross profit b/d	4,000

If the stock at the close of the period had been £1,000, then

TRADING ACCOUNT FOR THE YEAR ENDED 31ST DECEMBER, 19—

	£	£		£
Purchases	£12,000		Sales	16,000
Less Stock at close	1,000			
Cost of goods sold		11,000		
Gross profit c/d		5,000		
		£16,000		£16,000
			Gross profit b/d	5,000

Trial Balance

In double-entry book-keeping for every debit entry in the ledger there is a corresponding credit entry and vice versa. When the business pays out money, the Cash Account is credited and the asset or expense account debited. When the business receives money, the Cash Account is debited and the corresponding revenue account credited. Here are some of the transactions a business might enter into and the entries which would appear in the ledger to record them.

	Credit	*Debit*
Mr X. deposits £10,000 with his banker preparatory to starting a business	Capital A/c	Bank A/c
Mr X. buys the lease of a shop	Bank A/c	Lease A/c
Mr X. buys fixtures for shop	Bank A/c	Fixtures A/c
Mr X. buys stationery	Bank A/c	Stationery A/c
Mr X. pays wages	Bank A/c	Wages A/c
Mr X. buys goods for resale	Bank A/c	Purchases A/c
Mr X. sells goods for cash	Sales A/c	Bank A/c

The recording of both aspects of a transaction means that the total debit entries must equal the total of the credit entries, and this provides us with a very useful check on the accuracy of our book-keeping.

Preparatory to producing the accounts and Balance Sheet at the end of the financial period, it is common practice to draw up a trial balance. Using two columns, one for debit balances and the other for credit balances, we list all the ledger account balances and if the totals are not equal something is wrong. Listing the balances in this way serves another purpose. Being a summary of the ledger balances, the trial balance gives us most of the information we need to prepare the Trading and Profit & Loss Account and the Balance Sheet.

TRIAL BALANCE EXTRACTED FROM THE BOOKS ON 31ST DECEMBER, 19—

	Dr	Cr
	£	
Cash at Bank	1,000·00	
Purchases	620·00	
Sales		1,160·00
Sales returns	19·00	
Purchases returns		30·00
Stock, 1st Jan 19—	260·00	
Wages	110·00	
Rent, rates, etc.	64·00	
Plant & machinery	670·00	
Motor van	140·00	
Sundry debtors	425·00	
Salaries	62·00	
Commission	15·00	
Sundry creditors		218·00
Discount		9·00
Capital		1,968·00
	£3,385·00	£3,385·00

Do not worry if you do not understand some of the accounts listed. Try to identify those revenue accounts which will be closed by transfer to the Trading and Profit & Loss Account and those capital accounts which will remain open and appear in the Balance Sheet.

A trial balance can be extracted at any time.

OPENING STOCK

The closing stock at the end of one financial period is the opening stock of the next financial period. You will recall that to record closing stock we opened a Stock Account and debited it with the value at cost price of this stock. We have now to move forward one year and consider the financial accounts for the second year of trading which opens with unsold stock. The Stock Account opened to record closing stock remains open until the end of the financial year and because it is in the ledger at the time the trial balance is taken out, it will be one of the items in the trial balance. Often you are told this by the entry being dated the beginning of the period. (See trial balance above.) Opening Stock is always an item in the trial balance, whereas closing stock is an adjustment outside the trial balance.

STOCK ACCOUNT

(End of year 1) Dec 31	Trading Account		£ 1,800				

The corresponding credit entry was made in the Trading Account and reduced the Purchases charged to the Trading Account by the amount of unsold stock. (Refer to page 38.) At the end of year 2, purchases totalled £13,000 and Stock at close, a piece of information given to us outside of the trial balance, was valued at £1,200. This information enables us to calculate the cost price of goods sold, e.g.:

	£
Stock at the beginning of the period ...	1,800
Add Purchases	13,000
	14,800
Less Stock at close	1,200
Cost of goods sold	£13,600

The Trading Account is prepared as follows:

(1) At the end of year 2, close the Stock Account by transferring the balance to the Trading Account, viz.:

STOCK ACCOUNT

Year 1	Trading Account		£ 1,800	Year 2	Trading Account		£ 1,800

TRADING ACCOUNT FOR YEAR ENDED

Year 2	Stock at beginning of period		£ 1,800				

(2) Close the Purchases Account and transfer the balance to the Trading Account.

PURCHASES ACCOUNT

19— Dec 31	Balance		£ 13,000	19— Dec 31	Trading Account		£ 13,000

(3) An entry is made in the Stock Account to record stock at the close of the period.

STOCK ACCOUNT

			£				£
Year 1	Trading Account		1,800	Year 2	Trading Account		1,800
Year 2	Trading Account		1,200				

TRADING ACCOUNT FOR YEAR ENDED ...

	£
Stock at beginning of period	1,800
Purchases	13,000
	14,800
Less Stock at close	1,200
Cost of goods sold	£13,600

ILLUSTRATIVE EXERCISE 5.2

The following Trial Balance was extracted from the books of L. G. Archer on 31 December, 19—. Prepare a Trading Account and Profit and Loss Account for the year ended 31 December 19— and a Balance Sheet at this date.

		Dr	*Cr*
		£	£
C	Cash at bank	40,000	
R	Purchases	24,800	
R	Sales		46,400
R	Stock (1st Jan., 19—)	11,160	
R	Wages	4,400	
R	Rent and Rates	2,560	
C	Plant and Machinery	26,800	
C	Motor Lorry	5,600	
C	Sundry Debtors	17,000	
R	Salaries	2,480	
R	Commission	600	
C	Sundry Creditors...		8,720
R	Discount		360
C	Capital		79,920
		£135,400	£135,400

The value of the stock at 31 December, 19— was £12,400.

Notice:

(1) The stock at the beginning of the period is included in the Trial Balance whereas the stock at the close is outside the Trial Balance.

(2) Only the Revenue Accounts will be closed by transfer to the Trading and Profit and Loss Account—we have marked these with the letter R.

(3) The Capital Account balances marked with the letter C will be brought down in the Ledger and these will provide us with the information necessary to draw up a Balance Sheet.

(4) The item 'discount' is a revenue item and being a credit balance it is a gain. It represents discounts earned by Archer in consequence of paying his suppliers promptly.

(5) The Trading and Profit and Loss Account is for a period of time, in this case one year.

(6) The item 'commission' is an expense—money paid to a salesman. Had it been a credit balance it would have been a gain—money earned by Archer for selling goods or services for someone else.

TRADING AND PROFIT AND LOSS ACCOUNT FOR THE YEAR ENDED 31ST DEC. 19—

	£		£
Stock (1st Jan. 19—)	11,160	Sales	46,400
Add Purchases	24,800		
	35,960		
Less Stock (31st Dec., 19—)	12,400		
Cost of goods sold	23,560		
Gross Profit c/d	22,840		
	46,400		46,400
Wages	4,400	Gross Profit from Trading Account	22,840
Rent and Rates	2,560	Discount	360
Salaries	2,480		
Commission	600		
	10,040		
Net Profit c/d	13,160		
	23,200		23,200
Transferred to Capital A/c	13,160	Net Profit b/d	13,160
	£13,160		£13,160

BALANCE SHEET AS AT 31ST DECEMBER, 19—

	£	£	*Fixed Assets:*	£	£
Capital	79,920		Plant and Machinery	26,800	
Add Profit	13,160		Motor Lorry	5,600	
		93,080			32,400
Current Liabilities:			*Current Assets*		
Creditors		8,720	Stock	12,400	
			Debtors	17,000	
			Bank	40,000	
					69,400
		£101,800			£101,800

6

The Cash Book—Value Added Tax

WE have seen that one of the principal aims of book-keeping is to record transactions in the ledger in such a way as to allow the accountant, at the end of a trading period, to produce the financial statements we were considering in the last chapter. In this chapter we look at one of the important subdivisions of the ledger and afterwards examine in greater detail the making of entries in the ledger from books of original entry—that is, books in which transactions are first recorded before being posted to the ledger.

We begin with the Cash Book because money plays such a dominant role in our economy; every transaction at some stage involves money. That part of the ledger which is used to record the receipt and payment of money is separated from the rest of the ledger and contained in a book called the Cash Book. Basically there will be two accounts in the Cash Book—one to record dealings involving metallic and paper money and one to record dealings through a bank.

There is another way in which the Cash Book is different from other parts of the ledger. We say that a Cash Book is a book of original entry as well as being a Cash Account. This means simply that when a transaction involves cash we can make the entry directly in the Cash Account without having first to pass it through some other book.

Although the majority of transactions involving money will be done through the firm's bank, some coins and paper money will be wanted for the purchase of small everyday things for which payment could not be made by cheque. You are already familiar with a simple Bank Account in which payment of money into the bank is recorded on the left-hand side of the account and payments out on the right-hand side. A similar account can be kept for transactions involving coins and paper money. If we stored our cash in a cash box we would debit the Cash Account every time we put money into the box and would credit the Cash Account every time we took money out.

When more cash is wanted, a cheque will be cashed. The entries will be: credit the Bank Account with the sum withdrawn and debit the Cash Account with the cash received, viz.,

Bank Account

19—			£	19—			£
Jan 1	Balance	b/d	170·00	Jan 2	Cash		10·00

Cash Account

19—			£				
Jan 2	Bank		10·00				

Conversely, if we accumulate more money in our cash box than we need and wish to pay some of this money into the bank, we credit the Cash Account with the sum withdrawn and debit our Bank Account with the sum paid into our account, viz.,

Cash Account

19—			£	19—			£
Apr 1	Balance	b/d	60·00	Apr 2	Bank		50·00

Bank Account

19—			£				
Apr 1	Balance	b/d	190·00				
,, 2	Cash		50·00				

ILLUSTRATION 6.1

On 1st January 19— you have in your cash box £12·10
On 2nd January 19— £3·00 was paid to you by David Copperfield
On 15th January 19— you paid Oliver Twist £10·50
On 16th January 19— you paid £2·30 to Richard Carstone.

'You have in your cash box £12·10'. This item should be entered on the debit side because the money must have been received at some time and in fact is the amount which was in the cash box when the account was last balanced. A record of the existence of this money in the cash box is made by entering Balance £12·10 on the left hand side of the account.

Dr *Cash Account* Cr

		Fol.	£			Fol.	£
19—				19—			
Jan 1	Balance		12·10	Jan 15	Oliver Twist		10·50
2	David Copperfield		3·00	,, 16	Richard Carstone		2·30
				,, 16	Balance	c/d	2·30
		£	15·10			£	15·10
19—							
Jan 17	Balance	b/d	2·30				

POINTS TO NOTE CAREFULLY

Where an amount contains no pence, insert noughts in the pence column, e.g. £3·00. Write £3 and 10 pence £3·10, never £3·1; and similarly £3 and 50 pence must be written £3·50, never £3·5, and so on.

When an account is balanced, the total on the debit side should be on the same horizontal line as the total on the credit side. Draw double lines under totals.

The object of a Cash Account is to record all transactions in which cash is received or paid at the time of the transaction, and to show the balance in hand.

The account is closed periodically, and the balance brought down to the debit side on the same page or transferred to a new page.

When closed, the balance, together with the date of closing, and the words 'Balance c/d', are entered on the credit side. This balance is carried down and dated ready for the following day 'Balance b/d'.

Note that the process of balancing is really a summary of the account. Whereas *before balancing*, the amount on hand (£2·30) was shown by two entries on the debit side and two entries on the credit side, *after balancing* the amount on hand is shown by one entry.

Correct and careful ruling adds much to the appearance of a set of books.

Sometimes students grasp the idea better by reading the Account as follows:

(1) name of account,
(2) Dr,
(3) the matter in the details column,
(4) for.

Thus the item on 2nd January would read 'Cash Account is debtor to David Copperfield for £3·00'.

If there is any balance in a Cash Account, it must always fall on the *debit* side, because it is not possible to pay out more cash than is received.

Be particularly careful to place all figures in their proper places exactly under one another. Many errors in casting are traceable to carelessness in this respect.

The diagonal line drawn across the details column after the account has been balanced is for the purpose of preventing false entries.

Remember that all money which comes in is entered on the debit side, and all money which goes out is recorded on the credit side.

Cash Account (Simple Form) Exercises

(If more than one exercise is written on a page, leave three blank lines after each exercise. Be sure to indicate the number of each exercise. VAT is to be disregarded in the following exercises.)

EXERCISE 6.1

Employing a simple form of Cash Account as shown above, enter the following particulars. (All transactions are deemed to be cash transactions involving metallic and paper money.)

19—
Jan 3 Balance of cash in hand amounted to £18·80
„ 4 James Robson paid you £15·00 in settlement of his account
„ 16 Paid gas account, £10·75
„ 25 Remitted (paid) £6·10 to Stanley Martin
„ 26 Bought for cash, office furniture and fittings, £4·30
„ 28 Received £29·50 from Alfred Robertson & Co.
„ 29 Paid for trade expenses, £11·80
„ 30 Paid salaries, £25·00
„ 31 Thomas Yates paid you £7·50
„ 31 Paid rent, £9·50

Enter the cash balance on the credit side, rule off as shown in the illustration (page 6), and bring the balance down to the debit side.

EXERCISE 6.2

19—
Jan 1 Cash in hand, £250·00
„ 4 Paid £20·00 for motor licence
„ 5 Paid City Mills £192·00 for flour
„ 5 Received for cash sales, £50·00
„ 7 Paid Broachie & Son £77·00 in settlement of their account
„ 9 Received £10·25 from R. Jennings on account
„ 10 The Central Hotel paid their account, £12·75
„ 12 Cash sales, £14·00
„ 14 Paid Hazel & Brown, £129·70
„ 18 Received from C. L. Lloyd, £95·00
„ 29 Cash sales, £40·00

Enter the cash balance on the credit side, rule off, and bring the balance down to the debit side.

EXERCISE 6.3

19—
Mar 1 Cash in hand, £50·00
„ 2 Purchased and paid cash for office desk, £10·00 (enter 'Furniture & Fittings' in the details column)
„ 3 Cash sales amounted to £7·50
„ 9 Paid Caleb Barber, £20·00
„ 17 Received £20·00 from James Graham in settlement of his account
„ 17 Sent £24·00 to the Solid Construction Company on account
„ 19 Bought, for cash, 500 patent heel pads, £20·00
„ 29 Received £224·87½ for cash sales, and paid the Hardware Company £27·00 in settlement
„ 30 Paid rent of premises, £132·00
„ 31 Accepted the Caxton's Company estimate for the printing of 50,000 circulars at £750·00, and paid £50·00 on account

Enter the cash balance on the credit side, rule off neatly, and bring down the balance to the debit side.

EXERCISE 6.4

19—			£
Aug	1	Cash in hand	250·00
„	3	Paid Walter Lea	90·00
„	3	Received from N. Penny	10·50
„	4	William Pitt paid his account	1·5

,,	7	Received cash for goods sold by auction	34·12
,,	8	Cash sales	13·21
,,	8	Received from Mark Cook	230·00
,,	8	Purchases made in market	221·17
,,	9	Carriage on goods from market	10·11
,,	10	Purchased goods	56·37
,,	11	Cash sales	121·11
,,	13	Paid into bank	250·00

Enter the cash balance on the credit side, rule off neatly, and bring down the balance on the debit side.

EXERCISE 6.5

19—			£
Jan	1	Cash in hand	10·50
,,	3	Received from J. Smith	30·12
,,	4	Cash sales	120·25
,,	5	Paid Mrs Cutbush	14·16
,,	8	Bought goods for resale	25·80
,,	9	T. Ward paid his account	65·10
,,	10	Bought office chair	14·75
,,	11	Paid carriage on goods bought	5·50
,,	12	Cash sales	60·15
,,	15	Paid balance into bank except for £10·00	

Two-Column Cash Book

Most payments are made by cheque, i.e. an order written in legal form, requiring the banker to pay a specified sum of money as directed by the person signing the cheque. Another method of payment, now operated by the clearing banks, which is becoming increasingly popular, is payment by credit transfers. By this method a business man with several bills to settle merely lists the slips (see below) on forms supplied by the bank and sends them to his own branch with one cheque for the total.

CREDIT TRANSFER BANK GIRO

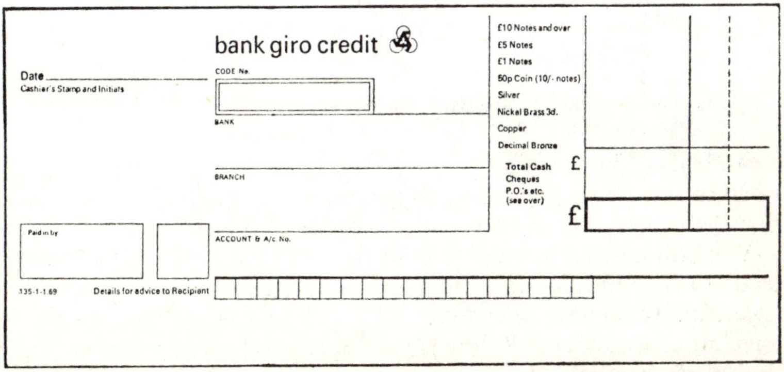
bank giro credit
Date
Cashier's Stamp and Initials
CODE No.
BANK
BRANCH
ACCOUNT & A/c No.
Paid in by
135-1-1.69
Details for advice to Recipient
£10 Notes and over
£5 Notes
£1 Notes
50p Coin (10/- notes)
Silver
Nickel Brass 3d.
Copper
Decimal Bronze
Total Cash £
Cheques
P.O.'s etc.
(see over)
£

At a later stage a deeper study of banks and banking will be made, but meanwhile it is sufficient to know that a business man becomes a customer of an ordinary commercial bank, and keeps a certain amount of money there, on the understanding that the banker will pay as directed by the signed cheques. This is a safe and convenient means of making and receiving payments. Certain payments could not be made by cheque. For example, workmen's wages must be paid in the coin and currency of the realm by virtue of the Truck Acts, 1831–1940. The Payment of Wages Act, 1960, however, enables wages to be paid in ways not authorized by the Truck Acts provided that certain conditions are satisfied. It would not be worth while to pay very small amounts by cheque, and there are many other items of expenditure in which coin and paper currency are necessary. We may therefore correctly assume that most business firms require to keep a Cash Account as well as a Bank Account, and these can be kept in the two-column Cash Book.

This can best be made clear by an illustration. (In this exercise V.A.T. is to be disregarded.)

ILLUSTRATIVE EXERCISE 6.2

Write up the Cash and Bank Accounts of M. Morrison, merchant, from the following particulars (key showing separate accounts and how they are combined in one account is shown on page 51).

19—			£
Feb	1	Cash in hand	30·00
,,	1	Balance at bank	250·00
,,	3	Received cheque from D. David	17·50
,,	3	Paid John Cleale by cheque	47·50
,,	3	Sold goods for cash	23·50
,,	4	Cashed cheque	30·00
,,	4	Paid sundry trade expenses by cash	1·52½
,,	4	Paid rent by cash	12·60
,,	4	Paid wages by cash	20·00
,,	4	Paid for office cleaning by cash	5·00
,,	4	Drew cash for personal expenses	20·00
,,	5	Received cash from Charles Gilbey	56·50
,,	6	Paid into bank	50·00

All cheques are paid into the bank on the same day.

Students of book-keeping in the early stages often become alarmed when they see elaborate rulings, apparently because of a misconception that the more ruling there is, the greater the complication.

You will be well advised to take the opposite view, that all ruling tends to simplification and clearness. If ruling had not achieved these objects, it would have been dispensed with long ago, for business people have no time to waste. Ruling is really the practical application of the time-worn counsel, 'A place for everything, and everything in its place'. With this idea in your mind, study the key to the Illustrative Exercise on page 51.

KEY TO ILLUSTRATIVE EXERCISE (page 50)

Dr *Cash Account* Cr

Date	Particulars		£	Date	Particulars		£
19—				19—			
Feb 1	Balance	b/d	30·00	Feb 4	Trade Ex.		1·52½
,, 3	Sales		23·50	,, 4	Rent		12·60
,, 4	Bank		30·00	,, 4	Wages		20·00
,, 5	C. Gilbey		56·50	,, 4	Office Clg		5·00
				,, 4	Drawings		20·00
				,, 6	Bank		50·00
				,, 6	Balance	c/d	30·87½
		£	140·00			£	140·00
19—							
Feb 7	Balance	b/d	30·87½				

Dr *Bank Account* Cr

Date	Particulars		£	Date	Particulars		£
19—				19—			
Feb 1	Balance	b/d	250·00	Feb 3	J. Cleale		47·50
,, 3	D. David		17·50	,, 4	Cash		30·00
,, 6	Cash		50·00	,, 6	Balance	c/d	240·00
		£	317·50			£	317·50
19—							
Feb 7	Balance	b/d	240·00				

Dr *Cash Book* Cr

Date	Particulars		Cash £	Bank £	Date	Particulars		Cash £	Bank £
19—					19—				
Feb 1	Balances	b/d	30·00	250·50	Feb 3	J. Cleale			47·50
,, 3	D. David			17·50	,, 4	Cash	c		30·00
,, 3	Sales		23·50		,, 4	Trade Ex.		1·52½	
,, 4	Bank	c	30·00		,, 4	Rent		12·60	
,, 5	C. Gilbey		56·50		,, 4	Wages		20·00	
,, 6	Cash	c		50·00	,, 4	Office Cleaning		5·00	
					,, 4	Drawings		20·00	
					,, 6	Bank	c	50·00	
					,, 6	Balances	c/d	30·87½	240·00
		£	140·00	317·50			£	140·00	317·50
19—									
Feb 7	Balances	b/d	30·87½	240·00					

The balance at the bank would be shown on the debit side of the Bank Account in the same manner as the balance of cash in the cash-box would be shown on the debit side of the Cash Account. Suppose a balance of £200 existed at the bank and the cash in hand had dwindled down to £4·00, the cash and bank balances would be shown as set out below.

Dr *Cash Book* Cr

Date	Details Column		Cash £	Bank £	Date	Details Column		Cash £	Bank £
	Balances		4·00	200·00					

You decide to draw £50·00 from the bank and place the money in your cash-box. Having done so, the transaction is recorded as follows.

Dr *Cash Book* Cr

Date	Details Column		Cash £	Bank £	Date	Details Column		Cash £	Bank £
	Balances		4·00	200·00		Cash	c		50·00
	Bank	c	50·00						

Notice that when the Bank Account is credited the entry is 'Cash' and when the Cash Account is debited the entry is 'Bank'. In double entry book-keeping there are always cross references of this kind to show in which accounts the corresponding debit or credit entries are to be found.

POSTING THE CASH BOOK

When we speak of posting the Cash Book, we mean making the corresponding debit and credit entries in the ledger necessary to complete the double entry.

ILLUSTRATIVE EXERCISE 6.3

Enter the following transactions in A. Thompson's two-column Cash Book and post to the Ledger.

19—			£
Feb	1	A. Thompson paid into the business, cash	20·00
		and into the business's bank account	500·00
,,	3	Received cheque from D. Cowan	10·10
,,	3	Paid A. Newman by cheque	5·60
,,	3	Bought stationery for cash	1·10
,,	4	Bought postage stamps for cash	2·00
,,	7	Paid rent by cheque	45·00
,,	10	Paid deposit on motor van by cheque	120·00
,,	12	Paid J. Johnson by cheque	25·90
,,	14	Cashed cheque	40·00
,,	17	Paid wages in cash	30·50
,,	18	Cash sales, banked the same day	52·00
,,	19	Paid sundry expenses in cash	3·10

Dr *Cash Book* (CB1) Cr

			Cash £	Bank £				Cash £	Bank £
19—					19—				
Feb 1	Capital	L1	20·00	500·00	Feb 3	A. Newman	L4		5·60
,, 3	D. Cowan	L2		10·10	,, 3	Stationery	L5	1·10	
14	Bank	c	40·00		,, 4	Postage	L6	2·00	
18	Cash Sales	L3		52·00	,, 7	Rent	L7		45·00
					,, 10	Motor Van	L8		120·00
					,, 12	J. Johnson	L9		25·90
					,, 14	Cash	c		40·00
					,, 17	Wages	L10	30·50	
					,, 19	Sundry Ex.	L11	3·10	
					,, 19	Balances	c/d	23·30	325·60
		£	60·00	562·10			£	60·00	562·10
19—									
Feb 20	Balances	b/d	23·30	325·60					

Ledger

Dr Capital Account (Personal A/c of A. Thompson: L1) Cr

							£
				19— Feb 1	Cash & Bank	CB1	520·00

Dr D. Cowan (L2) Cr

							£
				19— Feb 3	Bank	CB1	10·10

Cash Sales (L3)

Dr							Cr
				19—			£
				Feb 18	Bank	CB1	52·00

A. Newman (L4)

Dr							Cr
19—			£				
Feb 3	Bank	CB1	5·60				

Stationery Account (L5)

Dr							Cr
19—			£				
Feb 3	Cash	CB1	1·10				

Postage Account (L6)

Dr							Cr
19—			£				
Feb 4	Cash	CB1	2·00				

Rent Account (L7)

Dr							Cr
19—			£				
Feb 7	Bank	CB1	45·00				

Motor Vans Account (L8)

Dr							Cr
19—			£				
Feb 10	Bank	CB1	120·00				

J. Johnson (L9)

Dr							Cr
19—			£				
Feb 12	Bank	CB1	25·90				

Wages Account (L10)

Dr							Cr
19—			£				
Feb 17	Cash	CB1	30·50				

Sundry Expenses Account (L11)

Dr							Cr
19—			£				
Feb 19	Cash	CB1	3·10				

In practice the personal accounts of customers are usually kept in a separate Ledger called the 'Sales' or 'Sold' Ledger and the personal accounts of suppliers in the 'Bought' or 'Purchases' Ledger.

By taking out a Trial Balance we can prove the arithmetical accuracy of our posting.

Trial Balance—19th February, 19—

	Debit Balances	*Credit Balances*
	£	£
Capital		520·00
D. Cowan		10·10
Cash Sales		52·00
A. Newman	5·60	
Stationery	1·10	
Postage	2·00	
Rent	45·00	
Motor Vans	120·00	
J. Johnson	25·90	
Wages	30·50	
Sundry Expenses	3·1C	
Cash	23·30	
Bank	325·60	
	582·10	582·10

Value Added Tax

Value Added Tax (V.A.T.), introduced into Great Britain in 1973, is a tax charged (with certain exceptions) every time goods move from one business to another and every time a service is performed for a fee. The rate of tax can, of course, be varied by the Government, but for the purposes of illustration it is assumed in this book to be chargeable at a uniform rate of 10%. A trader must add 10% to the net invoice price of all chargeable goods or services sold (his *outputs*) and later remit this tax to the Customs and Excise. He can, however, reduce his tax liability by offsetting against these amounts the V.A.T. he himself has been charged by his suppliers on goods and services bought (his *inputs*). In some cases his taxable inputs will exceed his taxable outputs, and then he can claim a refund.

Under the VAT system, a taxable person must, for each tax period, summarize his records of output tax (including tax on any goods applied to personal use), tax due but not paid on imported or warehoused goods, deductible input tax, and tax adjustments affecting the amount due or repayable. These summaries must be entered in a special book, or ledger, to be known as the VAT Account, showing the tax due to the Customs & Excise, the tax deductible and the net amount for payment or repayment.

Some firms may choose to keep a day book to record cash sales, but work can be saved by simply packeting copies of each day's cash sale dockets or invoices and, from a pre-list, recording in a VAT column in the Cash Book the total VAT on the day's sales.

Cash Book

	Goods	VAT Rate	VAT	Cash	Bank	
19—			£		£	
Feb 3	Cash Sales £900·00	10%	90·00		990·00	

In posting this entry, £900 would be credited to the Sales Account and £90 to the credit of the VAT Account. The corresponding debit entry is the £990 in the bank column. The goods and VAT columns are memoranda columns only. A similar method might be employed to record those cash purchases upon which VAT has been paid and which is deductible from tax due. As it is necessary to distinguish between goods bought for re-sale and services (general business overheads including stationery, perhaps taxable at different rates), a further column for services is advisable.

Cash Book

			Goods	Services	VAT Rate	VAT	Cash	Bank
	19—		£			£		£
	Apr 2	Purchases	70·00		10%	7·00		77·00

ILLUSTRATIVE EXERCISE 6.4

D. Williams started business on 1st March, 19— with £500·00 in the bank and £50·00 **cash.** Record this and the following transactions in a two-column Cash Book with memoranda columns to record VAT.

				£
19—				
Mar	1	Paid to J. Gibson, cheque		42·00
,,	3	Cash sales retained in office ...	£50 + VAT £5	55·00
,,	4	Paid into bank		30·00
,,	7	Paid wages, cash		20·50
,,	8	Received from R. Robinson, cheque (paid into bank)...		40·15
,,	10	Paid rent by cheque		55·00
,,	15	Paid salaries by cheque		75·50
,,	15	Paid sundry expenses, cash ...	£2 + VAT 20p	2·20
,,	15	Paid into bank		30·00
,,	23	Cash sales paid into bank ...	£80 + VAT £8	88·00
,,	23	Paid W. Gayle, cheque		15·25
,,	29	Paid carriage, cash	£3 + VAT 30p	3·30
,,	31	Drew cheque for office cash		20·00

Post to the Ledger and take out a Trial Balance.

ILLUSTRATIVE EXERCISE

Possible ruling of a two column Cash Book to provide for V.A.T. memoranda colums.

Cash Book

Dr Cr

Date	Particulars	Goods	Services	VAT Rate	VAT	Fol.	Cash	Bank	Date	Particulars	Goods	Services	VAT Rate	VAT	Fol.	Cash	Bank
19—									19—								
Mar 1	Capital (D. Williams)					L1	£50·00	£500·00	Mar 1	J. Gibson					L5		£42·00
,, 3	Sales	50·00		10%	5·00	✓	55·00		,, 4	Bank					C	30·00	
,, 4	Cash					C		30·00	,, 7	Wages					L10	20·50	
,, 8	R. Robinson					L4		40·15	,, 10	Rent					L11		55·00
,, 15	Cash					C		30·00	,, 15	Salaries					L12		75·50
,, 23	Sales	80·00		10%	8·00	✓		88·00	,, 15	Sundry Expenses	2·00		10%	0·20	L13	2·20	
,, 31	Bank					C	20·00		,, 15	Bank					C	30·00	
									,, 23	W. Gayle					L20		15·25
									,, 29	Carriage		3·00	10%	0·30	L14	3·30	
									,, 31	Cash					C		20·00
									,, 31	Balances					c/d	39·00	480·40
	£	130·00			13·00		125·00	688·15		£				0·50		125·00	688·15
Apr 1	Balances	L2			L3	b/d	39·00	480·40						L3			

Notes: (1) Sales Account and VAT account (both sides) can be posted in total but sundry expenses and carriage (on the credit side of the Cash Book) must be posted separately.

(2) 'C' (for 'Contra') in Folio column indicates that the corresponding double entry is on the opposite side of the same account.

Capital Account (L1)

				19—			£
				Mar 1	Cash and Bank	CB1	550·00

Sales Account (L2)

				19—			£
				Mar 31	Sundries	CB1	130·00

VAT Account (L3)

19—	*Tax Deductible*		£	19—	*Tax Due*		£
Mar 31	Sundries		0·50	Mar 31	Sundries	CB1	13·00
,, 31	Balance	c/d	12·50				
			£13·00				£13·00
				Apr 1	Balance	b/d	12·50

R. Robinson (L4)

				19—			£
				Mar 8	Bank	CB	[illegible]0·15

J. Gibson (L5)

19—			£				
Mar 1	Bank	CB	42·00				

W. Gayle (L20)

19—			£				
Mar 23	Bank	CB	15·25				

Wages Account (L10)

19—			£				
Mar 7	Cash	CB	20·50				

Rent Account (L11)

19—			£				
Mar 10	Bank	CB	55·00				

Salaries Account (L12)

19—			£				
Mar 15	Bank	CB	75·50				

Sundry Expenses (L13)

19— Mar 15	Cash	CB	£ 2·00				

Carriage Outwards (L14)

19— Mar 29	Cash	CB	£ 3·00				

Trial Balance

	Dr £	Cr £
Capital		550·00
Sales		130·00
VAT		12·50
R. Robinson		40·15
J. Gibson	42·00	
W. Gayle	15·25	
Wages	20·50	
Rent	55·00	
Salaries	75·50	
Sundry Expenses	2·00	
Carriage outwards	3·00	
Cash	39·00	
Bank	480·40	
	£732·65	£732·65

In these exercises, VAT can be either included or ignored. Answers are given for both alternatives.

EXERCISE 6.6

Enter the following transactions in the appropriate columns of the Cash Book and post to suitable Ledger accounts. Extract a Trial Balance. (Cheques received are retained in the office except where otherwise stated.)

19—				£
Apr	1	Cash at bank		480·50
		Cash in hand		28·05
		Received cheque from J. Smith		92·10
,,	2	Cash purchases	£25 + VAT 2·50	27·50
		Cashed cheque for office cash		20·00
		Cash sales	£35 + VAT 3·50	38·50
,,	3	Paid into bank		120·00
		Received cheque from D. Dunn		28·20
		Sent cheque to J. Green		57·30
		Cash sales	£41 + VAT 4·10	45·10
,,	4	Paid into bank		62·50
		Bought stamps, cash		3·00
		Received cheque from A. Allen		42·60
,,	5	Gave cheque for typewriter (Office Furniture)	£50 + VAT £5	55·00
		Cash sales paid straight into bank	£68 + VAT £6·80	74·80
		Sent cheque to D. Dunn		115·30
,,		Received cheque from W. White and paid into bank		54·85

19—				£
Apr	6	Drew from bank for office cash		30·00
		Paid wages in cash		25·00
		Paid carriage in cash	£1·20 + VAT 12p	1·32
		Cash sales	£13 + VAT 1·30	14·30

Balance the accounts, bring down the balances and enter the following transactions.

19—				£
Apr	8	Received cheque from J. Roberts		39·60
		Paid into bank		40·00
		Paid cash for 2 office chairs	£5 + VAT 50p	5·50
,,	9	Sent cheque to J. Green		12·70
		Cash purchases paid by cheque	£34 + VAT 3·40	37·40
		Received cheque from J. Smith		27·15
		Cash sales	£38 + VAT 3·80	41·80
		Paid into bank		60·00
		Sent cheque to J. Green		42·10
,,	10	Received cheque from A. Allen		28·75
		Received cheque from W. White		35·15
		Both cheques paid into bank		
,,	11	Paid carriage in cash	£2·00 + VAT 20p	2·20
		Paid rates by cheque		79·30
		Received money order from K. Black		12·15
,,	12	Paid telephone account by cheque	£11 + VAT 1·10	12·10
		Cash sales	£73 + VAT 7·30	80·30
		Paid into bank		80·00
		Paid D. Dunn by cheque		137·15
,,	13	Drew cheque for office cash		30·00
		Paid wages in cash		26·15
		Paid cleaner in cash	£4 + VAT 40p	4·40

Extract a Trial Balance.

EXERCISE 6.7

19—				£
Jan	1	T. Robbins began business in fancy goods with	cash in hand	20·00
			cash at bank	600·00
,,	2	Bought goods and paid by cheque	£325 + VAT 32·50	357·50
		Sold goods for cash and paid into bank	£53 + VAT 5·30	58·30
,,	6	Cashed cheque		20·00
		Paid wages in cash		15·00
,,	11	Paid Farmer & Co. by cheque		100·00
		Paid cash for stationery	£3 + VAT 30p	3·30
,,	15	Cash sales, money retained in office	£65 + VAT 6·50	71·50
,,	21	Paid rent by cheque		25·00
,,	25	Paid L. Bedford, cheque		32·00
,,	26	Paid sundry expenses in cash	£7 + VAT 70p	7·70
,,	27	Paid cash for stationery	£4 + VAT 40p	4·40
,,	29	Paid wages in cash		10·00
,,	30	Received cheque from M. Rutland and retained in office		14·00

Enter these transactions in the appropriate columns of a two-column Cash Book, post to the Ledger and extract a Trial Balance.

7

Credit Buying-Purchases-Purchases Returns

WHENEVER a trader buys goods for resale, whether he pays immediately or buys on credit, it is the Purchases Account which is always debited. If the transaction is a cash one, he will credit his cash account; if he buys on credit, he will credit his supplier's account. In this chapter we are concerned solely with credit buying. The supplier's 'credit terms', that is, the time allowed by the seller between the dispatch of the goods and his customer's liability to pay for them, will vary according to the customs of the particular trade. One month is fairly common.

A shopkeeper will always be tempted to buy as much stock as possible on credit, for this is a cheap way of securing more capital. Provided that the shopkeeper remains sensitive of his customers' wants, and does not allow the attractiveness of the credit terms offered by different merchants to distort his judgement of what to buy, the shopkeeper will be able to make larger profits than would be possible if he restricted his buying of stocks to cash transactions only.

No trader, however, is willing to supply goods on credit until he is satisfied that the buyer is able to pay for them. The burden of proving 'credit trustworthiness' is upon the buyer, and he can do this most effectively by referring the seller to other traders with whom he, the buyer, has already had satisfactory credit dealings. Trade references, as these are called, are usually more acceptable than bank or personal references.

If the replies to the seller's enquiries are satisfactory, he will open an account for the shopkeeper, probably fixing a credit limit in the first instance, and arrange for any orders that have been given to be dispatched.

Let us follow a credit transaction through, step by step, from the time the order is placed until we finally record the details in our books of account.

It should be noted that suppliers' accounts are usually kept in a separate Purchases or Bought Ledger.

(*1*) *Placing the order*

Most firms use special order forms which are numbered serially and are under the control of persons authorized to buy stock on behalf of the business. In large undertakings there would probably be a buying department through which all such orders would pass. For the purpose of this example we shall assume that we are carrying on business as furniture retailers under the name of Thomas Hardy & Co. (remember that a sole trader who trades under a name which is not his true surname must register the business in accordance with the Business Names Registration Act, 1916).

ORDER **No. 62**

THOMAS HARDY & CO.
HIGH ST, OXBRIDGE

Date: 6th February 19–

To: The Benedict Supply Co. Ltd,
14 Middlesex Road, London, S.W.7

Please supply the following goods:

Catalogue No.	Description	Price
14D	6 Bookcases	£6.50 each
10C	4 Dining Room Chairs	£2.00 each

Delivery: As soon as possible
Per: British Railways

(Signed)
John James
Buyer

(2) *Action by supplier on receipt of the order*

If the goods are in stock, the supplier will arrange for their dispatch and will at the same time make out multiple copies of the invoice. One copy will go to the warehouse as authority for the issue of the goods; one may serve as a dispatch docket; another an advice note for inclusion in the package or crate; one copy will certainly go to the supplier's own accounts department so that our account is properly charged; and one copy will be the invoice, which is sent to us either with the goods or separately through the post.

INVOICE

Invoice No. 1264
Date 8 February 19--

The Benedict Supply Co., Ltd.,
14 Middlesex Road,
London, S.W.7

V.A.T. Registration No. 921 6421 64

To: Thomas Hardy & Co., High St., Oxbridge.

Consignee: Thomas Hardy & Co. Oxbridge

Delivery Note No. 1362

Terms: Strictly net one month

Order No.	Quantity	Goods	Cost £	V.A.T. rate	V.A.T. amount
62	6	Bookcases at £6.50	39.00	10%	3.90
	4	Dining Room chairs at £2 each	8.00	10%	0.80
		Total goods	47.00	10%	£4.70
		V.A.T.	4.70		
			£51.70		

Goods rec'd by	L. Scott
Qnty checked by	T. Hardy
Prices checked by	T. Hardy
Extensions checked by	L. Potts
Invoice pass by	J. James

Per: British Railways
Carriage: Paid

E. & O.E.

(3) *Action by us on receipt of the invoice*

It is the practice in many firms to stamp all incoming invoices with a rubber stamp; some firms attach a slip of paper called an 'invoice apron', to the invoice. As you will see from the specimen, the object of this stamp or apron is to ensure that no invoice is passed for payment until it has been certified by the Buyer and other persons concerned that the goods have been received and that the invoice is correct. Not until this has been done will the accounts department arrange for the transaction to be recorded in the books of account.

In the case of cash purchases, you will recall that it is possible to enter the transactions in the Cash Book directly, because the Cash Book is a book of prime entry as well as being part of the ledger.

Value Added Tax which is paid on purchases (inputs) can be set against VAT charged on sales (outputs) and it is important therefore that invoices for all purchases, whether for cash or on credit, are retained and properly filed. An invoice provides *prima facie* evidence that the VAT stated thereon has been paid. Note that where trade or cash discounts are allowed, VAT is calculated on the discounted figure. Invoices are required by law to be retained for a minimum period of three years.

When goods are bought on credit, we cannot make any entry in the Cash Book, for no money is immediately involved; the account which has given value is the account of the supplier, not the Cash Account, and his account must be credited accordingly. We do not do this directly, for it is a rule in double entry book-keeping that no entries are made direct to the Ledger. When stock-in-trade is bought on credit, a record is first made of each transaction in the Purchases or Bought Day Book, a subsidiary book used exclusively for assembling all credit transactions

PURCHASES DAY BOOK OR PURCHASES BOOK

Date	Invoice No.	Particulars	Ledger fol.	Details	Amount	VAT rate	VAT amount	Total
19—				£	£		£	£
Feb 8	1	Benedict Supply Co Ltd						
		6 bookcases at £6·50		39·00				
		4 dining chairs at £2 each		8·00	47·00	10%	4·70	51·70
			L1					
Feb 15	2	C. Clarke & Sons, Luton						
		12 tables—occasional at £10 each		120·00				
		1 writing table		40·00				
				160·00				
		Less 25% Trade Disc't		40·00	120·00	10%	12·00	132·00
	(Terms	strictly net one month)	L2					
			L11		£167·00		£16·70	£183·70
							L14	

of this kind preparatory to posting to the Ledger. Entries in this book are made from the invoices received from our suppliers. A simple Purchases Day Book might be as shown on p. 64.

It is usual to number incoming invoices and file them numerically for easy reference. There is little point in showing details of the invoices in the Day Book; if such information is required, it is easily obtainable from the invoices themselves and the practice nowadays is to omit these details, viz.

PURCHASES DAY BOOK

Date	Invoice No.	Particulars	Ledger Folio	Amount	VAT rate	VAT amount	Total
19—				£		£	£
Feb 8	1	The Benedict Supply Co. Ltd	L1	47·00	10%	4·70	51·70
Feb 15	2	C. Clarke & Sons—Luton	L2	120·00	10%	12·00	132·00
			L11	£167·00		£16·70	£183·70
						L14	

DAY BOOKS FOR ALTERNATE DAYS

It is sometimes advisable to keep separate Day Books for alternate days so that the ledger clerk can get on with posting the Ledger without interruption from persons wishing to make entries in the Purchases Day Books.

POSTING THE PURCHASES DAY BOOK

The personal accounts of the respective suppliers are credited with the net amounts of the invoices, including VAT, as shown in the Purchases Day Book, and at intervals the Purchases Day Book is totalled and the total cost of goods posted to the debit of the Purchases Account and the total of the VAT column to the debit of the VAT Account, thus completing the double entries. Notice how doing it this way saves work. Instead of debiting the Purchases Account and the VAT Account each time, these accounts are debited in total at the end of the week or month.

BOUGHT OR PURCHASES LEDGER

Dr — The Benedict Supply Company Ltd (L1) — Cr

				19—			£
				Feb 8	Purchases	PDB	47·00
				,,	VAT	,,	4·70

Dr — C. Clarke & Sons—Luton (L2) — Cr

				19—			£
				Feb 15	Purchases	PDB	120·00
				,,	VAT	,,	12·00

IMPERSONAL LEDGER

Dr — Purchases Account (L11) — Cr

19—			£				
Feb 28	Sundries	PDB	167·00				

Dr — VAT Account (L14) — Cr

19—	*Tax Deductible*		£		*Tax Due*		
Feb 28	Sundries	PDB	16·70				

Notes:

(1) When we post the total of the Purchases Day Book, we cannot refer to all the personal accounts in which the corresponding entries appear and so we use the word 'sundries'.

(2) The Purchases Day Book is not part of the Ledger, and therefore the double entry is not made until we have both debited and credited the appropriate accounts in the Ledger. Compare with the Cash Book, where an entry therein comprises one half of the double entry and all that is necessary is either to credit or to debit the relevant account in the Ledger.

SAVING PAPER WORK

An efficient firm will always be looking for new ways of reducing the volume of its paper work, and we shall now consider two methods whereby the work of recording credit purchases can be reduced.

(1) Where a firm pays its suppliers regularly each month

In this case both the Purchases Day Book and the personal bought Ledger accounts can be dispensed with. As the invoices are received, they are checked and filed alphabetically. When a supplier's statement is received, the invoices are removed from the file and, if in order, paid. These credit purchases are thereafter dealt with in the same way as cash purchases. The Bank Account is credited and the Purchases Account debited. If, at the end of the financial year, there are any unpaid invoices on the file, they must be totalled and the figure included in the Balance Sheet.

The VAT element must be shown separately in the Cash Book so that this amount can be debited to the VAT Account.

(2) Dispensing with the Purchases Day Book

Under this system, which is applicable to all businesses, whatever their size or payments policy, the invoices themselves are used as the posting media, having first been pre-listed (totalled on an adding machine). The totals are recorded in registers or departmental analyses books and posted to the debit of the Purchases Account and the VAT Account.

PAYING SUPPLIERS

Some time during the month following the dispatch of the order or orders, the supplier will send his customer a statement of account. This is simply a summary of the invoices for goods sent the previous month. After the statement has been checked with the Ledger, a cheque is made out and forwarded with the statement to the supplier.

STATEMENT

In A/C with:
THOMAS HARDY & Co.
HIGH STREET,
OXBRIDGE

A/C No. 2174
Date 1ST MARCH 19—

The Benedict Supply Co. Ltd.
14 Middlesex Road
London S.W.7
VAT Registration No. 921 6421 64

Date	O/No.	Inclusive of Value Added Tax	Dr	Cr	Balance
19—		BALANCE B/F			0·00
Feb 8	62	GOODS	51.70		51·70 DR

Terms: Strictly net, one month

The last figure in this column is the amount due

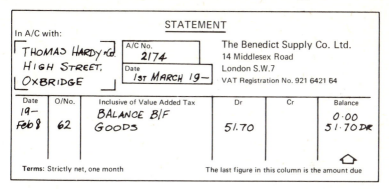

The Cash Book will, in due course, be written up from the cheque book counterfoils and the supplier's account debited with the amount of the payment, thereby clearing the account. Under the Cheque Act, 1957, a creditor need not give a receipt in respect of a payment by cheque unless expressly asked to supply one.

Dr *Cash Book* Cr

				19—			£
				Apr 1	Benedict Supply Co. Ltd	L1	51·70

PURCHASES LEDGER

Dr The Benedict Supply Co. Ltd (L1) Cr

19—			£	19—			£
Apr 1	Bank	CB	51·70	Feb 8	Purchases	PDB	47·00
				,, 8	VAT		4·70
			£51·70				£51·70

Purchases Returns or Returns Outwards

For various reasons goods may have to be returned to the seller, e.g. the merchandise may not correspond with the sample, more articles may be received than were ordered, or some goods become damaged in transit. The usual procedure in such cases is for the buyer to make out a debit note which, in addition to providing the necessary authority for the goods to leave the building, also ensures that an adjustment is made in the seller's personal account in the Bought Ledger. When the sellers credit note is received, details are entered in the Purchases Returns (or Returns Outwards) Book and from there posted to the Ledger. The Returns Outwards Book is kept in exactly the same way as the Purchases Day Book but when the ledger clerk comes to post it, he will debit the seller's personal account, for his account will now be receiving value and he will credit the Goods Account (called for this purpose the Returns Outwards Account, so that a separate record can be kept of goods returned to suppliers), for this account will be giving value.

DISPENSING WITH THE RETURNS OUTWARDS BOOK

What was said on page 66 (2) about dispensing with the Purchases Day Book applies equally to the Returns Outwards Book. The credit notes received from suppliers are then assembled, pre-listed and used as the posting media. In this way the copying of the details from the credit notes into a Returns Outwards Book is avoided.

ILLUSTRATIVE EXERCISE 7.1

M. Faregood, in business as a jeweller, received the following invoices, in respect of stock-in-trade purchased during March, 19—. (VAT 10%)

March 3	Sheffield Cutlery Co. Ltd 2 doz electro-plated spoons at £1·80 doz 1 canteen of cutlery at £7·00 6 doz fish knives at £2·00 doz	20% Trade Discount
March 5	Thomas Fairfield & Co. 4 doz wrist watches at £10·00 each	20% Trade Discount
March 12	P. C. Marchmont & Sons 2 pearl necklaces at £110·00 each 20% Trade Discount	
March 17	F. Douglas & Co. Ltd 1 tea set at £9·50	20% Trade Discount

Purchases Day Book

19—	Inv. No.			£	£	VAT rate	VAT £	Total £
Mar 3	27	Sheffield Cutlery Co. Ltd 2 dox electro-plated spoons at £1·80 doz 1 canteen cutlery at £7·00 6 doz fish knives at £2·00 doz		3·60 7·00 12·00				
				22·60				
		Less 20% Trade Discount	L1	4·52	18·08	10%	1·81	19·89
Mar 5	28	Thomas Fairfield & Co. 4 doz wrist watches at £10·00 each		480·00				
		Less 20% Trade Discount	L2	96·00	384·00	10%	38·40	422·40
Mar 12	29	P. C. Marchmont & Sons 2 pearl necklaces at £110·00 each		220·00				
		Less 20% Trade Discount	L3	44·00	176·00	10%	17·60	193·60
Mar 17	30	F. Douglas & Co. Ltd. 1 tea set at £9·50		9·50				
		Less 20% Trade Discount	L4	1·90	7·60	10%	0·76	8·36
			L10		£585·68		58·57	644·25

Returns Outwards Book

19—	C/N No.			£	£		£	£
Mar 18	36	Sheffield Cutlery Co. Ltd 1 canteen cutlery at £7·00 *Less* 20% Trade Discount Not in accordance with order	L1	7·00 1·40	5·60	10%	0·56	6·16
Mar 20	37	Thomas Fairfield & Co. 1 wrist watch at £10·00 *Less* 20% Trade Discount Unsatisfactory	L2	10·00 2·00	8·00	10%	0·80	8·80
			L11		£13·60		1·36	14·96

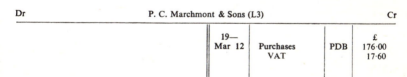

Bought Ledger

Dr **Sheffield Cutlery Co. Ltd (L1)** Cr

19—			£	19—			£
Mar 18	Returns	ROB	6·16	Mar 3	Purchases	PDB	18·08
,, 31	Balance	c/d	13·73		VAT		1·81
		£	19·89			£	19·89
				19— Apr 1	Balance	b/d	13·73

Dr **Thomas Fairfield & Co. (L2)** Cr

19—			£	19—			£
Mar 20	Returns	ROB	8·80	Mar 5	Purchases	PDB	384·00
31	Balance	c/d	413·60		VAT		38·40
		£	422 40			£	422·40
				19— Apr 1	Balance	b/d	413·60

Dr **P. C. Marchmont & Sons (L3)** Cr

				19—			£
				Mar 12	Purchases	PDB	176·00
					VAT		17·60

Dr **F. Douglas & Co. Ltd (L4)** Cr

				19—			£
				Mar 17	Purchases	PDB	7·60
					VAT		0·76

Nominal Ledger

Dr **Purchases Account (L10)** Cr

19—			£				
Mar 31	Sundries	PDB	585·68				

Dr **Returns Outwards Account (L11)** Cr

				19—			£
				Mar 31	Sundries	ROB	13·60

Dr **VAT Account** Cr

19—			£	19—			£
Mar 31	Sundries	PDB	58·57	Mar 31	Sundries	ROB	1·36
				Mar 31	Balance	C/d	57·21
		£	58·57			£	58·57
Apr 1	Balance b/d		57·21				

Trial Balance—31st March 19—

	Debit Balances	*Credit Balances*
	£	£
Sheffield Cutlery Co. Ltd		13·73
Thomas Fairfield & Co.		413·60
P. C. Marchmont & Sons		193·60
F. Douglas & Co Ltd		8·36
Returns Outwards Account		13·60
Purchases Account	585·68	
VAT Account	57·21	
	£642·89	£642·89

POINTS TO NOTE CAREFULLY

(1) Trade discount is shown, if at all, in the Purchases Day Book, never in a Ledger account.

(2) Only the net figure of each invoice is posted to the credit of the supplier's account.

(3) Goods returned to a supplier must be debited at the price originally charged. If an invoice was subject to a trade discount, this must be deducted from the catalogue price of items returned and the net figure debited to the supplier's personal account.

EXERCISE 7.1

The Muscovy Fur Co. keeps a simple detailed Purchases Day Book. Write up the Purchases Day Book of this company and post to the Ledger. (VAT 10%)

19—
Feb 1 Bought of The Riga Fur Trading Co. Ltd
4 dyed musquash coats @ £48·00 each
6 fox muffs @ £12·00 each
,, 6 Bought of Elliott & Simmons Ltd
10 stoles @ £20·00 each
Trade Discount 25%
,, 7 Bought of J. Robinson & Co. Ltd
3 silver grey squirrel muffs @ £9·00 each
2 fur-lined travelling rugs @ £25·00 each
,, 14 Bought of The Kaliningrad Trading Co. Ltd
1 sable stole @ £60·00
1 sable muff @ £8·00
Trade Discount 20%

,,	17	Bought of Henry Berlotski & Co. Ltd 10 bear muffs @ £9·00 each 3 fox muffs @ £11·00 each
,,	24	Bought of Jules Verne & Co. Ltd 15 squirrel ties @ £6·00 each
,,	27	Thomas & Hardy & Co. Ltd sold to The Muscovy Fur Co. 2 astrakhan muffs @ £6·00 each 1 skunk stole @ £10·00 1 special stole @ £75·00
,,	28	Purchased from J. Wilson & Co. 12 fur-lined men's overcoats @ £30·00 each 6 fur-lined jackets @ £12·00 each Trade Discount 25%

EXERCISE 7.2

J. Flower is in business as a wholesale confectioner. The following invoices, in respect of stock for resale, were received by him during the month of May, 19—.

				£
May	16	Holborn Confectionery Co. ...	£150 + VAT £15	165·00
,,	21	Lewisham Candy Stores Ltd	£194 + VAT £19·40	213·40
,,	22	The Sweeter Sweetmeat Co. Ltd	£27 + VAT £2·70	29·70
,,	27	J. Lloyd & Co. Ltd ...	£45 + VAT £4·50	49·50

(1) Enter in the appropriate book of original entry.
(2) Post to the Ledger.

EXERCISE 7.3

On 30th June, 19— the account of T. Atkins, in the Ledger of L. Simpkins, was as follows.

Dr T. Atkins Cr

19—			£	19—			£
June 5	Bank	CB	1,000·00	June 1	Balance	b/d	1,260·00
,, 12	Returns	ROB	7·50	,, 6	Purchases	PDB	500·00
,, 12	VAT	ROB	0·75	,, 6	VAT	PDB	50·00
				,, 29	Purchases	PDB	465·00
				, 29	VAT	PDB	46·50

(1) Balance this account and bring down the new balance for 1st July, 19—.
(2) Who owes to whom, and how much?
(3) In which Ledger accounts will the corresponding entries for 12th June and 29th June appear?

EXERCISE 7.4

The following credit notes were received by J. Johnson during the month of July, 19—. Enter these in Johnson's subsidiary book and post to the Ledger.

19—					£
July	7	C/N No. 12	L. Sullivan & Co.	£10·00 + VAT £1·00	11·00
,,	15	C/N No. 15	Thomas Edison & Co. Ltd	£5·20 + VAT 52p	£5·72
,,	23	C/N No. 23	T. Swanson	£12·80 + VAT £1·28	14·08

If J. Johnson decided to dispense with a Returns Outwards Book how might he process these credit notes to ensure that each supplier's account is properly debited and the Returns Outwards Account credited with the corresponding total sum.

8

Credit Selling — Sales Returns

WHEN goods are sold for cash, the Cash Account is debited with the receipt of the money and the Sales Account is credited (see page 39). You can, if it helps, look upon the Sales Account as a goods account which has yielded a benefit and is therefore credited, and the Cash Account as having received the benefit and so debited:

Cash Account

Sales	£1,000		

Sales Account

		Cash	£1,000

When goods are sold on credit, it is still the Sales Account which has yielded the benefit and so is credited, but this time it is the customer who has received the benefit and whose account is therefore debited:

Customer (debtor)

Sales	£400		

Sales Account

		Customer	£400

We are concerned in this chapter solely with the sale of goods on credit. The seller is now required by law to collect Value Added Tax on all sales which are subject to this tax. Some goods are exempt from the tax and the shopkeeper cannot therefore charge VAT although of course VAT may have been charged at different stages of their manufacture. Other goods are zero-rated, which means that they are subject to tax but the rate at the moment is zero.

Whereas VAT chargeable on inputs of zero rated supplies can be reclaimed, exempt supplies are outside VAT and input tax cannot be reclaimed in respect of them. All exports are zero rated.

In the illustrative exercises which follow, we have assumed that all sales are subject to the standard rate of 10%. The retailer will have paid VAT to the manufacturer or wholesaler when he bought the goods and can deduct this sum from the 10% he must collect from his own customers. The VAT Account will show, on the debit side, the tax he has paid to his suppliers and which is deductible from the VAT he must charge his own customers and which will appear on the credit side of the account.

GRANTING CREDIT

THE majority of traders who grant credit facilities to their customers do so either because (1) it is the usual way of doing business in their particular trade, or (2) it would place them at a serious competitive disadvantage if they did not.

Where a choice between selling for cash or giving credit exists, as is the case in most retailing establishments, the trader has to weigh carefully the advantages and disadvantages of credit trading. The most obvious advantage is that the trader will attract more customers and sell more goods if he offers credit facilities. But this is a service which has many drawbacks. A lot of capital will become tied up in book debts; additional office equipment will have to be installed; more clerks employed; more money spent on postage and stationery; and more factory or showroom space given up to non-profit earning activities. The costs may be considerable. Furthermore, there is always the danger that some debts will be irrecoverable. A trader can insure against making bad debts but it is often cheaper for him to set up his own credit control department. The main functions of such a department are the making of credit enquiries, the sanctioning of new orders, and the collection of overdue accounts.

TRADE PROTECTION AGENCIES

Many specialist firms exist to help traders with their credit control problems. Some, like the Mutual Communication Society for the Protection of Trade, are owned by members of a particular trade in a particular area. Other credit protection associations are independent and serve all industries. The M.C.S., by which name the Mutual Communication Society for the Protection of Trade is better known, is owned chiefly by the departmental stores of London. The Society maintains a register of the names of persons about whom members have enquired and it is possible, therefore, for a store to obtain information about a customer even when that customer is unable, or unwilling, to supply normal trade references. The success of the Society's activities depends largely upon the co-operation it receives from its members, who undertake to let it know immediately when customers' cheques are dishonoured, when communications are received from husbands disclaiming liability for their wives' debts, and of cases where further credit is not advised; this information is circulated quickly to all members. The Society will also provide its members with special reports on customers, submitted by its agents in the area in which the customer lives, when ordinary enquiries prove unfruitful. Debt collection is included amongst the many services provided by the Society for its members.

EQUIPPING A CREDIT CONTROL DEPARTMENT

In most businesses it is necessary to provide a system whereby orders received from customers can be quickly approved for credit purposes. Often a customer will want to take the goods away with him, and a card index or similar system for quick reference is essential. In addition, a well-equipped credit control department will have some or all of the following reference books: telephone directories, street directories, commercial directories, *Who's Who*, Stock Exchange Year Books, etc. If the customer is a joint stock company, information about its capital structure, the existence of any outstanding loans, the names of the persons responsible for its management, and other details can be obtained from an inspection of the company's file at the offices of the Registrar of Joint Stock Companies in City Road, London (search fee 5p). If the sale is likely to give rise to an unusual type of contract, it might be advisable to inspect the customer's file to ascertain whether the company has the necessary powers to make this particular kind of contract; a company can do only those things (1) which it is empowered to do by the objects clause of its Memorandum of Association, and (2) incidental to its main purposes.

A Credit Sale Transaction

In the previous chapter we followed through a credit purchase transaction from the time the order was placed to the final settlement of the supplier's account. We shall now do the same with a credit sale, but without reproducing the documents. For our example we shall take a small department store offering its customers credit facilities. The orders in most cases will be given verbally, and the shop assistant will make out a sales docket or invoice while the customer is present in the shop. When a customer wishes to take goods away with him, the detachable copies of the bill—one copy usually remains fixed in the assistant's counter book—are sent to the accounts department for sanction by the credit control department. If the customer's account is in order, the customer's copy is returned to the sales assistant, marked in some way to show that the sale has been approved, and this is then handed over to the customer with the goods. The copy which is retained in the accounts department is used to write up the Sales Day Book, or used as the posting medium.

Whereas the Purchases Day Book is written up from suppliers' invoices, which will vary in size, shape and format, the Sales Day Book is written up from copies of the firm's own invoices, which will be of uniform size and vary only as to the details written on them. The sales invoices are consequently much easier to file.

The Sales Day Book is written up in exactly the same way as the Purchases Day Book. The posting of the Sales Day Book, however, is the very opposite of the Purchases Day Book. The personal accounts of the customers are debited with the value of the goods received and the Goods Account (Sales Account) is credited with the total value given. Notice that the Purchases Account shows goods at cost price and the Sales Account goods at selling price.

ILLUSTRATIVE EXERCISE

Sales assistants employed by Ransford, Moore & Co., a small department store, made out the following account bills during the month of June, 19—. Enter these in the Sales Day Book of Ransford, Moore & Co. and post to the Ledger.

19—				Total £
June	1	Mrs B. Jarvis	£25·00 + VAT £2·50	27·50
,,	4	Mrs Wright-Bate	£10·00 + VAT £1·00	11·00
,,	8	Dr E. Potter	£27·00 + VAT £2·70	29·70
,,	12	K. Lack	£106·00 + VAT £10·60	116·60
,,	15	Mrs G. Gilbert	£40·00 + VAT £4·00	44·00
,,	16	T. Haswell	£19·00 + VAT £1·90	20·90
,,	23	Mrs Farmer	£3·00 + VAT 0·30	3·30
,,	26	Miss R. Foster	£14·00 + VAT £1·40	15·40

Sales Day Book or Sales Book

19—	Inv. No.			£	VAT £	Total £
June 1	1	Mrs B. Jarvis	L1	25·00	2·50	27·50
,, 4	2	Mrs Wright-Bate	L2	10·00	1·00	11·00
,, 8	3	Dr E. Potter	L3	27·00	2·70	29·70
,, 12	4	K. Lack	L4	106·00	10·60	116·60
,, 15	5	Mrs G. Gilbert	L5	40·00	4·00	44·00
,, 16	6	T. Haswell	L6	19·00	1·90	20·90
,, 23	7	Mrs Farmer	L7	3·00	0·30	3·30
,, 26	8	Miss R. Foster	L8	14·00	1·40	15·40
			L17	£244·00	£ 24·40	£268·40

Sales Ledger

Dr — Mrs B. Jarvis (L1) — Cr

19—			£	
June 1	Sales	SDB	27·50	

Dr — Mrs Wright-Bate (L2) — Cr

19—			£	
June 4	Sales	SDB	11·00	

Dr — Dr E. Potter (L3) — Cr

19—			£	
June 8	Sales	SDB	29·70	

Dr — K. Lack (L4) — Cr

19—			£	
June 12	Sales	SDB	116·60	

Dr — Mrs G. Gilbert (L5) — Cr

19—			£	
June 15	Sales	SDB	44·00	

Dr — T. Haswell (L6) — Cr

19—			£	
June 16	Sales	SDB	20·90	

Dr — Mrs Farmer (L7) — Cr

19—			£	
June 23	Sales	SDB	3·30	

Dr — Miss R. Foster (L8) — Cr

19—			£	
June 26	Sales	SDB	15·40	

Nominal Ledger

Dr Sales Account (L17) Cr

				19— June 30	Sundries	SDB	£ 244·00

Dr VAT Account Cr

				19— June	Sundries	SDB	£ 24·40

Ransford, Moore & Co. will send out statements of account at the beginning of July. Let us suppose that Dr E. Potter and T. Haswell pay their accounts on 10th July by cheque. The cheques are paid into the bank and the Cash Book written up from the paying-in slips. In due course, when the Cash Book is posted, the personal accounts of Dr E. Potter and T. Haswell will be credited and ruled off as paid, viz.

Dr *Cash Book* (CB1) Cr

19—				£	
July 10	Dr E. Potter	L3		29·70	
„ 10	T. Haswell	L6		20·90	

Sales Ledger

Dr Dr E. Potter (L3) Cr

19— June 8	Sales	SDB	£ 29·70	19— July 10	Bank	CB1	£ 29·70

Dr T. Haswell (L6) Cr

19— June 16	Sales	SDB	£ 20·90	19— July 10	Bank	CB1	£ 20·90

Sales Returns or Returns Inwards Book

This book is written up from copies of credit notes sent to customers who, for various reasons, have returned goods. A credit note may also be used when the seller wishes to reduce the amount originally charged to his customer's account, e.g. when the customer has been overcharged, or when the seller agrees to a reduction of price because the article sold is slightly soiled, etc. The Sales Returns Book is in the same form as the Sales Day Book. The posting involves crediting the appropriate personal account in the Sales Ledger and debiting the Sales Returns Account in the Nominal Ledger.

For instance, supposing Mrs Gilbert, in our previous example, returned faulty goods on 7th July, 19— valued at £4, and Mrs B. Jarvis sent back an unsatisfactory article valued at £3 on 10th July, 19—. The assistants receiving the goods would make out credit notes, sending, in each case, a copy to the customer and one to the accounts department. From the latter the Sales Returns Book or Returns Inwards Book would be written up as follows:

Returns Inwards Book

19—	C/N No.				£	£	£
July 7	7	Mrs G. Gilbert Goods faulty	L5		4·00	·40	4·40
,, 10	8	Mrs B. Jarvis Goods unsatisfactory	L1		3·00	·30	3·30
			L18	£	7·00	·70	7·70
						L20	

and then posted.

Dr — Mrs B. Jarvis (L1) — Cr

19—			£	19—			£
June 1	Sales	SDB	27·50	July 10	Returns	RIB	3·30

Dr — Mrs. G. Gilbert (L5) — Cr

19—			£	19—			£
June 15	Sales	SDB	44·00	July 7	Returns	RIB	4·40

Nominal Ledger

Dr — Returns Inwards Account (L18) — Cr

19—			£				
June 30	Sundries	RIB	7·00				

Dr — VAT Account (L20) — Cr

19—			£				
July 31	Sundries	RIB	0·70				

If trade discount was deducted from the catalogue price in the invoice, trade discount must also be deducted from the catalogue price in the credit note. Failure to do this will mean that the customer is credited with a larger amount than that with which he was originally charged.

We have now explained the uses of four very important books of original entry. A summary is given below to show which accounts are credited and which are debited when these books are posted to the Ledger. You can refer to this summary if in doubt, but it would be better if you were to try to envisage the actual transactions and decide which accounts are receiving value and which giving it.

Day Book	*Entered up from*	*A/cs debited*	*A/cs credited*
Purchases Day Book	Copies of suppliers' invoices	Purchases A/c and VAT A/c in total in Nominal Ledger	Personal A/cs of suppliers in Bought Ledger
Purchases Returns	Copies of suppliers' credit notes	Personal A/cs of suppliers in Bought Ledger	Returns Outwards A/c and VAT A/c in total in Nominal Ledger
Sales Day Book	Copies of own invoices	Personal A/cs of customers in Sales Ledger	Sales Account and VAT A/c in total in Nominal Ledger
Sales Returns	Copies of own credit notes	Sales Returns A/c and VAT A/c in total in Nominal Ledger	Personal A/cs of customers in Sales Ledger

It follows from this that the Purchases Account will always have a debit balance and the Sales Account a credit balance; the Returns Inwards Account will always have a debit balance and the Returns Outwards Account a credit balance. In subsequent exercises you may be given a list of Ledger balances without being told whether these have debit or credit balances, viz.

	£
Purchases	1,260·00
Sales	240·00
Returns Inwards	20·00
Returns Outwards	10·00

Goods returned by our customers could be debited in total to the Sales Account. There is nothing wrong with this, but if we were to do it this way we would have, at the end of the year, the figure for the net sales only; we would not know the total value of goods returned by customers during the year, which is information we might need to have. Similarly with goods returned by us to suppliers, we could credit the Purchases Account but most firms prefer to keep a separate account for goods returned to suppliers. The result is the same, but keeping separate accounts for returns gives more information.

EXERCISE 8.1

The following transactions took place between D.E., a wholesaler, and R.V., a retailer, during January, 19—. (Ignore VAT.)

Jan	1	Balance due to D.E. £100
,,	4	Goods sold to R.V. £180 less $33\frac{1}{3}\%$ trade discount
,,	11	Part of the above goods invoiced at £60 gross were returned by R.V.
,,	20	Goods sold to R.V. £120 less $33\frac{1}{3}\%$ trade discount
,,	27	R.V. sent a cheque to D.E. in settlement of the account due from him

Show the account of R.V. as it should appear in the books of D.E. at 31st January, 19—.

Associated Examining Board, G.C.E. 'O' level, 1958 (modified)

EXERCISE 8.2

How would the following documents be used in compiling accounting records:

(1) invoices received for purchases of stock-in-trade,
(2) credit notes received,
(3) bank paying-in slips,
(4) cheque book counterfoils,
(5) copies of credit notes sent out?

Associated Examining Board, G.C.E. 'O' level, 1962

EXERCISE 8.3

J. Kershaw, a wholesaler, sent out the following invoices to his customers during May, 19—.

				Total £
May	10	J.S.S. Ltd	£450 + VAT £45	495·00
,,	16	S. Sawyer	£120 + VAT £12	132·00
,,	21	Thomas Stone & Co.	£20 + VAT £2	22·00
,,	30	British Metals Ltd	£180 + VAT £18	198·00
,,	31	Excel Trading Co	£40 + VAT £4	44·00

Enter these in the appropriate subsidiary book and post to the Ledger. Take out a Trial Balance.

EXERCISE 8.4

F. Wade keeps the usual subsidiary books. He posts the totals to the relevant accounts in the Ledger each month.

The following are the monthly totals for the quarter ended 31st March, 19—.

	Jan	*Feb*	*Mar*
Sales Book	£2,147·00	£2,321·00	£2,629·00
Purchases Book	1,324·00	1,472·00	1,584·00
Sales Returns Book	32·00	41·00	26·00

Make the entries to record the above totals in Wade's Ledger for the quarter ended 31st March, 19—.

University of London, G.C.E. 'O' level, 1963 (modified)

EXERCISE 8.5

(1) State the transactions which gave rise to the entries on 10th May and 23rd May in the following account. (Assume VAT is included in the figures shown):

J. Rose (credit limit £300·00)

19—			£	19—			£
May 1	Balance	c/d	250·00	May 10	Returns	SRB	30·00
23	Sales	SB	175·00	,, 23	Bank	CB	95·00
				,, 31	Balance	c/d	300·00
			£425·00				£425·00
May 31	Balance	c/d	300·00				

(2) Why did Rose make a payment of £95·00 in partial settlement on 23rd May?

(3) What information is conveyed to you by the balance at 31st May?

University of London, G.C.E. 'O' level, 1967 (modified)

9

Cash Discounts — Petty Cash Book

In writing about the two-column Cash Book in an earlier chapter, we showed you how memoranda columns could be conveniently added to record VAT. We are now going to add further columns for the purpose of recording, on the debit side, the cash discounts we allow our customers, and on the credit side, the cash discounts our suppliers allow us. Like the VAT columns, these discount columns are not part of the ledger; they really comprise a book of original entry and the amounts shown in these columns must be posted twice in the same way that entries in other books of original entry are posted twice. For example, supposing T. Cousins, a customer, pays his account of £100 on 1st July, 19—, goods supplied on 10th June, 19—, and is allowed $2\frac{1}{2}\%$ cash discount for prompt payment. This payment would be recorded in the Cash Book as shown below and posted to T. Cousins's personal account in the Sales Ledger.

In this first part of the chapter we are concerned principally with cash discounts and so columns to record VAT are omitted.

Because the bank columns are a Ledger account, the entry of £97·50 in the Cash Book is posted once only, and this completes the double entry. Not so the entry in the discount column, for this column is not part of the Ledger. To complete the double entry, it has also to be posted to the debit of the Discounts Allowed Account.

Nominal Ledger

Dr — Discounts Allowed Account (L . . .) — Cr

19— July 1	T. Cousins	CB	£ 2·50	

The Discounts Allowed Account is a nominal account and debit balances on nominal accounts are losses. They can be regarded as the costs of a service provided by our customers whereby we get our money sooner than we could normally expect it. The customer's account is credited because he gives the service, and the Discounts Allowed Account is debited because this is the account in which the value of this service is recorded.

Cash Book (CB)

Dr | Cr

Date	Particulars	Fol.	Discount Allowed	Cash	Bank	Date	Particulars	Fol.	Discount Received	Cash	Bank
19—			£		£						
July 1	T. Cousins	L7	2·50		97·50						

Sales Ledger

T. Cousins (L7)

Dr | Cr

19—			£	19—			£
June 10	Sales	SDB	100·00	July 1	Bank	CB	97·50
					Discount	CB	2·50
		£	100·00			£	100·00

By totalling the 'Discounts Allowed' column when the Cash Book is balanced and posting the total to the debit of the Discounts Allowed Account, just as we do with the totals of the other subsidiary books, much work is saved. The word 'Sundries' or 'Total' must be used, since it is impossible, in a single entry, to refer to all the personal accounts in which the corresponding credit entries appear.

In the 'Discounts Received' column on the credit side of the three-column Cash Book we record the cash discounts our suppliers allow us. The personal accounts in our Bought Ledger are debited with the cash discounts, and the total of this column is posted at the end of the month to the credit of the Discounts Received Account. Balances on the credit side of nominal accounts represent gains. We may look at transactions of this kind as services which we render our suppliers. We credit the account in which we record the value of the service given and debit the supplier's account with the value of the service received.

A firm may decide to keep one Discount Account only. If so, it will debit this account with the monthly totals of discounts allowed to customers and credit it with the monthly totals of discounts received. Any balance on this account will be transferred at the end of the financial period to the Profit & Loss Account.

ILLUSTRATIVE EXERCISE 9.1

During August, 19—, L. Thomas, a sole trader, makes the following payments by cheque.

19—				
Aug 3	B. R. Trading Co. Ltd	£75	less 5%	cash discount
,, 5	A. Hyde & Co.	£100	,, 3¾%	,, ,,
,, 10	H. Simpson	£40	,, 2½%	,, ,,

During the same month he receives cheques from the following customers.

Aug 5	T. E. Brown	£40	less 1¼%	cash discount
,, 6	J. Forsaith	£50	,, 5%	,, ,,
,, 10	E. Thirkettle	£150	,, 2½%	,, ,,
,, 17	H. T. Smith	£10	,, 3¾%	,, ,,
,, 21	D. Rees	£82	,, 2½%	,, ,,

Enter these payments in a three-column Cash Book and post to the personal accounts in the Sales and Bought Ledgers. (For Cash Book see page 86)

Sales Ledger

Dr T. E. Brown (L1) Cr

	19—			£	
	Aug 5	Bank	CB	39·50	
		Discount	CB	0·50	

J. Forsaith (L2)

Dr				Cr			
				19—			£
				Aug 6	Bank	CB	47·50
					Discount	CB	2·50

Sales Ledger

E. Thirkettle (L3)

Dr				Cr			
				19—			£
				Aug 10	Bank	CB	146·25
					Discount	CB	3·75

H. T. Smith (L4)

Dr				Cr			
				19—			£
				Aug 17	Bank	CB	9·63
					Discount	CB	0·37

D. Rees (L5)

Dr				Cr			
				19—			£
				Aug 21	Bank	CB	79·95
					Discount	CB	2·05

Bought Ledger

B. R. Trading Co. Ltd (L11)

Dr				Cr			
19—			£				
Aug 3	Bank	CB	71·25				
	Discount	CB	3·75				

A. Hyde & Co. (L12)

Dr				Cr			
19—			£				
Aug 5	Bank	CB	96·25				
	Discount	CB	3·75				

H. Simpson (L13)

Dr				Cr			
19—			£				
Aug 10	Bank	CB	39·00				
	Discount	CB	1·00				

At the end of the month the totals of the discounts columns would be posted as shown on p. 87.

Dr *Cash Book* Cr

			Discounts Allowed	Cash	Bank				Discounts Received	Cash	Bank
19—			£		£	19—			£		£
Aug 5	T. E. Brown	L1	0·50		39·50	Aug 3	B. R. Trading Co. Ltd	L11	3·75		71·25
,, 6	J. Forsaith	L2	2·50		47·50	,, 5	A. Hyde & Co.	L12	3·75		96·25
,, 10	E. Thirkettle	L3	3·75		146·25	,, 10	H. Simpson	L13	1·00		39·00
,, 17	H. T. Smith	L4	0·37		9·63	,, 31	Balance	c/d			116·33
,, 21	D. Rees	L5	2·05		79·95						
		£	9·17		322·83			£	8·50		322·83
			(L23)						(L24)		
19—											
Sep 1	Balance	b/d			116·33						

Nominal Ledger

Dr Discounts Allowed Account (L23) Cr

19— Aug 31	Sundries	CB	£ 9·17				

Dr Discounts Received Account (L24) Cr

				19— Aug 31	Sundries	CB	£ 8·50

or, if only one Discounts Account is kept,

Dr Discounts Account (L . . .) Cr

19— Aug 31	Sundries	CB	£ 9·17	19— Aug 31	Sundries	CB	£ 8·50

Students are advised to work the following exercises, at least the first time, ignoring VAT (using the figures *before* tax). The answers at the back of the book have been worked on this basis. They may be reworked later including the VAT.

EXERCISE 9.1

D. Johnson began business as a stationer on 1st January, 19— with cash £200. (Enter 'Capital £200' in cash column in Cash Book.) His transactions during the month were:

				Total £
Jan	1	Paid cash for stock	£30·00 + VAT £3·00	33·00
,,	1	Paid into bank		150·00
,,	2	Purchased goods on credit from T. Sims	£20·00 + VAT £2·00	22·00
,,	4	Cash sales	£12·00 + VAT £1·20	13·20
,,	6	Sold goods on credit to K. Derwent	£5·50 + VAT 55p	6·05
,,	6	Bought goods on credit from K. J. & Co.	£16·00 + VAT £1·60	17.60
,,	7	Cash sales	£15·00 + VAT £1·50	16.50
,,	7	Paid T. Sims by cash less 2½% cash disc.		
,,	9	Received cheque from K. Derwent in settlement, less 2½% cash discount. (Cheque retained in office.)		
,,	10	Cash sales	£10·00 + VAT £1·00	11·00
,,	11	Bought goods from L. Stephen on credit	£30·00 + VAT £3·00	33·00
,,	13	Sold goods to R. Ransford on credit	£4·00 + VAT 40p	4·40
,,	13	Paid L. Stephen by cheque less 2½% cash discount.		
,,	14	Cash sales	£8·00 + VAT 80p	8·80
,,	18	Bought goods from F. Voulger on credit	£10·00 + VAT £1·00	11·00

Jan 22	Paid wages in cash		12·30
,, 24	Paid into bank		25·00
,, 25	Cash sales	£10·50 + VAT £1·05	11·05
,, 31	Received cheque from R. Ransford in settlement of his account less 2½% cash discount (cheque retained in office)		

Enter the above in appropriate books of original entry, post to the Ledger, and prepare a Trial Balance. Suggested ruling for each side of Cash Book:

Date	Particulars	Goods	Services	VAT	Fol.	Disc.	Cash	Bank

EXERCISE 9.2

The following transactions took place between D.E., a wholesaler, and R.V., a retailer, during January, 19—.

Jan 1	Balance due to D.E. £100
,, 4	Goods sold to R.V. £180 less 33⅓% trade discount + VAT 10%
,, 11	Part of the above goods invoiced at £60 gross were returned by R.V.
,, 20	Goods sold to R.V. £120 less 33⅓% trade discount + VAT 10%
Jan 27	R.V. sent a cheque to D.E. in settlement of the amount due from him less 2½% discount

Show the account of R.V. as it should appear in the books of D.E. at 31st January, 19—.

Associated Examining Board, G.C.E. 'O' level (modified)

EXERCISE 9.3

Turner is in business as a manufacturer and the following are his transactions with Smith for the month of January, 19—.

19—	
Jan 1	Balance due to Smith £430
,, 10	Bought from Smith 20 tons Xyncalia at £45 per ton, less 15 per cent trade discount + VAT 10%
,, 15	Paid amount due to Smith on 1st January less 5 per cent cash discount
,, 16	Returned to Smith 3 tons of Xyncalia as supplied on 10th for credit in full
,, 17	Bought from Smith 5 tons Coranium at £22·50 per ton + VAT 10%
,, 22	Sold to Smith 4 old pressing machines as scrap, for £220 the lot + VAT 10%
,, 28	Paid cheque to British Railways £5 for carriage on goods returned on 16th January, chargeable to Smith + VAT 10%
,, 31	Bought from Smith a supply of chemical waste for £50 + VAT 10%

You are asked:

(1) to prepare from the above information Smith's account as it would appear in Turner's Ledger, balancing it and bringing down the balance on 31st January,

(2) to state in which of Turner's subsidiary books you would expect to find recorded the transactions on (*a*) 10th, (*b*) 15th, and (*c*) 22nd January,

(3) to state how the double entry would be completed in respect of the sale to Smith on 22nd January.

R.S.A. (modified)

EXERCISE 9.4

Enter the following transactions in a columnar Cash Book and balance the account.

19—			£
Mar	1	Cash at bank	500·00
,,	1	Cash on hand	50·36
,,	3	Paid to J. Gibson, cheque (discount recd £3·50) ..	45·25
,,	5	Cash sales, cash (retained in office) £47·00 + VAT £4·70	51·70
,,	5	Paid into bank	40·00
,,	7	Paid wages, cash	15·33
,,	8	Recd from R. Jones, cheque (discount allowed him £1·12½) (paid into bank)	40·50
,,	10	Paid rent by cheque	40·15
,,	12	Paid salaries, cash..	15·33
,,	15	Paid W. Gay, cheque (discount recd from him £1·83)	35·15
,,	23	Drew from bank for office cash	25·00
,,	23	Paid wages, cash	18·52
,,	23	Paid expenses, cash £6·00 + VAT 60p	6·60
,,	29	Cash sales, cash (retained in office) £5 + VAT 50p ...	5·50
,,	31	Paid rent, cheque	15·00

EXERCISE 9.5

Enter the following transactions in a columnar Cash Book and balance the account.

19—			£
May	1	Cash at bank	900·00
,,	1	Cash in hand	50·00
,,	2	Paid R. Owen, cheque (discount recd £2·50)	78·50
,,	3	Paid wages in cash	15·16
,,	3	Paid rent, cheque	40·25
,,	3	Bought goods by cheque ... £36·00 + VAT £3·60	39·60
,,	5	Recd from A. Day, cheque (discount allowed him £4·00) (paid into bank)	92·26
,,	7	Paid G. Gray, cheque (discount recd £2·25)	50·50
,,	12	Cash sales banked ... ... £56·00 + VAT £5·60	61·60
,,	12	Bought goods by cheque ... £15·00 + VAT £1·50	16·50
,,	12	Recd rent, cheque (paid into bank)	10·18
,,	17	Paid salaries, cash..	25·00
,,	19	Drew cheque for office cash	40·00
,,	31	Paid R. Neil, cheque (discount recd £3·53)	50·19

The Petty Cash Book

Every business, in the course of a working day, pays out small sums in cash for postage, fares, stationery, and other sundry items. If these transactions are recorded in the main Cash Book, the latter soon becomes overloaded with numerous entries for small amounts which have then to be posted separately to the respective expense accounts in the Ledger. Moreover, if one single Cash Book is kept, the cashier's work cannot easily be subdivided, and bottlenecks may occur. These difficulties are largely overcome by keeping a separately bound book for small disbursements, called the Petty Cash Book. Kept in columnar form under suitable headings, the Petty Cash Book, like the main Cash Book, is a Ledger account as well as a book of original entry. The Cash Account columns in the main Cash Book, which the Petty Cash Book replaces, are then used to record, on the debit side, details of money paid into the bank and, on the credit side, details of items in respect of which one single cheque has been drawn; these columns cease to be part of the Ledger and are relegated to the role of memoranda columns. (Refer to page 91).

When a cheque is cashed for office use, the bank column in the main Cash Book is credited and the Petty Cash Book is debited with the sum cashed. The only debit entries in the Petty Cash Book will be those showing the receipt of funds from the bank, and consequently the debit side occupies one column only; most of the book is taken up with analysis columns on the credit side. This is understandable because a Petty Cash Book is used almost solely for recording cash that is paid out. The particulars column is shared by both the debit and credit sides.

No money should be paid out by the cashier unless he receives a proper document authorizing the payment. Petty cash vouchers, obtainable from most stationers, are generally used for this purpose and any receipts obtained in respect of these payments should be attached. The cashier will number these vouchers so that they can be filed numerically for easy reference, and these numbers will be noted in the Petty Cash Book against the entries to which they refer.

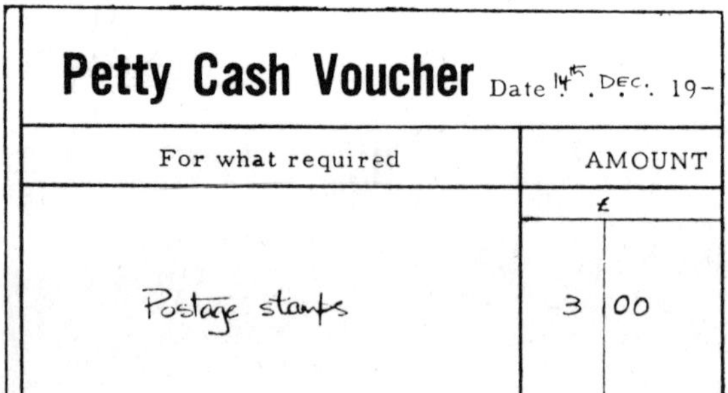

Petty Cash Voucher Date 14th. Dec. 19–

For what required	AMOUNT £	
Postage stamps	3	00
£	3	00

Signature L. Tomkins

Folio 1 Passed by T. Ford

Main Cash Book

Dr Cr

Date	Particulars		Discounts Allowed	Details	Bank	Date	Particulars		Discounts Received	Details	Bank
19—				£	£	19—				£	£
Mar 24	T. Crouch			10·60		Mar 25	Wages			100·00	
,, 24	D. Dawson			5·00	15·60	,, 25	Petty Cash			18·00	118·00

THE IMPREST SYSTEM

Under the imprest system, which is the one employed almost universally in business, the cashier starts each week, or other period, with a fixed sum, say, £20. If he has paid out £11 during the week, he produces vouchers for this sum so that a cheque can be drawn to bring the amount in his cash-box up to £20 again for the start of the new period. One advantage of this system is that the petty cash can quickly be checked at any time; when asked, the cashier must be able to produce cash, cash and vouchers, or vouchers totalling the imprest amount.

ILLUSTRATIVE EXERCISE 9.2

This illustrative exercise should be written out in full, even though the complete key is given. This will afford an opportunity for practice in careful ruling, and the general principle will be more thoroughly grasped in this way than if the details are merely read. The extra time and work involved will be well repaid later.

Record the following transactions in the appropriate books—Cash Book and Petty Cash Book, suitably ruled. Post to the Ledger and prove the posting by means of a Trial Balance. (Cash Book and Petty Cash Book on pages 93 and 94)

				Total
19—				£
Jan	1	Balance at bank		150·00
,,	1	Balance of petty cash on hand		20·00
		(The proprietor of the business should be credited with £170 capital which the above represent.)		
,,	3	Paid office cleaner	£2·00+ VAT 20p	2·20
,,	3	Bought stamps		0·60
,,	4	Paid for carriage	£0·50 + VAT 5p	0·55
,,	5	Paid R. Jones's account		0·50
,,	5	Bought memo pads	£0·60 + VAT 6p	0·66
,,	7	Paid postage		1·00
,,	7	Paid for cleaning	£3·00 + VAT 30p	3·30
,,	8	Bought string...	£0·70 + VAT 7p	0·77
,,	10	Paid carriage	£0·40 + VAT 4p	0·44
,,	10	Bought stamps		0·50
,,	10	Paid carriage	£0·20 + VAT 2p	0·22
,,	10	Paid cleaning...	£1·00 + VAT 10p	1·10
,,	11	Received from cashier amount necessary to make up imprest to £20		

Petty Cash Book

Dr Cr

Cash Received	Date	Details	Voucher No.	Total	Postage	Stationery	Carriage	Cleaning	Fol.	Ledger Account	VAT
£	19—			£	£	£	£	£		£	£
20·00	Jan 1	Balance									
	,, 3	Office Cleaner	1	2·20				2·00			0·20
	,, 3	Stamps	2	0·60	0·60						0·05
	,, 4	Carriage	3	0·55			0·50				
	,, 5	R. Jones	4	0·50					L4	0·50	
	,, 5	Memo Pads	5	0·66		0·60					0·06
	,, 7	Postage	6	1·00	1·00						
	,, 7	Cleaning	7	3·30				3·00			0·30
	,, 8	String	8	0·77		0·70					0·07
	,, 10	Carriage	9	0·44			0·40				0·04
	,, 10	Postage	10	0·50	0·50						
	,, 10	Carriage	11	0·22			0·20				0·02
	,, 10	Cleaning	12	1·10				1·00			0·10
				11·84	2·10	1·30	1·10	6·00		0·50	0·84
11·84	,, 11	Bank			(L1)	(L2)	(L3)	(L5)			(L7)
		Balance c/d		20·00							
31·84				31·84							
	19—										
20·00	Jan 12	Balance b/d									

Cash Book (CB1)

Dr | Cr

					£	19—					£
19— Jan 1	Balance	b/d			150·00	Jan 11	Petty Cash	1			11·84
						,, 11	Balance	c/d			138·16
				£	150·00					£	150·00
19— Jan 12	Balance	b/d			138·16						

Ledger

Dr Postage (L1) Cr

19—			£	
Jan 10	Petty Cash	PCB	2·10	

Dr Stationery (L2) Cr

19—			£	
Jan 10	Petty Cash	PCB	1·30	

Dr Carriage (L3) Cr

19—			£	
Jan 10	Petty Cash	PCB	1·10	

Dr R. Jones (L4) Cr

19—			£	
Jan 5	Petty Cash	PCB	0·50	

Ledger

Dr Cleaning (L5) Cr

19—			£	
Jan 10	Petty Cash	PCB	6·00	

Dr Capital (L6) Cr

19—			£
Jan 1	Bank	CB	150·00
„ 1	Petty Cash	PCB	20·00

Dr VAT (L7) Cr

19—			£	
Jan 10	Sundries	PCB	0·84	

Trial Balance—12th January, 19—

	Fol.	Dr £	Cr £
Postage	1	2·10	
Stationery	2	1·30	
Carriage	3	1·10	
R. Jones	4	0·50	
Cleaning	5	6·00	
Capital	6		170·00
Bank	CB	138·16	
Petty Cash	PCB	20·00	
VAT	7	0·84	
	£	170·00	170·00

POSTING THE PETTY CASH BOOK

At the end of the week or month the Petty Cash Book has to be balanced. We begin by totalling each of the analysis columns. Double lines are not drawn under the total in the 'Total' column because we have to make further entries before the Petty Cash Book is balanced. Each total in the analysis columns is posted to the debit of the appropriate expense account in the Ledger. One column, headed 'Ledger', needs a word of explanation. Occasionally money is paid out of petty cash in respect of real and personal accounts; these are then entered in the column headed 'Ledger'. Supposing, for example, we paid a supplier's account out of petty cash. We would enter this in the Ledger column and post this item to the debit of the supplier's account. Each item in this column is posted separately; we total this column only so that we can check our vertical additions with our cross totals. At this point we would remind students that petty cash items should be kept to a minimum. Moreover, despite what has just been said above, it is inadvisable to handle credit transactions through petty cash.

ANOTHER WAY OF DEALING WITH PETTY CASH

An alternative way of dealing with small payments is to treat the Petty Cash Book as a memorandum book only. Each item of expenditure is analysed, as with the Petty Cash Book, and when a cheque is drawn at the end of the period, the totals are entered in the details column on the credit side of the Cash Book and posted from there to the debit of the respective accounts in the Ledger.

Cash Book

Dr						Cr
	19—			VAT	£	£
	Jan 11	Postage	L1		2·10	
	,, 11	Stationery	L2	0·13	1·30	
	,, 11	Carriage	L3	0·11	1·10	
	,, 11	Cleaning	L5	0·60	6·00	
	,, 11	R. Jones	L4		0·50	
				0·84	11·00	11·84

As the student progresses with his book-keeping studies, he will discover that there are often alternative ways of doing things. This should not cause him any undue worry. If he understands the basic principles of double entry book-keeping, he will experience little difficulty in appreciating the respective merits of alternative procedures.

EXERCISE 9.6

Answer fully the following questions.
(1) What is the meaning of 'imprest' system?
(2) Why are small payments recorded in a separate book?
(3) Describe how a Petty Cash Book is balanced.

EXERCISE 9.7

Enter the following in the Petty Cash Book. Use analysis columns for (1) postage (2) telegrams, (3) travelling expenses, (4) stationery, (5) sundries, (6) VAT.

19—		
Apr	1	Petty cashier had £10 in hand
,,	2	Stamps £1·90, string 12p + VAT 1p, envelopes 52p +VAT 5p, bottle of glue 27p + VAT 3p
,,	3	Bus fares 7p, postage on parcel 14p, stamps 65p, telegram 52p
,,	4	Stamps 62p, telegram 37p, taxi 86p, bus fares 12p

On 6th April the amount expended was made good by the cashier; show this in closing the Petty Cash Book.

EXERCISE 9.8

Rule a columnar Petty Cash Book containing provision for the following headings: Postage, Telegrams, Carriage, Office Expenses, Stationery, Travelling, Salaries & Wages, Sundries and VAT. Record the undermentioned transactions. Bring down the balance as on 9th January, 19—, and enter the amount which should be received from the cashier to make up the amount of the 'imprest', viz. £50·00.

Transactions

				Total £
19—				
Jan	4	Received from the cashier a cheque (which was cashed) for £36·73, the amount required to make up the amount of the 'imprest', viz. ...	... ...	50·00
,,	4	Bought stamps...	... ...	2·50
,,	4	Paid office cleaner	£3·00 + 30p VAT	3·30
,,	5	Purchased stationery	50p + 5p VAT	0·55
,,	5	Paid for telegram	... ...	0·25
,,	5	Bought new office stool	£5·00 + 50p VAT	5·50
,,	6	Paid fares to Barnes	... ...	0·30
,,	6	Paid telephone account for December	£8·00 + 80p VAT	8·80
,,	7	Paid carrier's account...	£4·00 + 40p VAT	4·40
,,	7	Paid for insertion in Directory ...	£1·00 + 10p VAT	1·10
,,	7	Paid for return fare to Bedford ...	... ...	0·75
,,	7	Bought packing materials	£2·00 + 20p VAT	2·20
,,	8	Paid window cleaner	£1·50 + 15p VAT	1·65
,,	8	Bought pens and pencils	£3·00 + 30p VAT	3·30
,,	9	Paid wages	... ...	7·00
,,	9	Paid salary of office boy	... ...	8·00

EXERCISE 9.9

Draft a Petty Cash Book showing twenty items of expenditure in the week ending 7th March, 19—, in accordance with instructions that the total amounts spent on travelling, postage, printing and stationery, carriage, and general expenses will be required (incl. column for VAT).

Balance the book and show the amount received to bring the cash in hand to the original balance of £50·00.

R.S.A. Intermediate

EXERCISE 9.10

J. Tate, a wholesaler, has accounts in his ledger for Frobisher & Son and for T.X. Manufactures Ltd. On 1st December, 19— these accounts showed the following balances:

Frobisher & Son—debit balance	£420
T.X. Manufactures Ltd.—credit balance	£510

(1) Enter these balances in the accounts named.
(2) Make the entries which would arise *in these two accounts* from the following transactions and balance the two accounts at 31st December 19—:

19—
Dec 4 Paid cheque to T.X. Manufactures Ltd for the amount of their account less 5% cash discount.
,, 10 Received cheque (paid into bank) from Frobisher & Son for the amount of their account.
,, 12 Sold goods to Frobisher & Son at list price £300 less 20% trade discount + VAT 10%.
,, 15 Purchased 20 cases of goods from T.X. Manufactures Ltd at £16 per case plus 10% VAT. In addition, returnable cases were charged at 25p each + VAT 10%.
,, 18 Sent a credit note to Frobisher & Son for goods, list price £40 purchased on 12th December and returned.
,, 21 Received a credit note from T.X. Manufactures Ltd for the return of 11 empty cases charged at 25p each (+ VAT 10%) and 1 case of goods purchased on 15th December.

University of London G.C.E. 'O' level, 1967 (modified)

10
The Journal

At one time the only book of original entry was the Journal. In it were entered all transactions in debit and credit form. For example, a purchase of stock-in-trade valued at £56·00 from John Smith would be entered as follows.

				Dr	Cr
19—				£	£
Oct 4	Purchases Account	Dr		56·00	
	VAT A/c			5·60	
	John Smith				61·60

The account debited was always entered first, and the record showed the twofold effect of each transaction. When all transactions were journalized in this way, they had to be written four times, twice in the Journal and twice in the Ledger. The use of subsidiary books for Cash, Purchases, Sales and Returns enables the work of recording transactions to be subdivided and allotted to different employees; a saving of time and work is also effected, as there are fewer entries to make in the subsidiary books and Ledger. The double entry is completed by posting the totals of the subsidiary books. Although almost all the transactions of a business can be entered in the subsidiary books, there usually remain some miscellaneous items which must be entered in the Journal. What goes into the Journal is determined by the other subsidiary books used. One may summarize the position by saying that all transactions which cannot properly be entered in one of the other subsidiary books must be entered in the Journal.

Opening Entries

An important function which the Journal Proper, or General Journal, performs is that of recording opening entries. These entries consist of debit and credit balances. Supposing we owned a business for which, in the past, no proper books of account had been kept. In order to introduce a proper double entry system, it would be necessary to begin with opening entries in the Journal. However, we might not be able to do this until we had first assessed the worth of the business by listing its assets and liabilities. Thus:

Property Owned by the Business on 1st January, 19—

	£
Leasehold premises	2,000·00
Fixtures and fittings	500·00
Stock-in-trade	700·00
Money at bank	1,000·00
Cash in hand	50·00
	£4,250·00

Liabilities of the Business on 1st January, 19—

	£
J. Thompson (loan)	500·00
Proprietors (capital)	3,750·00
	£4,250·00

Very little rearrangement is required to set out these figures in the form of a Balance Sheet.

BALANCE SHEET AS AT 1ST JANUARY, 19—

Liabilities	£	*Assets*	£	£
Capital of Proprietors	3,750·00	*Fixed Assets*		
		Leasehold Premises	2,000·00	
J. Thompson (Loan)	500·00	Fixtures & Fittings	500·00	
				2,500·00
		Current Assets		
		Stock-in-Trade	700·00	
		Bank	1,000·00	
		Cash	50·00	
				1,750·00
	£4,250·00			£4,250·00

We know that assets are debit balances in the Ledger and liabilities are credit ones, and we might therefore be tempted to open accounts in the Ledger and straightway debit and credit these accounts with the values shown. If we were to do this, we would not only be violating an important double entry principle, namely, that entries are not made direct to the Ledger, but would be storing up trouble for ourselves in the future by making it difficult to locate errors and omissions. You will notice that the assets on the right are owned by the proprietors, except for the loan, which is, in a sense, a charge against the assets for the sum of £500. We could make single Journal entries for each of the assets, viz.

			Dr	Cr
19—			£	£
Jan 1	Leasehold Premises Dr		2,000	
	Capital			2,000

			Dr	Cr
19—			£	£
Jan 1	Fixtures & Fittings Dr		500	
	Capital			500

When we came to the loan, we should have to debit the proprietors' account, viz.

			Dr	Cr
19—			£	£
Jan 1	Capital Dr		500	
	Loan Account			500

In an examination a student might be given the assets and liabilities and be required to calculate the capital in the course of making the opening entries. It is useful to remember that *total assets less total liabilities equals capital.*

Instead of making entries to the Capital Account each time, as shown above, the entries in the Journal can be set out in such a way as to require only one posting to the Capital Account.

			Dr	Cr
19—			£	£
Jan 1	Leasehold Premises Dr	L1	2,000	
	Fixtures & Fittings	L2	500	
	Stock-in-Trade	L3	700	
	Bank	CB1	1,000	
	Cash	CB1	50	
	J. Thompson (Loan)	L4		500
	Capital	L5		3,750
	Being assets, liabilities and capital at this date			
			£4,250	£4,250

Having made the opening entries in the Journal, we have now to open accounts in the Ledger and debit and credit these with the sums shown. The word used when posting these entries is 'Balance'. As each item is posted to the Ledger, the page numbers of the Ledger must be inserted in the folio columns in the Journal. The letter 'J' for Journal is entered in the folio columns of the Ledger accounts.

Dr *Cash Book* (CB1) Cr

19--			£	£	
Jan 1	Balances	J	50·00	1,000·00	

If a Petty Cash Book were kept, the £50 would be debited to the Petty Cash Book. Note that the bank and cash balances are included in the opening entries in the Journal for the purpose of ascertaining the capital and recording it in one entry.

Ledger

Dr Leasehold Premises (L1) Cr

19—			£	
Jan 1	Balance	J	2,000·00	

Dr Fixtures & Fittings (L2) Cr

19—			£	
Jan 1	Balance	J	500·00	

Dr Stock-in-Trade (L3) Cr

19—			£	
Jan 1	Balance	J	700·00	

Dr J. Thompson (Loan Account) (L4) Cr

	19—			£
	Jan 1	Balance	J	500·00

Dr Capital Account (L5) Cr

	19—			£
	Jan 1	Balance	J	3,750·00

POSTING OTHER GENERAL JOURNAL ENTRIES

All transactions must first be entered in a book of original entry. The Journal must be used whenever there is no other suitable book of original entry. Since the latter entries will relate to a variety of matters, it is customary to add a short note of explanation after each entry. Supposing a business, keeping only the subsidiary books we have already discussed, received an invoice from British Railways for £5·50 for carriage of goods to a customer. As this is not an invoice in respect of the purchase of goods for resale, it could not be entered in the Purchases Day Book but would have to go through the Journal:

Journal

			Dr	Cr
19—			£	£
	Carriage Outwards Dr	L16	5·50	
	British Railways	L17		5·50
	Being cost of sending goods to customer			

and then be posted to the Ledger.

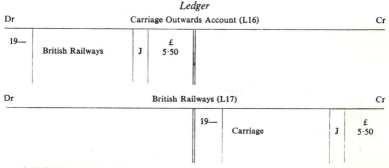

Ledger

Dr — Carriage Outwards Account (L16) — Cr

19—	British Railways	J	£ 5·50				

Dr — British Railways (L17) — Cr

				19—	Carriage	J	£ 5·50

A WORKED EXERCISE

On 1st May, 19— the balances in the Ledger accounts of J. F. Stone, a wholesale ironmonger, were as follows:

> stock-in-trade £3496·50; sundry debtors: L.X. Supplies Co. £167·28, W. Sawyer £282·24, F.S.S. Ltd £373·40; furniture and fittings £390; sundry creditors: Kitchen Equipment Co. £468·13, Hardware Manufacturers Ltd £332·15; cash at bank £381·36; petty cash £20.

(1) Ascertain Stone's capital and record the above position in the Ledger accounts.

(2) During the month of May Stone's business transactions as revealed by the original documents were as follows (VAT to be taken into account only where shown):

			Total £
Invoices sent to customers			
May 10	F.S.S. Ltd	£400·00 + VAT £40·00	440·00
„ 24	W. Sawyer	£197·00 + VAT £19·70	216·70

Invoices received			
May 16	Hardware Manufacturers Ltd (stock for resale)	£167·00 + VAT £16·70	183·70
„ 23	Kitchen Equipment Co. (stock for resale)	£184·00 + VAT £18·40	202·40
„ 30	British Railways (carriage on goods sent to customers)		16·10

		£	
Bank paying-in counterfoils			
May 9	Cheques:		
	L.X. Supplies Co. (discount allowed £8·36)	158·92	
	F. S. S. Ltd (discount allowed £18·67) ..	354·73	
			513·65
„ 30	Cheque: W. Sawyer	282·24	
	Cash: cash sales ... £246·00 + VAT £24·60	270·60	
			552·84

Cheque book counterfoils		
May 5	Kitchen Equipment Co.	468·13
	Hardware Manufacturers Ltd.	332·15
„ 10	Landlord (rent)	150·00
„ 12	S. W. Electricity Board (electricity)	21·11
	S. W. Gas Board (gas)	10·24
„ 25	S. W. Borough Council (rates for half year)	98·18
„ 31	Petty cash expenses refund	18·39½

Petty cash vouchers			
May 6	Postage for week		3·46
„ 13	„ „ „		2·97½
„ 15	Sundry office expenses ...	£4·00 + VAT £0·40	4·40
„ 20	Postage for week		3·14
„ 23	Electric light bulbs for office	£0·50 + VAT £0·05	0·55
„ 24	Office window cleaning ...	£0·70 + VAT £0·07	0·77
„ 27	Postage for week		3·10

Credit notes received			
May 27	Hardware Manufacturers Ltd (overcharge on invoice of 16th May)	£8·00 + VAT £0·80	8·80

You are required to record the above transactions in the books of original entry and post therefrom to the Ledger accounts.

(N.B. The Petty Cash Book should have analysis columns for Postage, Office Expenses and VAT. A Trial Balance is *not* required.)

University of London, G.C.E. 'O' level (modified)

General Journal

			Dr	Cr
19—			£	£
May 1	Stock-in-Trade Dr	L6	3,496·50	
	Sundry Debtors:			
	L.X. Supplies Co.	L1	167·28	
	W. Sawyer	L2	282·24	
	F.S.S. Ltd	L3	373·40	
	Furniture & Fittings	L7	390·00	
	Cash at Bank	CB	381·36	
	Petty Cash	PC	20·00	
	Sundry Creditors:			
	Kitchen Equipment Co.	L10		468·13
	Hardware Manufacturers Ltd	L11		332·15
	Capital	L5		4,310·50
	Being assets and liabilities at this date			
		£	5,110·78	5,110·78

(The capital is calculated by subtracting total liabilities from total assets.)

			Dr	Cr
19—			£	£
May 30	Carriage Outwards A/c Dr	L 27	16·10	
	British Railways			16·10
	Being carriage on goods sent to customers	L 12		

(Day Books page 110)

Petty Cash Book

Dr Cr

Cash Received	Date	Details	Voucher No.	Total	Postage	Office Expenses	VAT
£	19—			£	£	£	£
20·00	May 1	Balance J					
	,, 6	Postage	1	3·46	3·46		
	,, 13	,,	2	2·97½	2·97½		
	,, 15	Office Expenses	3	4·40		4·00	0·40
	,, 20	Postage	4	3·14	3·14		
	,, 23	Light Bulbs	5	0·55		0·50	0·05
	,, 24	Office Cleaning	6	0·77		0·70	0·07
	,, 27	Postage	7	3·10	3·10		
				18·39½	12·67½	5·20	0·52
18·39½	,, 31	Bank CB					
	,, 31	Balance c/d		20·00	(L24)	(L25)	(L28)
38·39½				38·39½			
	19—						
20·00	June 1	Balance b/d					

Cash Book

Dr

Date		Goods £	VAT £		Disc. £	Details £	£
19—							
May 1	Balance			J			381·36
,, 9	L.X. Supplies Co.			L1	8·36	158·92	
,, 9	F.S.S. Ltd			L3	18·67	354·73	
							513·65
,, 30	W. Sawyer			L2		282·24	
,, 30	Cash Sales	246	24·60			270·60	
							552·84
	£	246	24·60		27·03		1,447·85
		L8	L28		(L26)		
19— June 1	Balance b/d						349·64

Cr

Date		Goods £	VAT £		Disc. £	Details £	£
19—							
May 5	Kitchen Equipment			L10			468·13
,, 5	Hardware Mfg			L11			332·15
,, 10	Landlord (Rent)			L20			150·00
,, 12	S.W. Electricity			L21			21·11
,, 12	S.W. Gas Board			L22			10·24
,, 25	S.W. Borough Council			L23			98·18
,, 31	Petty cash			PC			18·39½
,, 31	Balance			c/d			349·64½
				£			1,447·85

General Ledge

Capital Account (L5)

Dr				Cr			
				19—			£
				May 1	Balance	J	4,310·50

Stock-in-Trade (L6)

Dr				Cr			
19—			£				
May 1	Balance	J	3,496·50				

Furniture & Fittings (L7)

Dr				Cr			
19—			£				
May 1	Balance	J	390·00				

Sales Account (L8)

Dr				Cr			
				19—			£
				May 30	Bank	CB	246·00
				,, 31	Sundries	SDB	597·00

Purchases Account (L9)

Dr				Cr			
19—			£				
May 31	Sundries	PDB	351·00				

Returns Outwards Account (L19)

Dr				Cr			
				19—			£
				May 31	Sundries	RDB	8·00

Rent Account (L20)

Dr				Cr			
19—			£				
May 10	Bank	CB	150·00				

Dr — Office Expenses (L25) — Cr

19—			£				
May 31	Petty Cash	PC	5·20				

Dr — Discounts Allowed (L26) — Cr

19—			£				
May 31	Sundries	CB	27·03				

Dr — Carriage Outwards (L27) — Cr

19—			£				
May 30	British Railways	J	16·10				

Dr — VAT Account (L28) — Cr

19—	*Tax Deductible*		£	19—	*Tax Due*		£
May 31	Sundries	PCB	0·52	May 31	Sundries	CB	24·60
,, 31	Sundries	PDB	35·10	,, 31	Sundries	SDB	59·70
,, 31	Balance	c/d	49·48	,, 31	Sundries	RDB	0·80
		£	85·10			£	85·10
				June 1	Balance	b/d	49·48

Sales Ledger

Dr — L. X. Supplies Co. (L1) — Cr

19—			£	19—			£
May 1	Balance	J	167·28	May 9	Bank	CB	158·92
					Discount	CB	8·36
		£	167·28			£	167·28

Dr — W. Sawyer (L2) — Cr

19—			£	19—			£
May 1	Balance	J	282·24	May 30	Bank	CB	282·24
,, 24	Sales	SDB	216·70				

Dr — F.S.S. Ltd (L3) — Cr

19—			£	19—			£
May 1	Balance	J	373·40	May 9	Bank	CB	354·73
					Discount	CB	18·67
			373·40				373·40
10	Sales	SDB	440·00				

Bought Ledger

Dr — Kitchen Equipment Co. (L10) — Cr

19—			£	19—			£
May 5	Bank	CB	468·13	May 1	Balance	J	468·13
				,, 23	Purchases	PDB	202·40

Dr — Hardware Manufacturers Ltd (L11) — Cr

19—			£	19—			£
May 5	Bank	CB	332·15	May 1	Balance	J	332·15
,, 27	Returns	ROB	8·80	,, 16	Purchases	PDB	183·70
,, 31	Balance	c/d	174·90				
			183·70				183·70
				June 1	Balance	b/d	174·90

Dr — British Railways (L12) — Cr

				19—			£
				May 30	Carriage	J	16·10

Sales Day Book

19—			£	VAT £	Total £
May 10	F.S.S. Ltd	L3	400·00	40·00	440·00
,, 24	W. Sawyer	L2	197·00	19·70	216·70
	Sales Account (credit)	L8	£597·00	£59·70	£656·70
				(L28)	

Purchases Day Book

19—			£	VAT £	Total £
May 16	Hardware Manufacturers Ltd	L11	167·00	16·70	183·70
,, 23	Kitchen Equipment Co.	L10	184·00	18·40	202·40
	Purchases Account (debit)	L9	351·00	35·10	386·10
				L28	

Returns Outwards Book

19—			£	VAT £	Total £
May 27	Hardware Manufacturers Ltd (overcharge on invoice of May 16)	L11	8·00	0·80	8·80
	Returns Outwards Account (credit)	L19	8·00	0·80	8·80
				L28	

SPECIAL POINTS TO NOTE

Be careful to keep the items in the Ledger in date order. Special attention to this point will be necessary when dealing with the Cash Book, Bill Books (to be referred to later), and the Journal.

In business posting is usually done from day to day, and this method should be followed from time to time when dealing with the exercises.

If Trade Discount is deducted from the invoice, see that it is also deducted from the returns.

THE ORDER OF POSTING

It is advisable to post the subsidiary books in the following order, keeping in mind what has been said above about entering items in the Ledger in date order:

(1) Journal opening entries,
(2) Purchases Day Book and Returns Outwards Book,
(3) Sales Day Book and Returns Inwards Book,
(4) Cash Book,
(5) Bill Books,
(6) remainder of Journal entries.

EXERCISE 10.1

James Maidment intends to open his books of account on a double entry basis from 1st January, 19—. His Balance Sheet on this date was as follows.

BALANCE SHEET AS AT 1ST JANUARY, 19—

		£			£
Capital		5,445·00	*Fixed Assets*		
	£		Leasehold Premises		2,000·00
Sundry Creditors:			Plant & Machinery		1,500·00
P. Scott	5·63		Fixtures & Fittings		475·00
O. Jones	100·00		Motor Vans		600·00
T. New & Co.	75·00				
		180·63	*Current Assets*		
			Stock-in-Trade		390·00
			Sundry Debtors:		
				£	
			T. Timpson	46·50	
			L. Bates	19·63	
					66·13
			Cash at Bank		582·00
			Cash in Hand		12·50
		£5,625·63			£5,625·63

Record the opening entries in the Journal and post to the Ledger.

EXERCISE 10.2

A. Patten's financial position on 1st July, 19— was as follows.

	£
Freehold premises	6,250·00
Fixtures and fittings	720·00
Stock-in-trade	2,432·50
Sundry debtors:	
L. Fenner	14·13
T. Townsend	121·21
A. F. C. Co.	82·73
T. Tilling	273·40
Sundry Creditors:	
Red Lion Supply Co.	198·23
Holborn Stores	482·34
Kingsway Trading Co.	181·36
Cash at bank	426·12
Petty cash	20·00

(1) Ascertain A. Patten's capital and record the above position in the Ledger accounts.

(2) The following transactions, as revealed by the original documents, took place during July (VAT to be taken into account only where shown).

				Total £
Invoices sent to customers				
July	2	A.F.C. Co.	£291·00 + VAT £29·10	320·10
,,	14	L. Fenner	£57·00 + VAT £5·70	62·70
,,	23	T. Tilling	£180·00 + VAT £18·00	198·00
Invoices received from suppliers				
July	14	Holborn Stores	£126·00 + VAT £12·60	138·60
,,	29	Kingsway Trading Co.	£298·00 + VAT £29·80	327·80
Credit notes sent to customers				
July	5	A.F.C. Co. (goods unsatisfactory)	£11·00 + VAT £1·10	12·10
,,	21	L. Fenner (goods damaged in transit)	£12·00 + VAT £1·20	13·20
Credit notes received				
July	20	Holborn Stores (goods not in accordance with sample)	£24·00 + VAT £2·40	26·40
,,	31	Kingsway Trading Co. (overcharge on invoice)	£4·00 + VAT 40p	4·40
Bank paying-in slip counterfoils				
July	10	Cheques:		
		T. Tilling (discount allowed £10)		263·40
		T. Townsend (discount allowed £8·21)		113·00
,,	11	Cheque: L. Fenner		14·13
,,	31	Cash: cash sales	£291·00 + VAT £29·10	320·10

Cheque book counterfoils

July	6	Red Lion Supply Co. (discount £7·10)		191·13
,,	7	Rent (landlord)		72·00
,,	10	Electricity		17·23
,,	12	Gas		21·19
,,	20	Rates (half year)		78·73
,,	30	Typewriter for office ...	£56·00 + VAT £5·60	61·60
,,	31	Petty cash expenses refund		12·04

Petty cash vouchers

July	4	Postage for week		1·15
,,	11	,, ,, ,, ...		2·53
,,	13	Stationery	£2·00 + VAT £0·20	2·20
,,	16	Sundry office expenses ...	£1·11 + VAT £0·11	1·22
,,	18	Postage for week		2·06
,,	25	,, ,, ,, ...		1·50
,,	30	Pencils and notebooks ...	£0·38 + VAT £0·04	0·42
,,	31	Postage for week		0·96

Record the above transactions in the subsidiary books and post therefrom to the Ledger accounts. Prepare a Trial Balance. Analyse petty cash expenditure under the following headings: Postage, Office Expenses, and Stationery.

EXERCISE 10.3

A firm manufactures radio and television sets and components. It is a standing rule of the firm that all payments below £5 are made through petty cash, and that payments of £5 and over are made by cheque. Name

(*a*) the subsidiary book through which the original record in respect of each of the following transactions would be put, and

(*b*) the document from which this record would be written up:

(1) a payment of £5·00 for a cash purchase of brass screws,
(2) a purchase on credit of 1,000 yards of copper wire,
(3) an allowance granted by the firm in respect of goods returned by a credit customer,
(4) a payment of £4·12 to British Road Services in respect of inward carriage,
(5) payment into the firm's bank of the day's total of cheques and cash received from various customers,
(6) a sale on credit of 50 television sets. (Ignore VAT).

Note: Your answer should be in tabulated form, as follows:

	(*a*)	(*b*)
(1)	....	....
(2)	....	....

and so on.

R.S.A. Elementary, 1959 (modified)

Journalizing as an Aid to Solving Book-keeping Problems

Theoretically all transactions can be entered through the Journal, and practice in this method is frequently used by teachers as an introduction to book-keeping, for the purpose of assisting students to grasp the full significance of double entry. Facility in making Journal entries is often materially helpful in solving book-keeping problems. To provide practice of this kind, the following exercises have been included.

EXAMPLES

Feb 1 Sold to Philip Boyd, Bedford Street, London, old machine £25·00. (ignore VAT).

In deciding how to journalize this, the mental process is as follows: what two accounts are affected? Answer: Philip Boyd and Plant & Machinery. The rule for personal accounts is *debit the receiver*, and as Philip Boyd is receiving the goods, his account is debited. Plant & Machinery Account is parting with value, and therefore it is credited. So the entry would be as follows.

				Dr	Cr
19—				£	£
Feb 1	Philip Boyd	Dr		25·00	
	Plant & Machinery				25·00
	Being sale of old machine				

Feb 3 Bought from Gibson and Steele 2 doz bentwood chairs £15·00. (ignore VAT).

What are the two accounts affected? Answer: Gibson & Steele and Furniture & Fixtures. The latter is a real account, and the guiding rule is *value coming in is debited.* The personal account rule, *debit the receiver and credit the giver*, applied to Gibson & Steele, shows that they are the 'givers', and therefore the entry would be:

				Dr	Cr
19—				£	£
Feb 3	Office Furniture	Dr		15·00	
	Gibson & Steele				15·00
	Being purchase of 2 doz bentwood chairs				

Feb 4 F. Foster, who owes £20·00, becomes bankrupt, and a first and final dividend of 25p in the £ is paid—£5·00.

What are the accounts affected here? Obviously Cash and F. Foster, because he has paid you one-quarter of the amount he owed, but you also have an intimation that you are not going to get any more. To follow out the book-keeping process, it will be necessary to make an entry to close the account of F. Foster, and to show that 75p for every £1 he owed has been lost to the business. The account which makes a record of this kind is a nominal account called 'Bad Debts', and this account is regulated by the rule *debit losses and credit gains*. The balance which will not be paid is debited to Bad Debts Account and F. Foster is credited.

			Dr	Cr
19—			£	£
Feb 4	Bad Debts A/c Dr		15·00	
	F. Foster			15·00
	Being 75p in the £ written off as irrecoverable			

The Ledger accounts, after posting, would appear as follows.

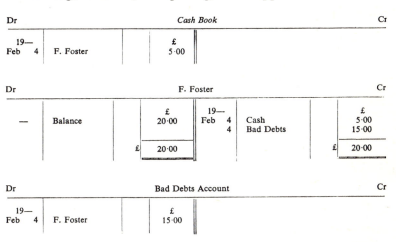

Dr *Cash Book* Cr

19—			£	
Feb 4	F. Foster		5·00	

Dr F. Foster Cr

			£	19—			£
—	Balance		20·00	Feb 4	Cash		5·00
				4	Bad Debts		15·00
		£	20·00			£	20·00

Dr Bad Debts Account Cr

19—			£	
Feb 4	F. Foster		15·00	

Feb 8 Credit interest on £1,455 capital at 5% per annum for one month—£6·06.

Pay careful attention to this entry. The interest is credited by the business to the proprietor, and therefore it is a loss to the business. The rule for nominal accounts is *debit losses and credit gains*. The transaction is recorded thus.

			Dr	Cr
19—			£	£
Feb 8	Interest Dr		6·06	
	Capital			6·06
	Being 5% per annum on £1,455 for one month			

This means that the business sustains a loss through having to pay interest, and the gain, which is recorded in the Capital A/c, is a gain to the proprietor of the business, who must be looked upon as distinct from the business.

Feb 8 Provide for £10 depreciation of machinery.

			Dr	Cr
19—			£	£
Feb 8	Depreciation	Dr	10·00	
	Machinery A/c			10·00

Depreciation is a loss in the value of an asset, and may be due to wear and tear, time, or obsolescence. In the Ledger the Depreciation Account is debited, and the total of this account is later transferred as a loss to the Profit & Loss Account. Machinery Account is credited with the amount of the depreciation, thereby reducing the book value of the machinery.

EXERCISE 10.4

Give the Journal entries necessary to record the following transactions (ignore VAT).

19—
Feb 8 Bought plant and machinery from Scotswood Engineering Co. for £1,000 on credit.
,, 9 T. Burke, a debtor owing £60, absconded, and his debt is written off as bad.
,, 16 Depreciation of plant and machinery 10% of cost (cost £6,000) and office furniture 5% of cost (cost £500).
,, 17 Bought office furniture from A. Bright & Co. £120·31 and gave in part exchange old furniture, for which an allowance of £32·00 was made.
,, 18 A. White, a creditor, charged interest £5 on his outstanding balance.
,, 22 Received from G.P.O. telephone account for £12·33.
,, 26 Bought office stationery of W. Simpson, £12·17.
,, 26 A. Cole, a debtor for £100, is charged interest £2·50.

EXERCISE 10.5

D. Tigg is in business as a wholesaler, and on 1st February, 19—, his assets and liabilities were:

Stock £1,800; office furniture £490; cash at bank £197; cash in hand £5.
Debtors: A. Jonas £40; M. Tapley £65.
Creditors: S. Gamp £78; B. Harris £90.

Entries in the respective day books during the period 1st to 15th February are summarized below. VAT at 10% to be added in respect of all sales and purchases of goods and services. (No VAT on wages or rent.)

Purchases		£	*Sales*		£	*Returns Inwards*		£
Feb 3	S. Gamp	150	Feb 2	A. Jonas	232	Feb 10	M. Tapley	25
,, 8	B. Harris	96	,, 8	J. Brick	195	,, 15	J. Brick	5
,, 14	M. Lupin	120						
		£366			£427			£30

Other transactions during the period were:

			£
Feb	1	Drew and cashed cheque for cash purposes	10·00
		Cash payments: wages	6·00
		sundry trade expenses	2·50
		drawings (D. Tigg)	5·00
,,	3	Sold to C. Dickins (for cash) office furniture	15·00
,,	4	Cash sales	75·00
		Paid to bank	50·00
,,	5	Paid by cheque to S. Gamp the amount due to him on 1st February less 5 per cent cash discount	
,,	6	Cash sales	80·00
		Received and banked a cheque from M. Tapley for ..	50·00
,,	7	Received and banked a cheque from A. Jonas for the amount due from him on 1st February less 2½ per cent discount for cash	
,,	8	Paid by cheque, rent	25·00
		Cash payments: wages	6·00
		sundry trade expenses	3·00
,,	9	Cash sales	99·00
		Paid to bank	70·00

			£
Feb	12	Paid to D. Tigg as drawings, a cheque for	25·00
,,	14	Received, and banked, a cheque from T. Pinch as loan	100·00
,,	15	Paid cheque, to M. Lupin, on account	50·00
		Banked all cash in hand except £5	

You are asked:

(1) to open the accounts of D. Tigg on 1st February by Journal entry,

(2) to enter the cash and bank transactions in a Columnar Cash Book,

(3) to post all entries, including the day books, to the appropriate Ledger accounts,

(4) to balance the personal accounts and Cash Book on 15th February, 19—, and extract a Trial Balance on that date.

Note: You are *not* required to include copies of the day books in your answer. Trading and Profit & Loss Account and Balance Sheet are *not* required.

R.S.A. (modified)

EXERCISE 10.6

F. Wade keeps the usual subsidiary books, a Cash Book and a Petty Cash Book with analysis columns. He posts the totals to the relevant accounts in the Ledger each month.

The following are the monthly totals for the quarter ended 31st March, 19—.

	Jan	*Feb*	*Mar*
	£	£	£
Sales Book	2,147	2,321	2,629
Purchases Book	1,324	1,472	1,584
Sales Returns Book	32	41	26
Discount allowed	67	72	69
Petty Cash Book (analysis columns)			
Office Expenses	6	4	2
Postage	4	5	6
Sundry Expenses	3	2	7

(1) Make the entries to record the above totals in Wade's Ledger for the quarter ended 31st March, 19—. (Ignore VAT.)
(2) State where the 'contra' entries would appear for the entries you have made in part (1).
(3) What rectifying entries would you make if it is subsequently discovered that a page of the Sales Book has been over-added by £10·00, and a petty cash payment in March of £1·50 for postage has been entered by mistake in the Sundry Expenses analysis column of the Petty Cash Book?

University of London, G.C.E. 'O' level (modified)

Journal-Closing Entries

At the end of the trading period the nominal accounts are closed by transfer to the Trading and Profit & Loss Accounts. The balances on these accounts represent losses and gains made by the business during the period, and when collected together in the Trading and Profit & Loss Accounts will show (1) what the gross profit is, and (2) what the net profit is for the period under review. The Trading and Profit & Loss Accounts are Ledger accounts and therefore subject to the rule that entries are not made direct thereto but must first pass through an appropriate subsidiary book. The entries made to record the transfer of the nominal account balances to the Trading and Profit & Loss Accounts are made in the General Journal and are called closing entries. Assume the following are the revenue accounts for T. Thomas, a sole trader, on 31st December, 19—.

Dr Purchases Cr

19—			£	19—			£
—	Balance		3,500·00	Dec 31	Trading A/c	J	3,500·00

Dr Sales Cr

19—			£	19—			£
Dec 31	Trading A/c	J	6,000·00	—	Balance		6,000·00

Dr Rent & Rates C

19—			£	19—			£
—	Balance	J	70·00	Dec 31	Profit & Loss A/c	J	70·00

Dr Lighting & Heating Cr

19—			£	19—			£
—	Balance		40·00	Dec 31	Profit & Loss A/c		40·00

Dr Wages Cr

19—			£	19—			£
—	Balance		120·00	Dec 31	Profit & Loss A/c		120·00

Dr			Stationery				Cr
19—			£	19—			£
—	Balance		25·00	Dec 31	Profit & Loss A/c	J	25·00

The closing entries in the Journal would be as follows.

		Dr	Cr
19—		£	£
Dec 31	Trading Account Dr	3,500·00	
	Purchases		3,500·00
	Sales Account	6,000·00	
	Trading Account		6,000·00
	Profit & Loss Account	255·00	
	Rent		70·00
	Lighting & Heating		40·00
	Wages		120·00
	Stationery		25·00
	Being transfer of balances to the Trading and Profit & Loss Accounts		
		£9,755·00	£9,755·00

Despite the rule about not making entries direct to the Ledger, an exception is often made in the case of closing entries. There is some justification for this. Such entries are made only at the end of the trading period, and little advantage is gained from making Journal entries. In examinations the student will probably be told whether closing entries are required.

11

Tabular or Columnar Book-Keeping

In this chapter we shall consider further uses of the columnar or tabular system of book-keeping.

Where a trader is marketing more than one product, or a retailer's shop consists of more than one department, it may be desirable to produce trading results on a product, or on a departmental basis. By suitably ruling the Purchases and Sales Day Books, the production of independent trading results is greatly facilitated.

ILLUSTRATION 11.1

Mr James Hardcastle, a dealer in electrical goods, including radio and television, wishes to keep the latter trading figures separate from those in respect of other merchandise. During August, 19— he made the following purchases on credit:

Aug 3 Bought of The General Wholesale Supply Co.
2 transistor radio sets at £10 each
4 electric toasters at £3 each
„ 6 Bought from Allied Manufacturing Corporation
2 doz Electric torches at 25p each
4 Electric razors at £3 each
(VAT 10%)

The entries would be made as follows:

Purchases Book

Date		Inv. No.	Fol.	Total	VAT	Electrical Goods	Radio & Television
19—				£	£	£	£
Aug 3	General Wholesale Supply Co	24	1	35·20	3·20	12·00	20·00
„ 6	Allied Mfg Corporation	25	2	19·80	1·80	18·00	
			£	55·00	5·00	30·00	20.00
					(L12)	(L10)	(L11)

and afterwards posted (1) to the personal accounts in the Bought Ledger,

Dr General Wholesale Supply Co. (Fol. 1) Cr

				19—			£
				Aug 3	Purchases	PDB	35·20

Dr Allied Manufacturing Corporation (Fol. 2) Cr

				19—			£
				Aug 6	Purchases	PDB	19·80

and (2) either to separate Purchases Accounts in the Ledger for each class of goods,

Dr Electrical Goods Account (Fol. 10) Cr

19—			£				
Aug 6	Sundries	PDB	30·00				

Dr Radio and television Goods Account (Fol. 11 Cr

19—			£				
Aug 6	Sundries	PDB	20·00				

Dr VAT Account (Fol. 12) Cr

19—			£				
Aug 6	Sundries	PDB	5·00				

or preferably to a Purchases Account in the Ledger in columnar form.

Dr Purchases Account (Fol. . . .) Cr

			Total	Electrical Goods	Radio & Television	
19—			£	£	£	
Aug 6	Sundries	PDB	50·00	30·00	20·00	

Dr VAT Account (Fol. 12) Cr

19—			£				
Aug 6	Sundries	PDB	5·00				

In practice, it is not necessary to rule up the credit side of the Purchases Account, for no entries would,.in the ordinary way, be made on that side. Where a single consignment contains goods of more than one class, any carriage charges which are payable are usually apportioned between the different classes of goods according to their relative values.

EXERCISE 11.1

Enter the following transactions in a tabular Purchases Book and post to the Ledger, using a tabular Purchases Account. The purchases are to be analysed under the following headings: Golf, Tennis, and Winter Sports (add VAT 10%).

19—	
Sep 14	Bought of Arctic Sports Co. Ltd 12 pairs of skis at £3 per pair 6 pairs of ice skates at £2 per pair.
15	Bought of The Wimbledon Supply Co. 6 tennis rackets at £4 each 6 doz tennis balls at £1 per ½ doz.
19—	
Sep 18	Bought of Northants Boot & Shoe Co. Ltd
,,	6 pairs ski boots at £3·50 per pair.
,, 21	Bought of L. Emerson & Co. 1 tennis net, £10.
,, 22	Bought of F. Tolley & Son 1 set of golf clubs, £60.
,, 23	Bought of S. Andrew & Co. 1 doz golf balls at 10p each.

We have dealt so far with Purchases only. The other subsidiary books would be ruled in the same way. However many columns are used for the analysis, the principles of double entry book-keeping are still strictly observed. For every debit entry there is a corresponding credit entry in the Ledger, and vice versa. The Cash Book is easily adapted to provide the details for posting to a columnar Purchases and columnar Sales Account. Thus, a business with three departments would incorporate three additional columns on both sides of the Cash Book, corresponding with its three departments. Below we show what the debit side would look like.

Dr *Cash Book* (Debit side only)

		LF	Discount	Cash	Bank	VAT	Dept *A*	Dept *B*	Dept *C*
19—			£	£	£	£	£	£	£
Jan 1	Balances	b/f		10·00	816·00				
	L. Bond & Co.		10·00		190·00				
	Sales			250·00		25·00	75·00	110·00	40·00
	S. Lloyd Ltd		2·50	97·50					
	Sales			200·00		20·00			
	Bank	c			360·00		90·00	60·00	30·00

Posting follows the ordinary rules. Entries on the debit side of the Cash Book are posted to the credit side of the corresponding account in the Ledger. For the purpose of departmental analysis, the cash sales figures are the important ones. Money received from credit customers is posted to the credit of their personal accounts in the Sales Ledger in the usual way. The departmental analysis is unaffected by payments in settlement of outstanding accounts; the departments concerned were credited with the sales when the goods were originally supplied.

EXERCISE 11.2

Enter the following transactions in the appropriate books of K. Ford and post to the Ledger. Use tabular book-keeping where possible.

The position of K. Ford's business on 1st January, 19— was as follows: Cash in hand £120; at bank £2,150; stock: *A* Dept £1,800, *B* Dept £2,200, *C* Dept £1,600; debtors: R. Ecol £120, J. Whittaker £240, T. Bingham £400; creditors: T. Thomas £600, D. Wright £400.

19—				VAT	£
Jan	2	Credit sales to R. Ecol		10%	
		(Dept *A* £90, Dept *B* £120)			210·00
		Credit sales to T. Bingham		VAT	21·00
		(Dept *A* £30, Dept *B* £80, Dept *C* £60)			170·00
,,	3	Paid T. Thomas by cheque (5% cash discount)		VAT	17·00
		Received cheque from T. Bingham £400 and paid into bank			
,,	6	Paid trade expenses, £11 (incl. VAT £1)			
		Paid wages, £100 cash			
,,	7	Drew cheque from bank for office cash			100·00
,,	8	Bought on credit from D. Wright goods for:			
		Dept *A*	£200		
		,, *B*	60		
		,, *C*	240		
			—		500·00
				VAT	50·00
,,	9	Paid D. Wright by cheque £380 (Discount £20)			
		Cash sales paid into bank:			
		Dept *A*	£600		
		,, *B*	450		
		,, *C*	300		
			—		1,350·00
				VAT	135·00
,,	10	Bought goods on credit from L. Cook & Sons for:			
		Dept *A*	£150		
		,, *B*	100		
		,, *C*	300		
			—		550·00
				VAT	55·00
,,	14	Bought stock-in-trade by cheque for:			
		Dept *A*	£400		
		,, *B*	380		
		,, *C*	120		
			—		900·00
				VAT	90·00

,, 15	Cash sales paid into bank:			
	Dept *A*	.. £480		
	,, *B*	.. 240		
	,, *C*	.. 400		
		—		1,120·00
			VAT	112·00
	Sold to R. Ecol on credit from Dept *A* ..			480·00
			VAT	48·00
,, 16	Received cheque from T. Bingham £178·50 (allowed discount £8·50)			
	Received cheque for £100 from R. Ecol on account (both cheques banked the same day).			
,, 17	Purchased stock-in-trade on credit from T. Thomas for:			
	Dept *A*	.. £600		
	,, *C*	.. 450		
		—		1,050·00
			VAT	105·00

Extract a Trial Balance.

EXERCISE 11.3

Using the accounts and books prepared for the previous exercise, record the following transactions and post to the Ledger. Extract a Trial Balance.

19—				£
Jan 20	Cashed cheque £200			
	Paid wages £150 and trade expenses £22 (including VAT £2)			
	Bought stock-in-trade on credit from A. Tucker & Sons for:			
	Dept *A*	..	£240	
	,, *B*	..	80	
	VAT	...	32	352·00
	Cash sales paid into bank:			
	Dept *A*	..	£480	
	,, *B*	..	360	
	,, *C*	..	160	
	VAT	...	100	1,100·00
,, 21	Returned goods to A. Tucker & Sons:			
	Dept *A*	..	£40	
	,, *B*	..	20	
	VAT	...	6	66·00
	Purchased stock-in-trade by cheque for:			
	Dept *B*	..	£350	
	,, *C*	..	280	
	VAT	...	63	693·00

Jan 21	Cash sales paid into bank:		
	Dept *A*	£520	
	,, *B*	360	
	,, *C*	320	
	VAT	120	1,320·00
,, 22	Paid A. Tucker & Sons their account less $3\frac{3}{4}\%$ cash discount		
	Sold goods on credit to T. Bingham:		
	Dept *A*	£600	
	,, *C*	90	
	VAT	69	759·00

Final Accounts in Tabular Form

If the revenue accounts are kept in columnar form, it is a simple matter to produce a Trading Account in a similar form. The preparation of a Profit & Loss Account in tabular form, however, requires the apportionment of expenses and gains on some predetermined basis.

In the case of a retail store, some expenses are easily apportioned departmentally, e.g. salaries and salesmen's commission, but other losses, such as rent, are apportioned according to a carefully worked out formula, which would normally take into account not only the amount of floor space occupied by the different departments but also the position of the departments within the building. Ground floor departments would probably be 'charged' a higher rent than departments on the sixth floor.

EXERCISE 11.4

Prepare the final accounts and Balance Sheet for the period ended 23rd January from the details given in the previous two exercises.

Stock at 22nd January was valued as follows:

Dept *A* £2,800, Dept *B* £1,800, Dept *C* £800.

Wages are to be apportioned as follows:

Dept *A* £100, Dept *B* £80, Dept *C* £70,

and trade expenses:

Dept *A* £6, Dept *B* £20, Dept *C* £4.

EXAMPLE OF TRADING AND PROFIT & LOSS ACCOUNTS IN COLUMNAR FORM

PRESTIGE DEPARTMENT STORE CO.

TRADING ACCOUNT FOR THE YEAR ENDED 31ST DECEMBER, 1963

Dr		Total	Dept *A*	Dept *B*	Dept *C*	Cr		Total	Dept *A*	Dept *B*	Dept *C*
		£	£	£	£			£	£	£	£
Stock (1st Jan, 1963)		1,200	600	300	300	Sales					
Purchases (*Less* returns)		22,800	11,400	6,000	5,400	(*Less* returns)		30,000	15,000	9,000	6,000
		24,000	12,000	6,300	5,700						
Less Stock (31st Dec, 1963)		1,830	1,200	600	30						
Sales at Cost		22,170	10,800	5,700	5,670						
Gross Profit transferred to Profit & Loss A/c		7,830	4,200	3,300	330						
	£	30,000	15,000	9,000	6,000		£	30,000	15,000	9,000	6,000

PROFIT & LOSS ACCOUNT FOR THE YEAR ENDED 31ST DECEMBER, 1963

Dr		Total	Dept *A*	Dept *B*	Dept *C*	Cr		Total	Dept *A*	Dept *B*	Dept *C*
		£	£	£	£			£	£	£	£
Rent		150	60	50	40	Gross Profit					
Heating & Lighting		30	10	10	10	from Trading A/c		7,830	4,200	3,300	330
Wages		1,600	600	550	450	Net Loss	c/d				185
Trade Expenses		42	20	12	10						
Carriage		21	10	6	5						
Net Profit	c/d	5,987	3,500	2,672	–						
	£	7,830	4,200	3,300	515		£	7,830	4,200	3,300	515
Net Loss	b/d				185	Net Profit	b/d	5,987	3,500	2,672	–

Note that the losses made by Dept C in the example above might have gone undetected for a long time had profits not been calculated departmentally from columnar records.

Columnar Purchases and Expenses Day Books

Where a day book is kept exclusively for Purchases, invoices relating to expenses, or matters not concerned with stock for resale, are then passed through the General Journal. But often it is more convenient to have a tabular form of Purchases Book for recording all inward invoices, whether they relate to purchases or expenses.

The posting of such a day book is straightforward. The suppliers' accounts are credited with the full amounts shown against their names in the total column. The totals of the other columns are posted periodically to the debit of the respective impersonal accounts. Items in the column headed 'Ledger' are posted separately; it is provided for transactions for which there is no other suitable column.

GOODS ON SALE OR RETURN OR APPROVAL

A book similar to the one on page 128 is often used to provide a permanent record of goods supplied on 'sale or return' or 'on approval'.

Goods sent to customers 'on approval' or 'on sale or return' are invoiced on special forms, making these transactions clearly distinguishable from ordinary credit sales. A copy of the invoice is sent to the accounts department, to enable entries to be made in the 'Sale or Return' Journal. If the goods are not returned within the stipulated time, the entry is extended to column (3) and the goods are then charged to the customer's account in the Sales Ledger. The double entry is completed by posting the total of this column periodically to the credit of Sales Account. Where the goods are returned within the agreed period, the entry in column (1) is extended to column (2), and no further action is necessary. (Note that a credit note is not made out because the goods have not been charged to the customer's account.) A book such as this will show at a glance what goods are still out on approval. At the end of the trading period, this information will be required to help determine the total value of the closing stock. Goods on 'sale or return' or 'on approval', and not yet charged to customers' accounts because the period of approval has not yet expired, are treated as part of the firm's closing stock. A note of warning is necessary here. All goods sent on 'sale or return' will be invoiced at selling price, but closing stock must be shown at cost price. Having, therefore, valued the goods still on approval at selling price, the accountant must reduce this sum to cost price. Some companies state their final stock figure at cost or current market price, whichever is the lower.

VAT

The basic tax point in respect of goods on sale or return or approval occurs when the customer adopts the transaction, which may be the date when he tells the supplier he has done so; or when the time-limit fixed for the return of the goods is up; or if there is no time-limit, at the end of twelve months.

Columnar Purchases Day Book

Date	Name	Inv. No.	Fol.	Total	VAT	Purchases: Dept *A*	Purchases: Dept *B*	Purchases: Dept *C*	Freight	Trade Expenses	Insurance	Ledger
19—				£	£	£	£	£	£	£	£	£
Jan 1	T. Tucker			22·00	2·00	10·00	7·00	3·00				
,, 8	R. Bate			5·00					5·00			
,, 15	L. Potts			2·75	0·25					2·50		

Date	Customer	(1) Goods Sent on Sale or Return: Total	VAT	Dept *A*	Dept *B*	Dept *C*	(2) Goods Returned: Total	VAT	Dept *A*	Dept *B*	Dept *C*	LF	(3) Goods Sold: Total	VAT	Dept *A*	Dept *B*	Dept *C*
19—		£	£	£	£	£	£	£	£	£	£	✓	£	£	£	*k*	£.
Jan 1	Smith & Co. Ltd	132	12	90	30		132	12	90	30							
	Wilson, John	22	2			20						1	22	2			20
	Grimond, Leslie	66	6	20	30	10	33	3	20		10	2	33	3		30	
,, 2	C. Robinson & Co.	176	16	40	100	20						3	176	16	40	100	20
	Remington, John	70				70						4	77	7			70

TABULAR BOOKS TO MEET PARTICULAR CONDITIONS

Opportunities for the useful employment of tabular records are practically unlimited, but there are some enterprises where, by reason of the particular services they market, the tabular method of book-keeping has special advantages. Hotels, and the services supplied by public utilities, such as electricity and gas, are good examples. The ruling of the 'Visitors' Ledger' which a hotel might keep is given below.

Visitors' Ledger

Date..........................

	Mr J. Jones	Mr L. Thomas	....	....	Daily Total
Debits					
Balance b/fwd					
Apartments					
Baths					
Service					
Breakfasts					
Luncheons					
Teas					
Dinners					
Suppers					
Wines					
Minerals					
Tobacco					
Stationery					
Newspapers					
Laundry					
Telephone					
VAT					
Total					
Credits					
Overcharges					
Ledger					
VAT					

From the examples given in this chapter, it will be seen that the intelligent use of columns in book-keeping, far from increasing the volume of work involved in keeping accounting records, often helps to reduce it. In some forms of tabular book-keeping, debits and credits may not always be in their customary places, and the application of double entry principles not always obvious. The student should, if he comes across examples of this kind, satisfy himself that the double entry has been made.

EXERCISE 11.5

Explain the principles of the columnar or tabular system of book-keeping. What are the advantages of this method?

EXERCISE 11.6

A retail business has two departments, *A* and *B*. Prepare a Trading and Profit & Loss Account in departmental form from the following Trial Balance, and a Balance Sheet as at 31st December, 19—. Apportion expenses on the basis of value of sales. (Ignore VAT.)

Trial Balance—31st December, 19—

		Dr	Cr
		£	£
Cash at Bank		950	
Cash in Hand		20	
Capital			10,000
Stock (1st January):	Dept *A*	4,000	
	Dept *B*	3,500	
Purchases:	Dept *A*	5,100	
	Dept *B*	4,900	
Sales:	Dept *A*		9,000
	Dept *B*		6,000
Debtors		6,000	
Creditors			2,600
Salaries		1,500	
Rent & Rates		480	
Electricity		105	
Discounts		75	100
Carriage on Sales		40	
Advertising		760	
Postage		30	
General Expenses		240	
		£27,700	£27,700

Stock at 31st December was valued at £4,600 (Dept *A*) and £4,000 (Dept *B*).

EXERCISE 11.7

D.A., a wholesale dealer in electrical goods, has two departments: (*a*) Radio and Television, (*b*) Electrical Sundries. During the period 7th to 13th January, 1958, he had the following credit transactions.

Jan 7 Purchased 6 television sets, No. 216, from E.M. & Co. Ltd, at £80 each, less trade discount of 25%.

,, 9 Sold 4 of the above sets, No. 216, to R.B. at £80 each, less trade discount of 10%.

,, 10 Purchased from R.M. & Co. Ltd, 1 doz electric irons at £3 each, less trade discount of 25%, 6 electric sweepers, No. 105, at £33 each, less trade discount of 33⅓%.

Jan 11 R.B. returned 2 of the television sets, No. 216, sold to him on 9th, as defective. Sent him a credit note. Returned the above 2 television sets, No. 216, to E.M. & Co. Ltd.

Add VAT at 10% in all cases.

Record the above transactions in columnar books of original entry and post to the Ledger.

G.C.E. 'O' level

EXERCISE 11.8

J.B. & Co. decide to sell all their goods on a sale or return basis. Suggest any modifications you would make in their book-keeping records. Give pro-forma rulings of subsidiary books and specimen entries to illustrate your answer.

G.C.E. 'A' level

EXERCISE 11.9

A. Avon's business is divided into two departments, A and B, and on 31 May 1971, the following balances are extracted from his books:

	Dept. A	Dept. B
	£	£
Purchases	4,600	6,240
Returns Inwards	120	240
Returns Outwards	56	98
Sales	5,400	9,040
Stock on 1 June 1970	1,800	2,160
Stock 31 May 1971	1,980	3,840

(i) Prepare on the columnar system Trading Account for the year ended 31 May 1971.

(ii) Express the Gross Profit as a percentage of turnover in respect of each Department and for the business as a whole.

Welsh Joint Education Committee, G.C.E. 'O' Level

EXERCISE 11.10

One of the subsidiary books kept by a firm of retailers is a columnar Purchases Book (or Bought Journal) in which the book-keeper enters all invoices received, whether for stock-in-trade purchased or for running expenses, etc.

The ruling of the book is as follows:

Date	Name	Folio	Amount	Analysis columns (1)	(2)	(3)	(4)	(5)
			£	£	£	£	£	£

The headings of the five analysis columns are: (1) Goods for re-sale, (2) Carriage, (3) Heating and lighting, (4) Other revenue expenditure, (5) Capital expenditure.

All invoices are entered in this subsidiary book and postings are made to the personal accounts involved. At the end of each month the analysis columns are totalled and the totals are posted to suitable real and nominal accounts.

In April 1971, the first month of a new accounting year, the invoices received were:

				£
Apr	2	Southside Garages Ltd	New delivery van	614·80
,,	6	Butterworth & Co. Ltd	Goods	525·00
,,	7	Borchester Weekly	Advertising...	5·25
,,	11	Southern Wholesalers Ltd	Goods	436·20
,,	16	British Road Services	For goods transported ...	4·75
,,	18	Office Supplies Ltd	Typewriter repaired ...	4·60
,,	24	Office Supplies Ltd	Stationery	12·30
,,	25	Southern Electricity Board	Quarterly bill for current consumed	69·60
,,	27	British Railways	For goods transported ...	3·25
,,	30	Southern Wholesalers Ltd	Goods	279·40

At April 1, there were no balances on any of the ledger accounts involved in these transactions apart from: Vehicles Account £723, Southern Wholesalers Ltd £748.

The firm made these payments, all by cheque, in April:

Apr 10 Paid Southern Wholesalers Ltd £748 less 2½% cash discount.
,, 18 Paid Southside Garages Ltd £614·80.
,, 25 Paid Office Supplies Co. Ltd £4·60.

You are asked to rule up the columnar Purchases Book, enter the invoices and make the postings to the appropriate ledger accounts. The ledger accounts should include the amounts posted from the Cash Book and should be balanced off where necessary. The entries in the Cash Book itself are *not* required. (VAT in this exercise is to be disregarded.)

Oxford Local Examinations G.C.E. 'O' Level 1971

12

Banking — Bank Reconciliation Statements

THERE are certain banking matters to which we must now turn our attention. When a firm opens a banking account, it makes a contract with its banker, and thereby establishes a debtor/creditor relationship with him. While the firm has funds in its banking account, the bank is its debtor, but, unlike an ordinary debtor, is not required, for obvious reasons, to seek out the firm and pay the debt. The bank agrees to look after its customer's money and to pay out such sums and to such persons as its customer shall from time to time instruct it to pay. The depositor, for his part, undertakes to make out his cheques carefully so as to minimize the risk of fraud and generally to conduct his account in a regular and proper manner.

There are two kinds of account which bankers' customers can open—a current account and a deposit account. With a current account, money can be drawn out at any time by cheque, whereas notice to the bank must be given if withdrawals from a deposit account are intended. The bank pays interest on money left on deposit but it is not usual to pay interest on current account balances. Indeed, the bank may charge its customer for looking after his current account, the amount being determined according to the average balance in the account and the number of entries made in the account over a period of time. Some banks make no charges to customers keeping minimum balances of £50 in their current accounts.

Paying Money into a Bank Account

A wise trader will keep as little cash as possible on his premises, and will pay all money, surplus to his daily cash requirements, into his bank account. Paying-in slips, which are used when money is paid into a bank account, are provided free by the customer's bank. They are often supplied in stapled book form, each page perforated to provide a copy which remains in the book, and from which the customer can write up the debit side of his Cash Book. The bank clerk receiving the money checks the money handed over with the paying-in slip, rubber stamps and initials both parts of the paying-in slip, removes the bank's copy and hands the paying-in book back to the customer.

The Cheque System

Of all the services provided by banks, none is more valuable, both to private persons and to the business community at large, than that of operating the cheque system. By means of it, a business man is able to pay large sums of money to his suppliers in distant parts of the country with no risk that the money will be lost in transit.

Cheques originated in the seventeenth century, when money would be deposited with goldsmith bankers for safe keeping. Instead of the depositors withdrawing money from the bank every time they wished to make a payment to a debtor, they would write to their banker and instruct him to make the payment for them. In the course of time it was more convenient to the bank to provide a standard letter of instruction, and thus the cheque came into being.

The cheque forms themselves are supplied free by the banks to their customers, upon receipt of an application form duly signed. Since the Bill of Exchange Act, 1882 defines a cheque as a bill of exchange drawn on a banker payable on demand, a post-dated cheque cannot be passed to a banker for collection, and a person who has accepted such a cheque must hold it until it matures.

A cheque does not derive its legal validity from its form and the printing thereon. An ordinary piece of paper addressed to a banker with whom the drawer has an account and signed by the drawer, is a cheque. Sir A. P. Herbert once wrote out a bill of exchange on an egg.

ENDORSEMENTS

At one time all cheques payable to order had to be endorsed (the payee had to write his name on the back) before the cheques could be paid into a bank account. This is no longer necessary by virtue of the Cheque Act, 1957, and the business community has been saved much work in consequence. Endorsements are still necessary when the payee wishes to transfer the payment to another person.

CROSSINGS

The effect of crossing a cheque, i.e. drawing two parallel transverse lines across it, is to make it payable only to a banker. The object is to prevent fraud by making it difficult for anyone other than the rightful person to cash it. Postal orders and money orders, although not negotiable instruments, may similarly be crossed, either by the person making the payment or by the person receiving the payment, and then like cheques, have first to be paid into a banking account. Some firms stamp all cheques and postal orders received through the post, with a rubber stamp bearing parallel transverse lines, whether these instruments are already crossed or not. In a large company, where money may not always be passed directly to the cashier, this is a wise precaution.

Cheques may be crossed either generally or specially. A general crossing means that the cheque is payable to a banker; a special crossing that it is payable to the particular banker whose name appears between the parallel transverse lines.

General Crossings

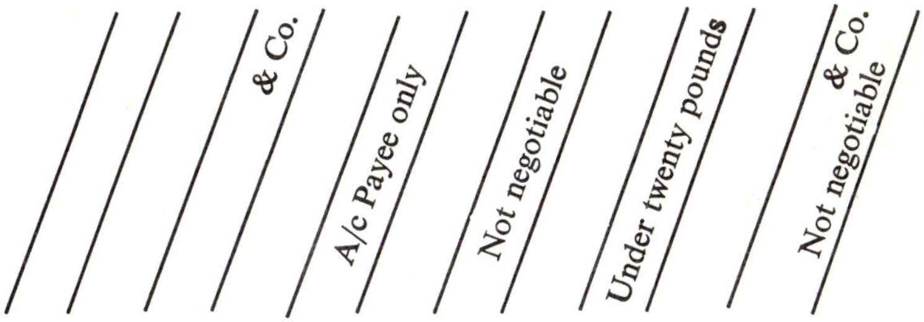

Special Crossings

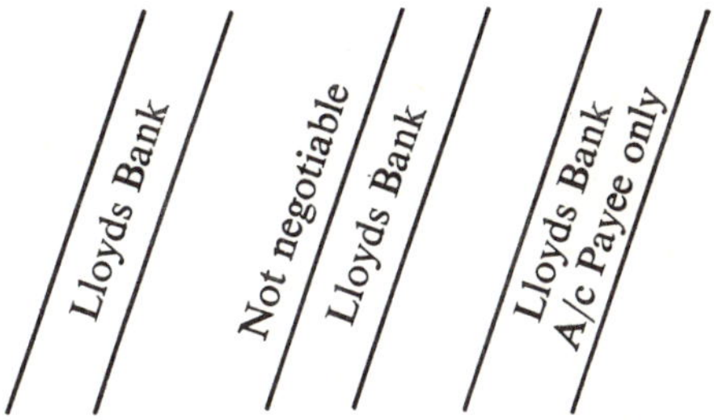

THE MEANING OF WORDS ADDED TO CROSSINGS

& Co.

Often written between the transverse lines but now only of historical interest. It has no practical significance.

A/c Payee only

A direction to the banker to pay the sum mentioned to the person named on the cheque and only to that person.

Under a Certain Amount, e.g. Under Twenty Pounds

Prevents the cheque being fraudulently altered to any sum appreciably larger than what the drawer intends to pay.

Not Negotiable

A cheque, unlike a postal order or money order, is a negotiable instrument. This means that if a person receives a cheque properly made out, for value and not as a gift, in good faith and without any notice of any defect in the title of the transferor, he gets a good legal title to the cheque and the drawer will be obliged to pay him, even though the person from whom he received it had stolen it, and had no proper legal title himself. When 'not negotiable' is written across the face of a cheque, the effect is to destroy this property of negotiability which cheques, in common with all bills of exchange, have. The purpose of writing 'not negotiable' on a cheque is to protect the drawer against theft or loss, and is a warning to anyone receiving the cheque that he will get no better legal title to the cheque than that possessed by the person from whom he receives it.

DISHONOURED CHEQUES

We have seen that when a trader receives cheques from his customers, he pays them into his banking account, debits his own Cash Book with the amounts paid in, and then completes the double entry by crediting the appropriate personal accounts in his Sales Ledger. If one of these cheques is dishonoured by non-payment, e.g. because the debtor has insufficient funds in his bank account to meet it, the cheque will be returned to the trader marked R/D (refer to drawer). Upon receipt of the dishonoured cheque, it is necessary to cancel the original entries in the trader's Cash Book and Sales Ledger. This is done by crediting the Cash Account (bank column) and debiting the customer's personal account. If cash discount was allowed, then a Journal entry is necessary to charge the customer with the discount allowed and cancel the entry in the Discounts Allowed Account. Suppose T. Ford, a customer, had a debit balance on his personal account of £100 on 20th January, 19—, which he settled two days later, deducting 5% cash discount. His account would appear as follows.

Dr T. Ford Cr

19—			£	19—			£
Jan 20	Sales	SDB	100·00	Jan 22	Bank	CB	95·00
					Discount	CB	5·00
		£	100·00			£	100·00

If now, on 30th January, the cheque was returned dishonoured, the Cash Book would be credited with £95 in order to cancel the Cash Book entry for 22nd January. To restore T. Ford's account to the original position, it would be necessary also to debit it with the £5 discount allowed. The credit entry for this would appear in the Discounts Allowed Account. On 30th January, T. Ford's account would look like this.

Dr T. Ford Cr

19—			£	
Jan 30	Bank (dishonoured cheque)	CB	95·00	
	Discount allowed	J	5·00	

Journal

				Dr	Cr
19—				£	£
Jan 30	T. Ford	Dr		5·00	
	Discount Allowed				5·00

OPEN AND BLANK CHEQUES

An open cheque is one which is not crossed. A blank cheque contains the signature of the drawer but does not mention an amount.

Bank Giro Credit Transfers

The making of payments by credit transfer was referred to earlier. The service is available to persons with or without banking accounts. For the business man the system offers the advantage that he does not have to sign numerous cheques, but just one cheque, which he attaches to a list giving the names of the persons to whom he wishes his bank to make payments, the payees' bankers, and the amounts to be paid.

As some suppliers prefer to be paid by cheque, and will object to accounts being settled by direct payment to their bankers, it is advisable to obtain the prior consent of the supplier to payment by credit transfer before paying his accounts by this method.

DIRECT DEBITS

These operate in a similar way to standing orders and are used where a customer wishes to make regular payments to a creditor. They differ from standing orders inasmuch as the debtor in the case of standing orders, gives instructions to his banker to make regular payments to specified persons, whereas, in the case of direct debits, the creditor is authorized to claim the payments from the debtor's banker.

Bank Statements

Banks are highly mechanized, and the statements their customers receive are invariably produced by computer or accounting machines on sheets of specially ruled paper. Very few banks now show the payees' names on these statements; the majority give only the cheque numbers, or rather, the last three figures of the cheque numbers.

Thomas G. Robinson In account with Blankshire Bank Ltd

Date	For Customer's Use	Debits		Credits	Balance
					37·67
27 Feb, —		54 16·00			21·67
28 Feb, —				CT* 146·32	167·99
2 Mar, —		SO* 5·65			
		SO 4·54			
		116 13·65			144·15

* CT stands for credit transfer
SO „ „ standing order

When money is paid into a bank account, it is credited to the customer's account and appears in the credit column of his bank statement, and when cheques are made out, they are debited to the customer's account and shown in the debit column. The last figure in the end column is the customer's balance. If the account has been overdrawn, the balance figure will usually be in red or marked 'OD' (for overdrawn).

Bank Reconciliation Statements

When bank statements are received, they must be checked with the firm's Cash Book. There are several reasons why the figure shown in the bank statement is unlikely to correspond with the balance shown in the Cash Book: (1) cheques which have been made out have not yet been presented for payment, (2) money paid into the bank has not yet been credited to the account, (3) certain payments, such as credit transfers, have been made direct to the bank and have not been recorded in the Cash Book, (4) the bank may have credited the account with dividends collected on behalf of its customer or with interest in respect of money held on deposit account, or (5) debited the account with interest on a bank loan.

The bank statement can still be checked with the Cash Book by allowing for these differences and this is the purpose of drawing up a Bank Reconciliation Statement. To illustrate this, we will take the Bank Statement and the Cash Book of T. Ford, a one-man business. (Refer to page 140.)

As we check the Bank Statement with the Cash Book, we tick off corresponding items, remembering that, although we have assumed that Cash Book and Bank Statement were in agreement at the beginning of October, in practice this is rarely the case. However, had there been a difference, we would have had in our Cash Book the previous Bank Reconciliation Statement to help us.

There are two items in the statement which do not appear in T. Ford's Cash Book, namely the standing order of £10 for 21st October and the credit transfer of £40 for 26th October. These should be entered in the Cash Book before preparing the Bank Reconciliation Statement. There would be no problem in finding out to what these payments refer. We will assume the £10 is a payment made by T. Ford to the Moreton Insurance Co. Ltd, and the £40 a payment received from one of his customers of the name of J. Lewis. (Refer to page 141.)

We could start with our Cash Book balance and reconcile it with the balance shown in the Bank Statement. The more usual way is to begin with the Bank Statement and work to the Cash Book, and this is what we shall do. This statement would be entered on a separate page in the Cash Book after the October postings.

BANK RECONCILIATION STATEMENT

	£	£
Balance as per Bank Statement		167·50
Add amounts not credited:		
T. Jones	25·00	
L. Brown	45·25	70·25
		237·75
Deduct cheques outstanding:		
G.P.O.	5·50	
F. Rout	41·00	46·50
Balance as per Cash Book		£191·25

If the four unticked entries above appeared in the next Bank Statement, Ford would tick them off in the above reconciliation statement when preparing the new one; it would not be necessary for him to look for these items in the Cash Book. If the cheque of £5·50, sent to the G.P.O. on 5th October, was lost in the post, Ford would find, the next time he prepared a Bank Reconciliation Statement, that this item appears again amongst the cheques outstanding. Eventually, if the cheque is not found, Ford will have to instruct his bank to cancel the cheque, and he will then have another cheque sent to the G.P.O.

Dr *T. Ford—Cash Book* Cr

Date			Disc. All. £	Details £	Bank £	Date				Disc. Recd £	Details £	Bank £
19—						19—						
Oct 1	Balance				√164·00	Oct 5	G.P.O.	402				5·50
,, 11	Cash				√50·00	,, 17	W. Smith	403				√10·00
,, 17	N. Thomas			√10·00		,, 19	L. Blundell	404		0·62		√25·00
,, 17	F. Lucas			√5·00		,, 24	District Stores	405				√20·00
					15·00	,, 26	R. T. L. Ltd	406				√36·50
,, 24	T. Jones		1·25		25·00	,, 28	F. Rout	407				41·00
,, 26	L. Brown				45·25	,, 31	Balance		c/d			161·25
		£	1·25		299·25					0·62		299·25
19— Nov 1	Balance	b/d			161·25							

Bank Statement of T. Ford

Date	For Customer's Use	Debits			Credits	Balance
Oct 1 —						164·00
Oct 11 —					√50·00	214·00
Oct 17 —					√15·00	229·00
Oct 18 —		√403	10·00			219·00
Oct 21 —		√404	25·00			194·00
Oct 21 —		SO	10·00			184·00
Oct 25 —		√405	20·00			164·00
Oct 26 —		√406	36·50			127·50
Oct 26 —					CT40·00	167·50

Dr *T. Ford—Cash Book* **Cr**

19—					£	19—					£
Nov 1	Balance	b/d			161·25	Nov 1/Oct 21	Moreton Assurance Co. SO				10·00
Nov 1/Oct 26	J. Lewis CT				40·00		Balance	c/d			191·25
		£			201·25			£			201·25
19—											
Nov 1	Balance	b/d			191·25						

THE BANK RECONCILIATION STATEMENT WHEN THERE IS AN OVERDRAFT

In this case cheques paid in and not yet credited to the customer's account must be deducted, because they will reduce the amount of the overdraft, and cheques outstanding must be added, because these will increase the amount of the overdraft.

EXERCISE 12.1

In March, 1959, K. Port received the following statement from his bank.

K. Port in account with the Northlands Bank Ltd

Date		*Debit*	*Credit*	*Balance*
1959		£	£	£
Feb 1	Balance			762
8	Clarke	18		744
„ 12	Sunds		15	759
„ 16	„		118	
	Gee & Cooks	150		727
„ 22	U.D.C.	86		641
„ 26	Wages	95		546
„ 28	Cheque unpaid	15		
	Charges	4		527

K. Port's Cash Book for the month of February, 1959, showed entries as below.

1959		£	1959		£
Feb 1	Balance at Bank brought forward	762	Feb 6	T. Clarke ..	18
„ 12	Johnson	15	„ 12	Gee & Cooks ..	150
„ 16	Snaithe	118	„ 19	Urban District Council ..	86
„ 28	Warner	216	„ 26	Gas Board ..	22
				Wages	95
			28	Murray	109
				Balance c/fwd ..	631
		£1,111			£1,111

From the above information prepare a statement in proper form reconciling the balance shown by the Cash Book with that shown by the Bank Statement on 28th February, 1959.

R.S.A. (Elementary),

EXERCISE 12.2

(1) How would the following documents be used in compiling accounting records:
   (*a*) invoices received for purchases of stock-in-trade,
   (*b*) credit notes received,
   (*c*) bank paying-in slips,
   (*d*) cheque book counterfoils,
   (*e*) copies of credit notes sent out?

Associated Examining Board, G.C.E. 'O' level, 1962 (modified)

(2) Show, by means of Journal entries, the book-keeping record for the following in the books of J. Brown, a trader.
  (*a*) J. Williams, a debtor for £72, was unable to pay his debt, and this amount was written off.
  (*b*) A cheque from W. Fraser for £26·35 was returned by the bank marked 'refer to drawer'.
  (*c*) £3 interest charged on bank overdraft had not been entered in the accounts.

Associated Examining Board, G.C.E. 'O' level, (*modified*)

(3) What is a Balance Sheet? In what ways does it differ from a Trial Balance?
(4) Explain concisely the following terms:
trade discount, credit note, statement.

EXERCISE 12.3

On 31st May, 19— the debit balance in J. Carr & Sons' Bank Account as shown in the Cash Book was £370·40. The Bank Statement at that date showed a credit balance of £409·51.

On checking the Bank Statement against the Cash Book, the following differences were found.

(1) Interest due on Westshire County Council Loan £36·75 had been collected by the bank during the month but not entered in the Cash Book.
(2) A standing order, £12·85, payable each 20th May for fire insurance premiums, had been paid by the bank but not entered in the Cash Book.
(3) Two cheques drawn on 30th May and entered in the Cash Book, one for £16·39 and one for £84·18 had not yet been presented for payment.
(4) On 31st May a cheque for £85·36 had been entered in the Cash Book and paid into bank after the Bank Statement had been collected from the bank.

Show your calculation of the balance that should appear in the Cash Book, and then prepare a Bank Reconciliation Statement.

Associated Examining Board, G.C.E. 'O' level, (*modified*)

EXERCISE 12.4

On 31st May, 19—, the Cash Book of W. Ball showed a balance at bank amounting to £6·27.

Ball's Bank Statement showed a debit balance of £22·27 on 31st May, 19—.

You are given the following information.

(1) A cheque drawn in favour of J. B. Ord on 20th May for £67·41 appeared correctly in the Bank Statement but had been entered in the Cash Book as £68·36.
(2) Cheques amounting to £148·00 entered in the Cash Book on 31st May were not credited by the bank until 1st June.
(3) A standing order of £14·00 for an insurance premium payable on 20th May had been paid by the bank but not entered in the Cash Book.
(4) On 20th May, J. Wells, a customer, had paid £57·00 into Ball's account in full settlement of his debt but no entries had been made in Ball's books.
(5) Cheques drawn in favour of creditors £75·51 and entered in the Cash Book were not presented for payment until 1st June.

Prepare statements showing:

(*a*) the balance that would appear in the Cash Book after the necessary corrections have been made,
(*b*) the reconciliation of the corrected balance with the balance shown on the Bank Statement.

Associated Examining Board, G.C.E. 'A' level (*modified*)

EXERCISE 12.5

On 31st May, 1971, B. Barclay's Bank Statement showed he had a balance at the bank of £230. On comparing the Statement with the Cash Book, he found that the following entries on the Statement had not been entered in his Cash Book: payment of insurance premium by standing order £25; dividend on an investment paid direct to the Bank £15.

He also found the following entries in the Cash Book had not yet appeared on the Statement; cheques drawn up to 31st May, 1971, £616; cheques paid up to 31st May, 1971, £405.

Prepare a Bank Reconciliation Statement so as to show the bank balance according to the Cash Book on 31st May, 1971.

Welsh Joint Education Committee G.C.E. 'O' Level

EXERCISE 12.6

On 31st December, M. Langley's Cash Book indicated a balance with his bank of £5,500. The bank statement gave a different balance, and enquiries showed that the following items were relevant:

(*a*) Cheques drawn but not presented totalled £250 in value.
(*b*) The debit side of the Cash Book had been undercast by £50.
(*c*) Some remittances had not been credited by the bank—the amount totalled £325.

Calculate the balance shown on the Bank statement—use a suitable statement to provide details of your working.

Southern Universities Joint Board G.C.E. 'O' Level

13

Reserves and Provisions-Bad Debts

ONE of the questions which the owners of a business, or their representatives, must consider at the end of the financial period is what proportion of the profits they will distribute and what proportion they will retain in the business.

Ploughing back profits into the business has always been one of the principal ways small businesses have employed to enable them to grow and prosper. But profits may not only be retained to ensure adequate working capital for future development; they may be kept in the business to provide for known liabilities which cannot be calculated with accuracy at the moment.

The expression 'provisions' means an amount retained (or written off) to provide for depreciation in the value of assets, e.g. plant and machinery, motor vans, etc.; or retained to provide for anticipated losses or contingencies which are certain to accrue but which cannot be ascertained with accuracy, e.g. bad debts, or losses incurred and not yet paid, e.g. wages, rent, etc. Thus we speak of provisions for depreciation, and provisions for bad and doubtful debts, and the term 'reserve' is used to mean other profits retained in the business. They will consist largely of undistributed profits or surplus assets.

In the chapter on company accounts, we shall see that reserves may be classified according to whether they are *capital* reserves or *revenue* reserves. The main difference between the two is that a capital reserve is accumulated in a certain way and is not available for distribution through the Profit & Loss Account, whereas a revenue reserve consists mainly of undistributed profits. These matters need not worry us unduly at the moment.

Provisions and reserves can be distinguished in other ways.

(1) *Provisions are charges against profits.* The net profits of a business cannot be properly calculated without first taking all actual and anticipated losses into account. *Reserves are appropriations of profit.*
(2) *Provisions* are usually *shown in the Balance Sheet as deductions from the assets to which they refer. Reserves are shown on the liabilities side of the Balance Sheet* with the owner's interests.

In both cases, whether creating a provision or a reserve, one account is debited (Profit & Loss in the case of provisions, Appropriation Account in the case of reserves), and the Provisions Account or Reserve Account credited.

EXAMPLE 13.1

Supposing that at the end of the financial year, 31st December, 19—, debtors totalled £10,000 and we wished to make a provision for Bad Debts of £1,000. The entry in the Profit & Loss Account would appear as follows:

Dr PROFIT & LOSS ACCOUNT FOR THE YEAR ENDED 31ST DECEMBER, 19— Cr

	£	
Provision for Bad Debts	1,000·00	

Dr Provision for Bad & Doubtful Debts Account Cr

				£
	Dec 31	Profit & Loss A/c		1,000·00

and in the Balance Sheet:

BALANCE SHEET AS AT 31ST DECEMBER, 19—

		£	£
	Fixed Assets	—	
		—	
	Current Assets		
	Debtors	10,000	
	Less Provision for Bad & Doubtful Debts	1,000	
			9,000

The creation of a reserve takes place after the net profit has been ascertained and carried down to an appropriation account.

Dr Appropriation Account Cr

			£				£
	Reserve Account		1,000·00		Net Profit from Profit & Loss A/c		5,000·00

Reserve Account

Dr					Cr
			Appropriation A/c		£ 1,000·00

BALANCE SHEET AS AT ——

	£	
Capital	—	
Reserve	1,000·00	

Bad Debts

We are now ready to consider in more detail some of the provisions which are made at the end of the financial period. A business which gives its customers credit is almost sure to make some bad debts. When it becomes certain that an outstanding account will not be paid, there is little point in continuing to show it as an 'asset' in the Sales Ledger. It is therefore transferred, without waiting until the end of the financial year, to the Bad Debts Account.

EXAMPLE 13.2

Assume L. Robinson owes us £100 in respect of goods supplied on credit on 1st February, 19—, and that on 3rd June, 19— he is adjudicated bankrupt. His liabilities total £62,000; his assets are nil.

This is a case where the debt should be transferred immediately to the Bad Debts Account. The entry in the General Journal would be as follows:

Journal

			Dr	Cr
19—			£	£
June 4	Bad Debts Account Dr		100·00	
	L. Robinson			100·00
	Being debt irrecoverable and written off			

and posted to the Ledger accounts as follows.

L. Robinson

Dr							C
19—			£	19—			£
Feb 1	Sales		100·00	June 4	Bad Debts		100·00

Bad Debts Account

Dr				Cr
19—			£	
June 4	L. Robinson		100·00	

At the end of the year, the Bad Debts Account will be closed by transfer to the Profit & Loss Account and set off against profits, with the other losses.

Let us now suppose that on 1st November, 19— our customer, L. Robinson, comes into possession of sufficient funds to enable him to pay all his creditors. The receipt by us of the money would be recorded on the debit side of the Cash Book in the ordinary way. When we came to post this entry to the Ledger, two courses would be open to us. We could either (1) credit the Bad Debts Account, or (2) reverse the entry made on 4th June by a Journal entry, thus transferring the amount back again to L. Robinson's account. The second method is preferred, since this is the only way we could obtain a complete history of these transactions in L. Robinson's account in the Sales Ledger. A credit controller should have available all the relevant facts which are likely to affect his judgement in deciding whether to allow L. Robinson credit in the future.

To give effect to the events just described the following entries would be necessary.

Journal

			Dr	Cr
19—			£	£
Nov 1	L. Robinson Dr		100·00	
	Bad Debts A/c			100·00
	Being bad debt recovered and written back			

Bad Debts Account

Dr							Cr
19—			£	19—			£
June 4	L. Robinson		100·00	Nov 1	L. Robinson (B/D recovered)		100·00

L. Robinson

Dr							Cr
19—			£	19—			£
Feb 1	Sales		100·00	June 4	Bad Debts		100·00
Nov 1	Bad Debts		100·00	Nov 1	Bank		100·00

In the case just described the decision to write the debt off as bad was taken prematurely and so was a mistake. Transferring the debt back to the customer's account corrected this mistake. Now let us consider the procedure where a debt written off as bad in one financial period is collected in a subsequent period.

Dr T. Smith Cr

1970 Jan 1	Balance		£ 100·00	1970 June 2	Bad Debts		£ 100·00

The financial year ends on 31st December. Smith paid the debt on May 2, 1972.

Procedure

Debit Smith's account with £100 and credit Bad Debts Recovered account with £100.

Debit the Cash Account on May 2nd with the £100 received from Smith and credit Smith's account.

At the end of 1972 close Bad Debts Recovered Account by transfer to the Profit & Loss Account.

Dr T. Smith Cr

1972 May 2	Bad Debts Recovered		£ 100·00	1972 May 2	Cash		£ 100·00

Dr Bad Debts Recovered Account Cr

1972 Dec 31	Profit & Loss Account		£ 100·00	1972 May 2	T. Smith		£ 100·00

PROVISION FOR BAD DEBTS

Apart from those debts which are written off to the Bad Debts Account during the year, some of the debts outstanding at the end of the year will also be irrecoverable, but it will not be possible to say, when preparing the final accounts, which these will be. Provision has therefore to be made to the extent of the sum of the debts considered doubtful. Two methods of calculating this figure are employed in practice. One is for the accountant to go through the Sales Ledger, noting those accounts which, in his opinion, are unlikely to be recovered. In doing this he will have regard to the age of the debt. The longer it has been outstanding the less likely it is that it will be paid. If there are many active accounts, this takes a very long time, and so instead he might take a percentage of the total debtors, the percentage being based on the trader's experience of the proportion of his debts which usually prove to be bad.

In calculating the net profit of a business, the expenses of the period should be matched with the income of that period. A bad debt is an expense but it is not always possible to match it with the period of the sale; the fact that the debt is bad may only become apparent in a subsequent period. A provision for bad debts is an estimate of the expenses arising from debts being irrecoverable; it is a device the Accountant employs to overcome this difficulty of matching income with expenses.

EXAMPLE 13.3

The figure for debtors, as shown in the Trial Balance drawn up on 31st December, 19—, is £10,560. You are required to create a Provision for Bad & Doubtful Debts equal to 5% of the debtors, and to show how the entries will appear in the Profit & Loss Account, Ledger and Balance Sheet.

Dr PROFIT & LOSS ACCOUNT FOR THE YEAR ENDED 31ST DECEMBER, 19— Cr

	£	
Provision for Bad & Doubtful Debts (5% of £10,560)	528·00	

Dr Provision for Bad & Doubtful Debts Account Cr

				£
	19— Dec 31	Profit & Loss A/c		528·00

BALANCE SHEET AS AT 31ST DECEMBER, 19—

		£	£
	Fixed Assets	—	
	Current Assets		
	Debtors	10,560	
	Less Provision for B & D Debts	528	
			10,032

The Provision for Bad & Doubtful Debts Account has a credit balance, but instead of showing this on the liabilities side of the Balance Sheet, we show it as a deduction from the debtors on the assets side.

Next time a Trial Balance is extracted, the Provision for Bad and Doubtful Debts Account will appear among the credit balances.

INCREASING AND REDUCING THE AMOUNT OF THE PROVISION FOR BAD DEBTS

Sometimes students are given a Trial Balance which includes a provision for bad debts, and are then instructed, in drawing up the final accounts, to increase the provision, or to reduce it.

EXAMPLE 13.4

Extract from Trial Balance

	Dr	Cr
		£
Provision for Bad Debts		500·00

The Bad Debts provision is to be increased to £1,000.

To give effect to this instruction, we must debit the Profit & Loss Account with £500 and credit the Provision for Bad Debts Account with £500. The entries would appear in the two accounts as follows.

PROFIT & LOSS ACCOUNT FOR THE YEAR ENDED ——

Dr			Cr
	£	£	
New Provision for Bad Debts	1,000		
Less Old Provision	500		
	—	500	

Provision for Bad & Doubtful Debts Account

Dr		Cr		
				£
		Balance	b/d	500
		Profit & Loss A/c		500

EXAMPLE 13.5

The facts are the same as stated in the Example 13.4 except that the provision is to be reduced to £300.

Instead of debiting the Profit & Loss Account, this time we must credit the Profit & Loss Account with £200. This sum now becomes available for distribution. The Provision Account is debited.

PROFIT & LOSS ACCOUNT FOR THE YEAR ENDED ——

Dr	Cr		
		£	£
	Old Provision for Bad Debts	500	
	Less New Provision	300	
		—	200

Dr **Provision for Bad & Doubtful Debts Account** Cr

		£			£
Profit & Loss A/c		200	Balance	b/d	500
Balance	c/d	300			
		£500			£500
			Balance	b/d	300

MISCELLANEOUS POINTS TO NOTE

(1) When a debt which has been written off as bad in a previous period is subsequently collected, its receipt is treated as an unexpected gain in the books of account.

(2) There is more than one way of dealing with bad debts and provision for bad and doubtful debts. For example, instead of closing the Bad Debts Account by transfer to the Profit & Loss Account, it may be closed by transfer to the Provision for Bad Debts Account. The effect on the final accounts will, however, be the same.

(3) The first time a provision for bad debts is created, this item will not appear in the Trial Balance because the account is opened after the Trial Balance is extracted; it will be included in subsequent lists of Ledger balances.

(4) When the student is required to prepare final accounts from a Trial Balance, each item in the Trial Balance will appear once only either in a final account or in the Balance Sheet. Thus, if there is an item 'Sundry Debtors £10,000' in the Trial Balance, this item will appear only in the Balance Sheet. Any instructions appended to the Trial Balance, e.g. to create a provision for bad and doubtful debts, will involve *two* entries in the final accounts —in this case in the Profit & Loss Account and again in the Balance Sheet as a deduction from the debtors. This is so with all adjustments which have to be made preparatory to drawing up the final accounts.

EXAMPLE 13.6

Jack Swan carries on business as a wholesaler. On 31st March, 19— the following Trial Balance was extracted from his books.

Trial Balance

	Dr	Cr
	£	£
Plant & Machinery	4,860	
Fixtures & Fittings	400	
Wages	2,610	
Office Salaries	1,030	
Bad Debts	600	

Returns Inwards and Outwards	350	340
Carriage on Sales	146	
Discounts Allowed and Received	70	230
Sundry Debtors & Creditors	4,700	3,610
Purchases and Sales	18,720	30,180
Cash in Hand	180	
Cash at Bank	900	
Rent and Rates	620	
Stock (1st April)	6,234	
Capital		7,060
	£41,420	£41,420

Prepare Trading and Profit & Loss Accounts for the year ended 31st March, 19— and a Balance Sheet at that date. The stock on hand at 31st March, 19— was valued at £6,200. A provision for bad and doubtful debts is to be created equal to 5% of the debtors.

TRADING AND PROFIT & LOSS ACCOUNTS FOR YEAR ENDED 31ST MARCH, 19—

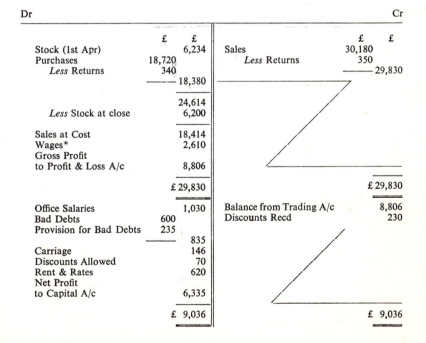

Dr	£	£		£	Cr £
Stock (1st Apr)		6,234	Sales	30,180	
Purchases	18,720		*Less* Returns	350	
Less Returns	340				29,830
		18,380			
		24,614			
Less Stock at close		6,200			
Sales at Cost		18,414			
Wages*		2,610			
Gross Profit to Profit & Loss A/c		8,806			
		£ 29,830			£ 29,830
Office Salaries		1,030	Balance from Trading A/c		8,806
Bad Debts	600		Discounts Recd		230
Provision for Bad Debts	235				
		835			
Carriage		146			
Discounts Allowed		70			
Rent & Rates		620			
Net Profit to Capital A/c		6,335			
		£ 9,036			£ 9,036

* See paragraph 1, Chapter 20

BALANCE SHEET AS AT 31ST MARCH, 19—

	£	£			£	£
			Fixed Assets			
Capital	7,060		Plant & Machinery		4,860	
Add Profits	6,335		Fixtures & Fittings		400	
		13,395				5,260
Current Liabilities			*Current Assets*			
Creditors		3,610	Stock		6,200	
			Debtors	£4,700		
			Less Provision for Bad Debts	235		
					4,465	
			Cash at Bank		900	
			Cash in Hand		180	
						11,745
		£17,005				£17,005

EXERCISE 13.1

A company makes a provision for doubtful debts of 5% on debtors and a provision at the rate of 2½% for discount on debtors.

On 1st January, 1964 the balances standing in the relevant accounts were provision for doubtful debts £672 and provision for discount on debtors £319.

(1) Enter the balances in the appropriate accounts.

(2) During 1964 the company incurred bad debts £1,480 and allowed discounts £3,289. On 31st December, 1964 debtors amounted to £12,800. Show the entries in the appropriate accounts for the year 1964, assuming that the company's accounting year ends on 31st December, 1964.

Associated Examining Board, G.C.E. 'A' level, 1965

EXERCISE 13.2

The sundry debtors of T. Smith & Co. total £6,000 at the close of the year (31st December, 19—). Three debts amounting to £742 are considered doubtful, and it is desired to create a provision equal to the amount of the doubtful debts. Show:

(1) the Journal entries necessary to create the provision,
(2) the appropriate Ledger entries,
(3) how the item 'Sundry Debtors' will appear in the Balance Sheet.

EXERCISE 13.3

An extract from the Trial Balance of G. Risborough & Co. at the end of the financial year, 31st March, 1965, is as follows.

Trial Balance

	Dr £	Cr £
Sundry Debtors	12,780	
Bad Debts	250	
Provision for Bad & Doubtful Debts		1,000

It is decided to reduce the provision to £800. Show:

(1) the Journal entry necessary to give effect to this decision,
(2) how this item will appear in the Profit & Loss Account and Balance Sheet.

EXERCISE 13.4

The present provision for bad debts in the books of G. Raleigh is £670. On 31st December, 1964 it is desired to adjust this figure so that it represents 5% of the outstanding debts. At 31st December, 1964 these total £16,380. Give the Journal entry to achieve this, and show the relevant entries in the Profit & Loss Account and the Balance Sheet.

EXERCISE 13.5

The sundry debtors of W. Cox & Co. amount to £12,500. Make a provision for bad debts of 4% and a provision for discounts on debtors of 2½% and show the item for sundry debtors as it should appear in the Balance Sheet.

EXERCISE 13.6

Give the entries required to create a provision for discounts on creditors of 2½%, the sundry creditors standing at £10,000 on 31st December.

Provisions for Cash Discounts

The argument used in support of the creation of provisions for discounts allowed and discounts received is that where it is customary to allow and to receive cash discounts, figures for debtors and creditors will be incorrect in the Balance Sheet unless the provisions are created. There is a considerable difference of opinion amongst accountants on the need for such provisions. A point to remember is that where these provisions are made, stock on hand should be shown in the Balance Sheet at the discounted cost. And, further, that where provisions for both doubtful debts and discounts allowed are to be made, the provision for discounts is calculated on the net figure, that is, after the doubtful debts have been deducted from the figure of the debtors.

EXAMPLE 13.7

Sundry debtors at 31st December, 19— stood at £5,000. Show the entries necessary to create (1) a provision for bad and doubtful debts equal to 5% of the debtors, and (2) a provision for discounts of 2½%.

Journal

Date	Particulars		Fo.	Dr	Cr
19—				£	£
Dec 31	Profit & Loss A/c	Dr		368·75	
	Provision for Bad Debts				250·00
	,, ,, Discounts				118·75
	Being 5% provision for Bad Debts and 2½% ,, ,, Discounts				

Dr — Provision for Bad & Doubtful Debts — Cr

		19—			£
		Dec 31	Profit & Loss A/c		250·00

Dr — Provision for Discounts on Debtors — Cr

		19—			£
		Dec 31	Profit & Loss A/c		118·75

PROFIT & LOSS ACCOUNT FOR THE YEAR ENDED 31ST DECEMBER, 19—

Dr — Cr

	£	£	
Provisions for			
Discounts	118·75		
Doubtful Debts	250·00		
		368·75	

BALANCE SHEET AS AT 31ST DECEMBER, 19—

		£	£	£
	Current Assets			
	Debtors		5,000·00	
	Less Provisions for			
	Doubtful Debts	250·00		
	Discounts	118·75		
			368·75	
				4,631·25

Whilst it is wise to provide for all contingent losses, and probably prudent to create a provisions account for discounts allowed, there is less justification for opening a provisions account for discounts received. These are gains, and although losses ought to be anticipated, it is often considered imprudent to anticipate gains. However, where it is done, the entries are the reverse of those shown above. In the Balance Sheet, the provision for discounts received would appear as a deduction from sundry creditors.

14

Provision for Depreciation

A REGISTERED COMPANY must keep such books of account as are necessary to give a true and fair view of the state of its affairs. Although this provision in the Companies Act, 1948 was intended, among other things, to protect persons who might be persuaded to invest money in a public company, every efficiently run enterprise, whatever its form of organization, will seek to keep its books of account in a manner which will give reliable information about the state of its affairs.

A 'true and fair' view demands a proper valuation of the assets in the Balance Sheet. As we have already seen, it is customary, before producing the final accounts, (1) to draw up an inventory of unsold stock, and (2) to provide for debts which might not be recoverable, and thus to show 'Debtors' in the Balance Sheet at a figure more closely representing the true worth of this asset. We must now consider other assets, such as machinery, delivery vans, etc., which suffer a permanent decrease in value in the course of trading.

Plant and machinery, office fixtures, delivery vans, loose tools, are bought for the purpose of earning an income, and the loss which arises from their use must be set off against this income. If this loss in value, or 'depreciation', as it is called, is not provided for, assets will be overvalued in the Balance Sheet, and resources may not be available when needed.

Depreciation and Obsolescence

The loss through depreciation which will be set off annually against the income earned will depend upon (1) the estimated life of the machine, and (2) the possibility of its becoming obsolete before it actually wears out.

An operative's output is governed by the efficiency of his machine. If, in a certain printing establishment, for example, a machine minder is looking after a machine capable of printing 10,000 copies an hour, this man's output will be twice as great as that of a similar skilled machine minder whose machine can print only 5,000 copies an hour. Labour costs will be twice as great in respect of this operation in the case of the second printing press. Even though this second machine has not worn out, it will probably pay the company to scrap the machine and install a more efficient one in its place. 'Obsolescence', as the resulting loss is called, occurs most frequently in the mass production industries, and in those where the operations are largely repetitive.

Where a machine is not likely to become obsolete, the useful life of the machine, and the consequent total loss through depreciation, is not difficult to compute. If, for example, a machine costing £1,000 is likely to have a useful life of ten years and to have a scrap value of £100 at the end of it, depreciation will amount to £900 over ten years. How this loss is apportioned annually over this period is a question of policy. We shall consider some of the ways it can be done.

METHOD 1 STRAIGHT LINE METHOD

The method whereby an asset is depreciated by equal instalments each year until the cost of the asset is extinguished is termed the 'fixed instalment' or 'straight line' method. In the example just given, the machine would be depreciated at the rate of £90 a year. We will show the accounts as they would appear in the Ledger, assuming the machine was bought on 1st January, 19—1.

Dr Machinery Account Cr

19—1 Jan 1	Cash	CB	£ 1,000·00				

Dr Provision for Depreciation (Machinery) Cr

19—1 Dec 31	Balance	c/d	£ 90·00	19—1 Dec 31	Depreciation	J	£ 90·00
19—2 Dec 31	Balance	c/d	180·00	19—2 Jan 1	Balance	b/d	90·00
				Dec 31	Depreciation		90·00
		£	180·00			£	180·00
19—3 Dec 31	Balance	c/d	270·00	19—3 Jan 1	Balance	b/d	180·00
				Dec 31	Depreciation		90·00
		£	270·00				270·00
				19—4 Jan 1	Balance	b/d	£270·00

BALANCE SHEET AS AT 31ST DECEMBER, 19—3

		£	£
	Fixed Assets		
	Machinery at cost	1,000·00	
	Less Depreciation	270·00	
			730·00

A registered company must show fixed assets in the Balance Sheet at cost less the total depreciation provision to date; it is usual, therefore, to continue to show the asset at cost and to keep a cumulative depreciation provision account similar to the one above.

An alternative method to the above is for the Machinery Account to be credited yearly with the fixed instalment and a Depreciation Account debited; the latter is then closed at the end of the year by transfer to the Profit & Loss Account.

Journal

				Dr	Dr
19—1				£	£
Dec 31	Depreciation Account	Dr		90·00	
	Machinery Account				90·00
	Being depreciation at £90 per annum				

Dr — Machinery Account — Cr

19—1			£	19—1			£
Jan 1	Cash	CB	1,000·00	Dec 31	Depreciation	J	90·00
				,, 31	Balance	c/d	910·00
		£	1,000·00			£	1,000·00
19—2							
Jan 1	Balance	b/d	910·00				

Dr — Depreciation Account — Cr

19—1			£	19—1			£
Dec 31	Machinery	J	90·00	Dec 31	Profit & Loss A/c	J	90·00

Although, in describing the cumulative provision method, the Journal entries and the Depreciation Account have not been shown, it should be understood that both are required. The basic difference between the two methods is that under the first the Provision Account is credited and no entry is made in the Machinery Account, whereas under the second, the Machinery Account itself is credited. In both cases the Depreciation Account is closed by transfer to the Profit & Loss Account or Manufacturing Account at the end of the financial period.

METHOD 2 THE REDUCING INSTALMENT (OR FIXED PERCENTAGE) METHOD

One objection to the fixed instalment method of depreciation is that whereas the amount charged to revenue each year is the same, the costs for repairs and renewals tend to increase as the machine gets older. Under the method we are about to describe, the same percentage is deducted each year from the written down value, thus causing the depreciation to be heaviest when the machine is new and repair costs are small, and lightest when the machine is older and costs more to maintain. A percentage must be chosen which will reduce the asset to its expected scrap value over the period of the machine's useful life. 20% depreciation in the case of a machine costing £1,000 will reduce the sum to £107 at the end of ten years. Note that under the reducing instalment method, the depreciation at the end of the first year is £200 as compared with £90 under the fixed instalment method.

The formula for arriving at the percentage is:

$$A = P(1-r/100)^n \quad \text{or} \quad r = 100(1-\sqrt[n]{[A/P]})$$

where A = estimated scrap value
P = original cost to be depreciated
r = rate of interest per cent
n = estimated life of asset in years.

EXAMPLE 14.1

The G.H.A. Co. purchase a machine on 1st January, 19— costing £2,500 fo cash. They decide to write this down at the rate of 20% per annum. Show the entries in the Machinery Account from the date of purchase to 1st January, 19—.

Dr Machinery Account Cr

19—1			£	19—1			£
Jan 1	Cash	CB	2,500·00	Dec 31	Depreciation A/c	J	500·00
				,, 31	Balance	c/d	2,000·00
		£	2,500·00			£	2,500·00
19—2				19—2			
Jan 1	Balance	b/d	2,000·00	Dec 31	Depreciation A/c	J	400·00
				,, 31	Balance	c/d	1,600·00
		£	2,000·00			£	2,000·00
19—3				19—3			
Jan 1	Balance	b/d	1,600·00	Dec 31	Depreciation A/c	J	320·00
				,, 31	Balance	c/d	1,280·00
		£	1,600·00			£	1,600·00
19—4				19—4			
Jan 1	Balance	b/d	1,280·00	Dec 31	Depreciation A/c	J	256·00
				,, 31	Balance	c/d	1,024·00
		£	1,280·00			£	1,280·00
19—5							
Jan 1	Balance	b/d	1,024·00				

METHOD 3 REVALUING THE ASSETS

There are some assets in the business for which the methods of depreciation already explained are hardly suitable, e.g. bottles, package materials, loose tools, patterns, models, cattle, etc. For these, the method of stocktaking and valuing is often employed. The Trading or Manufacturing Account is debited with the old value and credited with the new. Another way is to debit the Profit & Loss Account with the difference arising from the revaluation and credit the Asset Account. If the particular asset has increased in value, the Profit & Loss Account is credited and the Asset Account debited. Where the fluctuation in value is likely to be temporary, as in the case of investments, it might be advisable to carry the difference to a Reserve Account and leave the Asset Account as it is.

In a previous chapter it was pointed out that the sum charged by way of depreciation represents the value of the services rendered by the different assets. A criticism sometimes made of the method of periodical revaluation is that very unequal annual sums may be charged to the Profit & Loss Account, although the value of the services provided by these assets is approximately the same each year.

EXAMPLE 14.2

A motor van purchased on 1st January, 19— for £670 is valued at £450 on 31st December, 19—. Show the entries in the books to record this loss.

Journal

			Dr	Cr
19—			£	£
Dec 31	Depreciation Account Dr		220·00	
	Motor Vans Account			220·00
	Being amount of depreciation on revaluation of asset			

Motor Vans Account

Dr							Cr
19—			£	19—			£
Jan 1	Cash	CB	670·00	Dec 31	Depreciation A/c	J	220·00
				„ 31	Balance	c/d	450·00
		£	670·00			£	670·00
19—							
Jan 1	Balance	b/d	450·00				

Dr — Depreciation Account — Cr

19—			£	
Dec 31	Motor Vans A/c	J	220·00	

The Depreciation Account, which will also include depreciation of other assets, is closed by transfer to the Profit & Loss Account.

METHOD 4 SINKING FUND METHOD

Under this method, the asset remains on the books at its original cost, but each year a fixed sum is debited to the Profit & Loss Account and a similar amount of cash invested in securities. When it becomes necessary to replace the asset, the securities are sold to provide the purchase money.

EXAMPLE 14.3

A machine costing £1,000 is estimated to have a life of four years and a scrap value of a negligible sum after this period. It is decided to provide for replacement of the machine by means of a sinking fund (5% compound interest). Show the Machinery Account, the Sinking Fund Account, and the Sinking Fund Investment Account.

From sinking fund tables we can calculate the annual instalment to be invested at 5% compound interest, viz.

$$1{,}000 \times 0{\cdot}232012 = £232{\cdot}01$$

Each year this sum is debited to Profit & Loss Account and credited to Sinking Fund Account. A similar sum will be invested and debited to Sinking Fund Investment Account. At the end of each year, the interest received will be debited to the Cash Account and credited to the Sinking Fund Account. The cash invested in the second year will be the instalments plus the interest earned from investment of the first instalment. The accounts are set out below.

Dr — Machinery Account — Cr

Year 1			£	*Year 4*			£
Jan 1	Cash		1,000·00	Dec 31	Sinking Fund A/c		1,000·00

(EXTRACT FROM THE) BALANCE SHEET AS AT 31ST DECEMBER (END OF YEAR 1)

	£		£
Liabilities		*Assets*	
Sinking Fund A/c	232·01	Sinking Fund Investment A/c	232·01

Dr Sinking Fund Account (or Depreciation Fund Account) Cr

Date	Particulars		£	Date	Particulars		£
Year 1				*Year 1*			
Dec 31	Balance	c/d	232·01	Dec 31	Profit & Loss A/c		232·01
Year 2				*Year 2*			
Dec 31	Balance	c/d	475·62	Jan 1	Balance	b/d	232·01
				Dec 31	Cash (interest)		11·60
				31	Profit & Loss A/c		232·01
			475·62				475·62
Year 3				*Year 3*			
Dec 31	Balance	c/d	731·41	Jan 1	Balance	b/d	475·62
				Dec 31	Cash (interest)		23·78
				„ 31	Profit & Loss A/c		232·01
			731·41				731·41
Year 4				*Year 4*			
Dec 31	Machinery A/c		1,000·00	Jan 1	Balance	b/d	731·41
				Dec 31	Cash (interest)		36·57
				„ 31	Profit & Loss A/c		232·02
		£	1,000·00			£	1,000·00

Dr Sinking Fund Investment Account (or Depreciation Investment Account) Cr

Date	Particulars		£	Date	Particulars		£
Year 1				*Year 1*			
Dec 31	Cash		232·01	Dec 31	Balance	c/d	232·01
Year 2				*Year 2*			
Jan 1	Balance	b/d	232·01	Dec 31	Balance	c/d	475·62
Dec 31	Cash		243·61				
			475·62				475·62
Year 3				*Year 3*			
Jan 1	Balance	b/d	475·62	Dec 31	Balance	c/d	731·41
Dec 31	Cash		255·79				
			731·41				731·41
Year 4				*Year 4*			
Jan 1	Balance	b/d	731·41	Dec 31	Cash (on realization of investment)		1,000·00
Dec 31	Cash		268·59				
		£	1,000·00			£	1,000·00

The final sum of £268·59 would not of course be invested.

Note that other terms for Sinking Fund Account are Depreciation Fund Account, Amortization Fund Account or Redemption Fund Account. This method is often used in the case of leases of property.

The sinking fund formula is:

$$P = \frac{A(R^n - 1)}{R - 1} \text{ or } A = \frac{P(R-1)}{R^n - 1}$$

where A = the annual sum to be paid into the fund

P = the cost of the asset to which the sinking fund has to accumulate

R = the rate of interest in the form $1 + \frac{r\%}{100}$ i.e., if $r = 5\%$, $R = 1{\cdot}05$

n = number of years.

EXERCISE 14.1

Fortune Ltd owns freehold premises valued at £100,000 and the lease of adjoining premises. The lease was originally purchased for £18,000, and each year thereafter the company had transferred an appropriate amount to a leasehold redemption fund and invested an equivalent amount in outside securities.

On 31st December, 19–1 there was a balance of £5,100 on the leasehold redemption fund and a balance of the same amount on the Leasehold Redemption Fund Investment Account.

(1) Show the balances in the appropriate accounts at 31st December, 19–1.

(2) On 1st January, 19–2 the company concentrated its work in the freehold premises and sold the lease of the adjoining premises for cash £23,000. Legal and other costs were £490, and there were dilapidations, £1,400, which the company had to pay. These amounts were paid by cheque.

On 30th December, 19–1, the securities in the Leasehold Redemption Fund Investment Account were sold for £6,500.

Make the necessary entries in the Ledger accounts and close the relevant accounts at 1st January, 19–2.

Associated Examining Board, G.C.E. 'A' level

WORKED EXERCISE 14.4

The balances in the Ledger of a wholesale business on 31st December, 19–1 included plant and machinery £10,000 and office furniture £800. Open Ledger accounts and depreciate plant and machinery at 10% per annum and office furniture at 5%. Show how the assets would appear in the Balance Sheet.

Dr — Plant & Machinery Account — Cr

19–1			£	19–1			£
Jan 1	Balance	c/d	10,000·00	Dec 31	Depreciation		1,000·00
				,, 31	Balance	c/d	9,000·00
		£	10,000·00			£	10,000·00
19–2							
Jan	Balance	b/d	9,000·00				

Dr — Office Furniture Account — Cr

19–1			£	19–1			£
Jan 1	Balance	b/d	800·00	Dec 31	Depreciation		40·00
				, 31	Balance	c/d	760·00
		£	800·00			£	800·00
19–2							
Jan 1	Balance	b/d	760·00				

Dr Depreciation Account Cr

19–1			£	19–1			£
Dec 31	P & Mchy	J	1,000·00	Dec 31	Profit & Loss A/c	J	1,040·00
31	Office Furniture	J	40·00				
		£	1,040·00			£	1,040·00

BALANCE SHEET AS AT 31ST DECEMBER, 19–1

	Fixed Assets	£	£	£
	Plant & Machinery	10,000		
	Less depreciation	1,000	9,000	
	Office Furniture	800		
	Less depreciation	40	760	9 760

WORKED EXERCISE 14.5

A.B. started business as a manufacturer on 1st January, 19–1. He installed machinery and plant at a cost of £15,000.

On 1st May, 19–2 he purchased additional machinery for £2,800 and paid £200 for installation.

On 1st July, 19–3 he sold for £1,600 a machine installed on 1st January, 19–1, at a cost of £3,000.

A.B. closes his books on 31st December in each year. It is his practice to write off 20% of the cost of machinery each year (including the year of purchase).

Show A.B.'s Plant & Machinery Account for the years 19–1, 19–2, 19–3.

Associated Examining Board, G.C.E. 'O' level (modified)

Dr Plant & Machinery Account Cr

19–1			£	19–1			£
Jan 1	Cash		15,000·00	Dec 31	Depreciation		3,000·00
				„ 31	Balance	c/d	12,000·00
		£	15,000·00			£	15,000·00
19–2				19–2			
Jan 1	Balance	b/d	12,000·00	Dec 31	Depreciation		3,600·00
May 1	Cash (plant)		2,800·00	„ 31	Balance	c/d	11,400·00
1	Cash (installation)		200·00				
		£	15,000·00			£	15,000·00
19–3				19–3			
Jan 1	Balance	b/d	11,400·00	July 1	Cash (sale of plant)		1,600·00
				Dec 31	P & L A/c (loss on sale)		200·00
				„ 31	Depreciation		3,000·00
				„ 31	Balance	c/d	6,600·00
		£	11,400·00			£	11,400·00
19–4							
Jan 1	Balance	b/d	6,600·00				

or alternatively (see first paragraph on page 166).

Dr **Plant & Machinery Account** Cr

19–1			£	19–1			£
Jan 1	Cash		15,000·00	Dec 31	Depreciation		3,000·00
Dec 31	Depreciation to date	c/d	3,000·00	31	Plant & Mchy at cost	c/d	15,000·00
		£	18,000·00			£	18,000·00
19–2				19–2			
Jan 1	Plant & Mchy at cost	b/d	15,000·00	Jan 1	Depreciation to date	b/d	3,000·00
May 1	Cash (plant) £2,800 Cash (installation) £200		3,000·00	Dec 31	Depreciation		3,600·00
Dec 31	Depreciation to date	c/d	6,600·00	,, 31	Plant at cost	c/d	18,000·00
		£	24,600·00			£	24,600·00
19–3				19–3			
Jan 1	Plant at cost	b/d	18,000·00	Jan 1	Depreciation to date	b/d	6,600·00
Dec 31	Depreciation to date	c/d	8,400·00	July 1	Cash (sale of plant)		1,600·00
				Dec 31	P & L A/c (loss on sale)		200·00
				,, 31	Depreciation for year		3,000·00
				,, 31	Plant at cost	c/d	15,000·00
		£	26,400·00			£	26,400·00
19–4				19–4			
Jan 1	To Plant at cost	b/d	15,000·00	Jan 1	Depreciation to date	b/d	8,400·00

Notes.

(1) A full year's depreciation has been deducted on 31st December, 19–2 in respect of the machine bought in May that year; this is common practice.

(2) No depreciation has been deducted in 19–3 in respect of the machine sold in 19–3.

In some small businesses it is the practice to show the machinery at cost as a debit balance in the Plant & Machinery Account and the cumulative depreciation as a credit balance in the same account. Whilst this method is not recommended for examination purposes unless specially required, there are advantages in showing the machinery at cost, and the total depreciation to date, in the one account.

OTHER METHODS OF DEPRECIATION

Depletion Method

This is used where the asset is a wasting asset such as a quarry or mine. In this case it is common practice to write off the expired capital value by way of depreciation. Depreciation is often tied in with the operation of a sinking fund.

Machine-Hour Method

The cost of the machine is, under this method, divided by the total operating hours estimated for the machine's effective life, thus giving an hourly rate for depreciation. In making the calculation an allowance is made for the estimated scrap value of the machine.

Sale of Fixed Assets

A machine or other similar asset is estimated to have, for depreciation purposes, a profitable working life of so many years and a certain scrap value at the end of this time. If an asset is sold before, or at the end of, its useful life, the price obtained, i.e. its market value, may be very different from the written down value of the asset. The question is how to deal with these so-called profits and losses on the sale of fixed assets.

In practice, it is usual to depreciate an asset for a full year in the year of purchase, even though the asset has not been owned for a full year, and not to depreciate it at all in the year the asset is sold. Any small 'profit' and 'loss' on sale is then adjusted through the Depreciation Account.

ILLUSTRATION 14.6

A machine costing £1,000 on 1st May, 1960, and having an estimated life of 10 years and a scrap value at the end of this period of £100, is sold on 12th July, 1965 for £600. (The financial year ends on 31st December.)

Dr Machinery Account Cr

1960 May 1	Cash		£ 1,000	1965 July 12	Disposal of Fixed Asset A/c		£ 1,000

Dr Provision for Depreciation (Machinery) Cr

1965 July 12	Disposal of Fixed Asset A/c		£ 450	1960 Dec 31	Depreciation		£ 90
				1961 Dec 31	Depreciation		90
				1962 Dec 31	Depreciation		90
				1963 Dec 31	Depreciation		90
				1964 Dec 31	Depreciation		90
		£	450			£	450

In this example we shall deal with the profit on sale through the Depreciation Account by first opening a Disposal of Fixed Asset Account, to which the balances on the Machinery Account and the Accumulated Depreciation Account (Provision for Depreciation Account) are transferred, viz.

Disposal of Fixed Asset Account

Dr				Cr			
19—			£	19—			£
July 12	Machinery A/c		1,000	July 12	Provision for Depreciation		450
12	Depreciation A/c (Surplus on disposal of machinery)		50	12	Cash		600
		£	1,050			£	1,050

Depreciation Account

Dr				Cr			
				19—			£
				July 12	Disposal of Fixed Asset A/c		50

If an asset is sold at less than its written down figure, the difference is of course debited to Depreciation Account.

Any exceptional profits or losses on the sale of fixed assets ought to appear separately in the final accounts.

EXERCISE 14.2

From the following Trial Balance prepare a Trading Account, Profit & Loss Account, and a Balance Sheet, as at 31st December, 19—.

Trial Balance—D. Gerrard

	Dr	Cr
	£	£
Stock (1st January)	452	
Plant & Machinery	560	
Furniture & Fittings	280	
Sundry Debtors	295	
Sundry Creditors		442
Drawings	50	
Purchases	1,675	
Sales		2,587
Returns Outwards		35
Returns Inwards	73	
Manufacturing Wages	381	
Carriage Outwards	27	
Discount (balance)		58
Bad Debts (debit P & L A/c)	89	
Insurance	54	
Trade Expenses	13	
Rates & Taxes	107	
Commission	36	
Cash at Bank	196	
Cash in Hand	34	
Capital (D. Gerrard)		1,200
	£4,322	£4,322

10% depreciation to be written off plant and machinery, 7½% depreciation to be written off furniture and fittings. Stock on hand, 31st December, valued at £432.

EXERCISE 14.3

From the following list of balances draw up the Trial Balance of E. W. Rowcroft as at 31st December, 19—, and then prepare Trading Account, Profit & Loss Account for the 6 months and Balance Sheet at 31st December 19—.

	£
E. W. Rowcroft, Capital Account	3,500
Purchases	4,080
Heating & Lighting	20
Drawings	82
Sales	7,000
Returns Outwards	70
Machinery & Plant	1,300
Discounts Received	27
Land & Buildings	1,100
Returns Inwards	116
Rent & Rates	32
Fixtures & Fittings	222
Repairs	118
Trade Expenses	124
Horses & Carts	288
Sundry Creditors	1,029
Wages	1,526
Commission Received	90
Carriage Outwards	39
Cash at Bank	19
Sundry Debtors	230
Carriage Inwards	31
Stock, 1st July	2,389

The stock on 31st December was valued at £1,275.

When preparing the Trading Account, Profit & Loss Account and Balance Sheet, you are required to depreciate the machinery and plant by 10% per annum.

15

Other Provisions and Adjustments

THE dates of the financial year for which a business produces its accounts are at the discretion of its owners. Some firms choose the ordinary calendar year, 1st January to 31st December; others adopt, approximately, the Government's fiscal year. But whichever period is chosen, it is essential that only the income and the expenditure relating to the particular period are included in the Trading and Profit & Loss Accounts.

Outstanding Liabilities

In previous exercises we have assumed that all expenses for the period for which accounts have been prepared have passed through the books. In practice this is rarely the case. Usually certain expenses, such as rents, wages, salaries, lighting and heating, telephone, etc., have accrued but have not yet been paid, and so do not appear in the nominal accounts. If a firm's financial year, for example, ends on a Wednesday, and it normally pays wages in arrear on Fridays, it will owe, on the last day, wages for Monday, Tuesday, and Wednesday (assuming the firm is working a five day week), and the final accounts will be misleading if provision is not made for this outstanding liability. And again, supposing a firm's rent is payable quarterly in arrear, and the final quarter, at the time of balancing the books, is due but unpaid, the final quarter's rent must still be charged against the year's income. The method usually adopted is to debit the appropriate revenue account in the period to which the charge belongs and credit the same revenue account in the following period. As we shall see, any credit balance appearing in a revenue account after the closing of the books represents a liability, and must be shown as such in the Balance Sheet.

ILLUSTRATION 15.1

At 31st March the following debit balances appear in the Trial Balance of a trader.

Rent	£450
Gas & Electricity	£50

A quarter's rent (£150) is due but not yet paid. There is an outstanding debt in respect of gas, £9·12. Show how these revenue accounts will appear in the books when they are finally closed and the accrued charges brought into account.

Dr Rent Account Cr

19—			£	19—			£
Mar 31	Balance	b/d	450·00	Mar 31	Profit & Loss A/c		600·00
„ 31	Provision for accrued rent		150·00				
		£	600·00			£	600·00
				19—			
				Apr 1	Provision for accrued rent		150·00

Dr Gas & Electricity Account Cr

19—			£	19—			£
Mar 31	Balance	b/d	50·00	Mar 31	Profit & Loss A/c		59·12
31	Provision for accrued gas		9·12				
		£	59·12			£	59·12
				19—			
				Apr 1	Provision for accrued gas		9·12

These credit balances will appear in the Balance Sheet on the liabilities side as follows.

BALANCE SHEET AS AT 31ST MARCH——

	£	£	
Current Liabilities			
Accrued Charges			
Rent	150·00		
Gas	9·12	159·12	

POINTS TO NOTE

(1) In the example above, the amount charged to the Profit & Loss Account is the full amount for the services of accommodation and gas provided during the year. This is as it should be.

(2) When these outstanding charges are paid in the following period, the Cash Book will be credited and the revenue accounts debited, thus discharging these liabilities.

(3) The above method of dealing with accrued charges is applicable to all cases where expenses have accrued but are unpaid at the end of the financial period, e.g. telephone, salaries, etc.

(4) Where final accounts are to be prepared from a Trial Balance, the adjustments, e.g. to provide for a quarter's rent which is due and unpaid, will not have been passed through the books, and such items will appear both in the Profit & Loss Account and the Balance Sheet.

PROFIT & LOSS ACCOUNT FOR THE YEAR ENDED 31ST MARCH, 19—

Dr | Cr

	£	£	
Rent	450·00		
Add rent accrued	150·00		
		600·00	
Gas & Electricity	50·00		
Add gas accrued	9·12		
		59·12	

BALANCE SHEET AS AT 31ST MARCH, 19—

	£	£	
Current Liabilities			
Accrued Charges:			
Rent	150·00		
Gas	9·12	159·1	

Payments in Advance

The converse of an accrued charge is a payment in advance. Supposing a firm which prepares its final accounts on 31st December paid six months' rates in advance the previous October, half this sum would relate to the following financial period and should therefore be borne by that period. The accounts must be adjusted to ensure that the charge is properly apportioned between the two financial periods. The nominal account is credited in the current period with the amount paid in advance, thus reducing the sum for rates transferable to the Profit & Loss Account, and the nominal account debited in the following period. Any debit balance remaining on a revenue account, after the final accounts have been prepared, will appear in the Balance Sheet as an asset.

ILLUSTRATION 15.2

The Trial Balance of a trader included a debit balance of £200 on Rates Account at 31st December, 1964. This sum included £50 in respect of the quarter 1st January, 1965 to 31st March, 1965. Show the nominal account at 31st December, 1964, when the books are closed.

Dr — Rates Account — Cr

1964			£	1964			£
Dec 31	Balance	b/d	200	Dec 31	Rates paid in advance	c/d	50
				„ 31	Profit & Loss Account		150
			£ 200				£ 200
1965							
Jan 1	Rates paid in advance		50				

BALANCE SHEET AS AT 31ST DECEMBER, 1964

	Current Assets	£
	Payments in advance	50

Deferred Revenue Expenditure

This refers to expenditure incurred in one financial period but from which a company will derive benefits over more than one period. The expense is allocated to succeeding periods instead of being charged wholly against the income for the year in which it was incurred. In the books of account, the method for dealing with deferred revenue expenditure is the same as that for recording payments in advance.

ILLUSTRATION 15.3

A firm whose financial year extends from 1st January to 31st December paid, on 1st January, 1964, £18,000 in respect of advertising. It was decided to spread this cost evenly over a period of three years. Show how the entries would appear in the Advertising Account for the first year.

Dr Advertising Account Cr

1964			£	1964			£
Jan 1	Cash	CB	18,000	Dec 31	Proportion of cost	c/d	12,000
				,, 31	Profit & Loss A/c		6,000
		£	18,000			£	18,000
1965							
Jan 1	Balance	b/d	12,000				

The sum carried down will show in the Balance Sheet as an asset; it represents the value of advertising services available to the business.

Where payments are made in advance, as in our earlier example of Rates, it is usual to record the Trial Balance figure in the Profit & Loss Account, and to show the payment in advance as a deduction.

PROFIT & LOSS ACCOUNT FOR THE PERIOD ENDED 31ST DECEMBER, 1964

Dr Cr

		£	
Rates	£200		
Less unexpired period	50		
		150	

PACKING MATERIALS, STATIONERY, AND CATALOGUES

At the end of the financial period, only the materials actually consumed should be charged to the Trading and Profit & Loss Accounts. The value of the stocks of materials of the kind listed above, remaining at the end of the year, should be credited to the particular account and debited in the same account for the following period as with payments in advance. These stocks in hand will show in the Balance Sheet.

PROPRIETOR'S DRAWINGS OF CASH AND STOCKS FOR PERSONAL USE

When the owner withdraws cash for personal use, the Cash Book is credited and the proprietor's Drawings Account debited. If stock-in-trade is taken by the owner for his personal use, it is usual to debit his Drawings Account with the cost price of the goods taken and credit the Purchases Account. The owner would be liable to pay VAT on the value of the goods withdrawn.

WORKED EXERCISE 15.4

On 1st January, 1961, W. Ord started business as a wholesale confectioner. The following were amongst the balances extracted from his books on 31st December, 1961. From this information prepare Ord's Trading and Profit & Loss Accounts for the year ended 31st December, 1961.

	£
Purchases	11,377
Sales	13,475
Returns Inwards	242
Returns Outwards	268
Carriage on Purchases	47
Advertising	110
Motor Van Expenses	155
Vanman's Wages	652
Office Expenses	104
Bad Debts	79
Insurances	26
Heat & Light	30
Interest on Loan	21
Discounts Allowed	337
Discounts Received	210
Rent & Rates	365
Rent of Premises Sub-let	104

You are given the following additional information.

(1) Stock in hand at 31st December, 1961, was valued at £898.
(2) A motor van which cost £660 is to be depreciated by 15% on cost.
(3) Provide £105 bad debts.
(4) A half year's interest £21 is due on the loan.
(5) A demand for rates for the half year ending 31st March, 1962, £56 had been received but not paid.
(6) Insurance £6 is prepaid.
(7) £12 is owing to Crossways Garage Ltd for maintenance and repair of the motor van.

Associated Examining Board, G.C.E. 'O' level, Principles of Accounts

TRADING AND PROFIT & LOSS ACCOUNT FOR THE YEAR ENDED 31ST DECEMBER, 1961

Dr					Cr
	£	£		£	£
Purchases	11,377		Sales	13,475	
Less Returns	268		*Less* Returns	242	
		11,109			13,233
Carriage		47			
		11,156			
Less Stock at close		898			
Cost of Goods sold		10,258			
Gross Profit to Profit & Loss A/c		2,975			
	£	13,233		£	13,233
Advertising		110	Gross Profit from Trading Account		2,975
Rent & Rates	365		Discounts Received		210
Add rates due	28		Rent (from sub-letting)		104
		393			
Office Expenses		104			
Insurances	26				
Less unexpired	6				
		20			
Heat & Light		30			
Bad Debts	79				
Provision for Bad Debts	105				
		184			
Interest on Loan	21				
Add interest due	21				
		42			
Discounts Allowed		337			
Motor Van Exps	155				
Add accrued charge	12				
		167			
Vanman's Wages		652			
Depreciation of motor van (15% of £660)		99			
Net Profit transferred to Capital		1,151			
	£	3,289		£	3,289

EXERCISE 15.1

The following entries appeared in the Trial Balance taken from the books of P. Wilson on 31st December, 1964.

	Dr
Insurance Account	£120
Rent Account	240

Insurance prepaid comes to £25 and rent due totals £120. Show the Ledger accounts with adjustments when the books are finally closed.

EXERCISE 15.2

J.B. is a haulage contractor. From the following Trial Balance extracted on 31st December, 1962 and the notes attached prepare J.B's Trading and Profit & Loss Accounts for the year ended 31st December, 1962 and a Balance Sheet on that date

	£	£
Capital ..		10,000
Drawings	2,100	
Motor Vehicles	5,200	
Sundry Debtors	650	
Sundry Creditors		230
Furniture & Fixtures ..	240	
Freehold Premises	7,000	
Revenue from Haulage Contracts ..		11,400
Office Wages & Salaries	900	
Light & Heat ..	190	
Motor Vehicle Expenses:		
Drivers' Wages	3,600	
Licences & Insurance	210	
Running Expenses ..	1,880	
Maintenance Expenses	320	
Bank Overdraft		1,000
Petty Cash in Hand ..	30	
Rates ..	220	
Office Expenses	90	
	£22,630	£22,630

Notes:

(1) On 1st January, 1962 an old lorry purchased on 1st January, 1958 for £1,000 and depreciated annually at 20% on cost had been sold for £240 and a new lorry purchased costing £1,100. The only entries made in the books were for the sale of the old lorry at £240 and the purchase of the new lorry at £1,100.

(2) Motor vehicles are to be depreciated by £1,800.

(3) The Rates Account included a payment of £96 representing rates for the half year 1st October, 1962 to 31st March, 1963.

(4) It was decided that £200 of the total motor vehicle expenses is attributable to J.B'.s private purposes.

(5) Lorry drivers' wages accrued and unpaid amounted to £40.

Associated Examining Board, G.C.E. 'O' level, Principles of Accounts, 1963

EXERCISE 15.3

The figures of the following Trial Balance were extracted from the books of W. Walker, a wholesale provision merchant, on 31st December.

	£	£
Capital ..		17,874
Lease (to run 10 years from 1st January) ..	5,000	
Advertising	127	
Motor Vans	927	
Purchases	68,485	
Postage	138	
Lighting & Heating ..	91	
Wages ..	2,837	
Rates & Water	101	
Telephone	34	
Furniture & Fittings ..	1,104	
Sales ..		73,498
Returns Inwards and Outwards	56	392
Bad Debts	26	
Insurance	192	

	£	£
Debtors	4,882	
Creditors		8,405
Cash in Hand	352	
Balance with Bank	3,792	
Stock at 1st January	12,025	
	£100,169	£100,169

Prepare Trading and Profit & Loss Accounts for the year ending 31st December, 19—, and Balance Sheet at that date. In preparing the accounts, the following matters should be taken into consideration.

(1) The stock at 31st December was valued at £10,787.
(2) An appropriate amount of depreciation should be written off the lease.
(3) 20% per annum on cost (£1,250) should be written off motor vans.
(4) £100 is to be reserved as a bonus to the staff.
(5) Make a provision for bad debts of £300.
(6) 10% per annum should be written off furniture and fittings.

Indicate in the accounts the rate of gross profit earned on the sales.

R.S.A.

EXERCISE 15.4

(a) The following trial balance was extracted from W. Tate's books on 30th April 19—.

	£	£
Capital		3,146
Drawings	1,300	
Sales		9,703
Purchases	7,178	
Sales returns and allowances	193	
Purchases returns and allowances		141
Rent, rates and insurance	870	
Sundry expenses	203	
Stock (1 January 19—)	1,924	
Trade debtors	1,947	
Trade creditors		2,103
Cash at bank	988	
Furniture and fittings	490	
	£15,093	£15,093

During the month of May information from the following documents was passed through the books.

	£	£
Invoices sent to customers		2,156
Invoices received from suppliers for stock-in-trade		1,609
Credit notes sent to customers		52
Credit notes sent by suppliers		46
Bank paying-in slips:		
Cash sales	296	
Receipts from trade debtors	1,887	
Premium bond winnings	100	
		2,283

Cheques drawn:	£	£
Rent	100	
Trade creditors	1,974	
Sundry expenses	42	
Drawings	250	
New fittings	35	
		2,401

Draft Tate's trial balance as it would appear on 31st May 19—.
Note: All calculations *must* be shown adjacent to the trial balance.

(b) What 'difference' would be caused in a trial balance by the following errors? You are to state which side of the trial balance would be *in excess* of the other side and by how much and to present your answer in the following form.

Item	Debit in excess of credit by	Credit in excess of debit by
	£	£
(i)		
(ii)		

and so on.

If there is no effect on the agreement of the trial balance write the words 'no effect'.

(i) £16 paid for motor vehicle expenses was credited to motor vehicles account.
(ii) The monthly total of the postages column in the petty cash book £6·25 was posted to the postages account as £5·30.
(iii) Some old office filing cabinets were sold for cash £7 and this amount was included in the cash sales posted to the sales account.
(iv) Discount received £324 was credited to the discount account as £234.

University of London, G.C.E. 'O' level, Principles of Accounts, 1968 (modified)

16
Partnership Accounts

So far we have confined our attention to the books of account of a one-man business. The owner of such an undertaking may employ other people to help him, but he alone owns its assets and he alone is responsible for its liabilities. Yet an organization of this kind is not without its advantages. The one owner has complete control; he does not have to consult anyone before he acts, and so can act quickly. What profits the business makes are all his.

Numerically there are more sole traders than any other kind of business, but generally they are very small organizations. Not all of them will, however, remain small. Many of the present-day public companies began as one-man businesses, and a number of existing small ones will probably develop into substantial enterprises within the course of the next decade or two. Marshall, the distinguished economist, likened different business units to a forest in which there are always some young trees growing up and some old ones decaying and passing away.

The successful sole trader is unlikely to remain a sole trader for long. The reason is that expansion calls for additional capital, which it is often beyond the means of the sole trader to find. This new money is needed to provide additions to premises, to finance bigger stocks, to buy more machinery, and to expand credit facilities to customers. Although the commercial banks are always ready to lend money on security for short periods, they are not normally willing to finance a long term investment of the kind we are contemplating.

One method by which the sole trader can obtain additional long term capital is by converting his business into a partnership. This way he not only secures the additional finance he needs, but he and his fellow partners are able to specialize in the different functions of management. One partner can, for example, supervise the buying, one can concentrate on the problems of marketing the firm's product, and another can assume responsibility for the financial control of the business. Greater efficiency is thereby achieved. The sole trader, in return, must relinquish some control, and, of course, share the profits with his co-partners.

There is not a great deal of difference between keeping the books of account of a sole trader and those of a partnership. What differences there are stem from the fact that the existence of a number of joint owners means that separate capital accounts must be kept, profits must be apportioned, and the individual partners' financial interests in the business properly calculated and recorded. Before going into these various matters, it will pay us to examine some of the implications of forming a partnership.

The Partnership Act, 1890 defines a partnership as 'the relation which subsists between persons carrying on a business in common with a view of profit'. The law does not require the partnership agreement to be made in any special way. It can be made orally, but this would be unwise. Men's memories are short, and disputes between the partners over what was actually agreed would inevitably occur. Usually the contract is made in writing, or in writing under seal, and the document sets out the respective rights and duties of the partners in accordance with what was agreed between them. A deed of partnership, or partnership agreement, would cover such points as:

(1) the firm name, i.e. the name under which the business will be carried on,
(2) the amount each partner is required to contribute to the capital of the firm,
(3) the ratio in which profits and losses are to be shared,
(4) whether partnership salaries are to be paid,
(5) whether interest is to be paid on capital, and at what rate,
(6) the machinery for settling any disputes which may arise.

If there is any matter for which the partnership agreement does not provide, then the provisions of the Partnership Act, 1890 apply. This specifies, for example, that in the absence of an agreement to the contrary: (1) profits and losses are to be shared equally among the partners, irrespective of their Capital; (2) no interest is to be allowed on partners' Capital; (3) no interest is to be charged on drawings; (4) the books of the firm are to be kept at the principal place of business and that the partners are to have free access to inspect and copy them; and (5) no salaries are to be paid to partners.

The deed of partnership or partnership agreement regulates the domestic or internal relations of the partners. As to the partnership's external relationships, i.e. its relationship with the outside world, though a partnership is not a separate legal entity, as a registered company is, yet a partnership may have a 'firm name', and the partners be known collectively as the 'firm'. Both sole traders and partnerships must register under the Registration of Business Names Act, 1916 if the firm's name does not consist of the proprietors' true surnames. The full names of the owners must appear in all catalogues, circulars, and business letters of the firm.

Another point to remember with regard to the external relationship is that every partner is an agent of the firm, and his other partners, for the purpose of the business of the partnership. Accordingly, if a partner, acting within the limits of his ostensible authority, buys goods on behalf of the firm, his co-partners will be liable in just the same way as any other principal is liable for contracts made by an agent acting with apparent authority.

Under the Limited Partnership Act, 1907 one or more partners can limit their liability to the sum they have agreed to subscribe to the capital of the partnership. They are not permitted to participate in the actual management of the business, and there must be at least one general partner whose liability is unlimited. Such partnerships must register with the Registrar of Joint Stock Companies. Because of the greater advantages of the private limited liability company, limited partnerships are rare.

The ordinary partnership form of organization is most common in the professions, where members are prohibited by law from limiting their liability by registering as limited liability companies. But it seems likely, now that the status of exempt private company has been abolished by the Companies Act, 1967 and companies must file accounts with their annual returns, that some undertakings, particularly those which attach more importance to secrecy about their financial affairs than they do to the advantages of limited liability, will change to the partnership form of organization. Furthermore tax considerations will influence the decision as to whether the business is to be a partnership or a registered joint-stock company.

The Capital Accounts of the Partnership

In the books of account of the sole trader there is one capital account, and it is usual to credit this account with profits earned and debit it with drawings. The sole trader is a creditor of the business to the extent of the balance shown on the credit side of his capital account. With a partnership, capital accounts are opened for each partner, and each is a creditor for the credit balances shown in these accounts. The partnership agreement will usually state the amount of capital each partner is to contribute. The sums are not always equal, for some partners may have the money and others the skill and experience. Where capital is contributed by the partners in unequal amounts, provision is sometimes made in the partnership agreement for interest to be paid on capital at a fixed rate of interest. In these cases, it is usual to leave the capital accounts credited with the original capital contributed. They thus remain unaltered, and profits and losses are credited and debited to separate current accounts opened for each partner.

ILLUSTRATION 16.1

T. York and R. Rutland are in partnership. T. York contributed £2,000 and R.

Rutland £1,000 as capital. The partnership agreement provides that interest at 5% per annum shall be paid on capital before distribution of profits, which are to be shared in the ratio of T. York $\frac{2}{3}$ and R. Rutland $\frac{1}{3}$. T. York drew out £200 and R. Rutland £300 respectively on 1st July, 1964 on account of profits. The profits at the end of the year (31st December, 1964) came to £1,650.

Show the capital and current accounts of the partners on 31st December, 1964, and show also how these would appear on the liabilities side of the Balance Sheet at this date.

T. York's Capital Account

Dr				Cr			
				1963			£
				Jan 1	Balance	b/d	2,000

R. Rutland's Capital Account

Dr				Cr			
				1963			£
				Jan 1	Balance	b/d	1,000

T. York's Current Account

Dr				Cr			
1964			£	1964			£
July 1	Cash	CB	200	Dec 31	int. on Capital	J	100
Dec 31	Balance	c/d	900	„ 31	Share of profits $\frac{2}{3}$	J	1,000
		£	1,100			£	1,100
				1965			
				Jan 1	Balance	b/d	900

R. Rutland's Current Account

Dr				Cr			
1964			£	1964			£
July 1	Cash	CB	300	Dec 31	int. on Capital	J	50
Dec 31	Balance	c/d	250	„ 31	Share of profits $\frac{1}{3}$	J	500
		£	550			£	550
				1965			
				Jan 1	Balance	b/d	250

BALANCE SHEET AS AT 31ST DECEMBER, 1964

	T. York	R. Rutland	Total
	£	£	£
Capital Accounts:	2,000	1,000	3,000
Current Accounts:			
Interest on Capital	100	50	
Share of profits	1,000	500	
	1,100	550	
Less Drawings	200	300	
	900	250	1,150

Profit & Loss Appropriation Account

Since all the profit of a sole trader's business belongs to the one owner, it can be transferred directly from the Profit & Loss Account to the proprietor's capital account. But in the partnership accounts, it is desirable to show separately and in detail how the profit is disposed of between the different interests. The net profit is therefore carried down to an Appropriation Account.

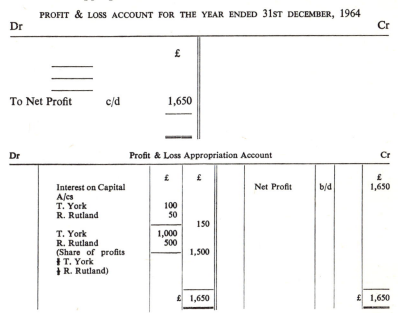

PROFIT & LOSS ACCOUNT FOR THE YEAR ENDED 31ST DECEMBER, 1964

Dr			Cr
		£	
To Net Profit	c/d	1,650	

Dr		Profit & Loss Appropriation Account						Cr
		£	£					£
	Interest on Capital A/cs				Net Profit	b/d		1,650
	T. York	100						
	R. Rutland	50						
			150					
	T. York	1,000						
	R. Rutland	500						
	(Share of profits ⅔ T. York ⅓ R. Rutland)		1,500					
		£	1,650				£	1,650

The partners' current accounts are credited with interest on capital and an Interest on Partners' Capital Account debited with the corresponding amount. This latter account is closed at the end of the trading period by transfer to the appropriation section of the Profit & Loss Account. The Appropriation Account is debited and the partners' current accounts credited with their respective shares of the remaining profits.

When Sole Traders Combine to Form a Partnership

Occasionally two or more sole traders in a similar trade will agree to form a partnership. The separate sets of books previously kept by the sole traders are then replaced by one set of books for the partnership. The opening entries in the partnership Journal, to give effect to this, can be made from the combined Balance Sheets of the sole traders. Let us suppose that L. Payne and J. Cooper are in business as sole traders and that their respective Balance Sheets on 31st December, 1964 were as follows.

BALANCE SHEET OF L. PAYNE AS AT 31ST DECEMBER, 1964

	£		£	£
Capital Account	7,810	*Fixed Assets*		
		Freehold Premises	5,000	
		Plant & Machinery	2,000	
				7,000
Current Liabilities		*Current Assets*		
Creditors	1,100	Stock-in-Trade	800	
		Debtors	400	
		Cash at Bank	700	
		Cash in Hand	10	
				1,910
	£8,910			£8,910

BALANCE SHEET OF J. COOPER AS AT 31ST DECEMBER, 1964

	£		£	£
Capital Account	10,000	*Fixed Assets*		
		Freehold Premises	7,000	
		Plant & Machinery	1,600	
				8,600
Current Liabilities		*Current Assets*		
Creditors	370	Stock-in-Trade	600	
		Debtors	500	
		Cash at Bank	650	
		Cash in Hand	20	
				1,770
	£10,370			£10,370

The new Balance Sheet for the partnership on 31st December, 19— would be as follows.

BALANCE SHEET AS AT 31ST DECEMBER, 19—

	£	£		£	£
Capital Accounts:			*Fixed Assets*		
J. Cooper	10,000		Freehold Premises	12,000	
L. Payne	7,810		Plant & Machinery	3,600	
		17,810			15,600
Current Liabilities			*Current Assets*		
Creditors		1,470	Stock-in-Trade	1,400	
			Sundry Debtors	900	
			Cash at Bank	1,350	
			Cash in Hand	30	
					3,680
		£19,280			£19,280

ILLUSTRATION 16.2

Flower agreed to take Rose into partnership as from 1st July, 19— On that day the following balances were extracted from their books.

	Flower	Rose
	£	£
Freehold Premises	6,000	4,600
Machinery & Tools	2,700	1,400
Stock of Materials	850	450
Stock of Finished Goods	1,450	950
Cash at Bank	800	—
Bank Overdraft	—	765
Cash in Hand	30	20
Sundry Creditors	2,340	1,270
Rates & Insurance prepaid	50	40
Sundry Debtors	1,630	970
Provision for Bad Debts	130	—
Current Accounts, credit balances	40	55

Rose was to pay off the amount of his bank overdraft out of his private funds and to make a provision for bad debts of £105.

The terms of the partnership were:

(*a*) interest on capital to be allowed at 5% per annum;

(*b*) Rose was to act as manager of the business and receive a bonus of 15% of profits after charging interest on capital. The remainder of the profits to be divided equally between Flower and Rose.

(1) Draft the opening Balance Sheet of the new firm as at 1st July, 19—.

(2) On 31st December, 19— the net trading profit for the half year, before charging interest on capital and Rose's bonus was £4,830. Draft the Profit & Loss Appropriation Account for the half year.

University of London, 'O' level, Principles of Accounts, 1961 (modified)

The separate Balance Sheets of Flower and Rose, after Rose has paid off his bank overdraft and made a provision for bad debts of £105, would be as follows.

FLOWER'S BALANCE SHEET AS AT 1ST JULY, 19—

	£			£	£
Capital Account	11,000	*Fixed Assets*			
		Freehold Premises		6,000	
Current Account	40	Machinery & Tools		2,700	8,700
Current Liabilities		*Current Assets*			
Sundry Creditors	2,340	Stock of Materials		850	
		Stock of Goods		1,450	
		Debtors	£1,630		
		Less Provision	130		
				1,500	
		Rates and Insurance prepaid		50	
		Cash at Bank		800	
		Cash in Hand		30	
					4,680
	£13,380				£13,380

ROSE'S BALANCE SHEET AS AT 1ST JULY, 19—

	£			£	£
Capital Account	7,000	*Fixed Assets*			
		Freehold Premises		4,600	
Current Account	55	Machinery & Tools		1,400	
					6,000
Current Liabilities		*Current Assets*			
Creditors	1,270	Stock of Materials		450	
		Stock of Goods		950	
		Debtors	£970		
		Less Provision	105		
				865	
		Rates & Insurance prepaid		40	
		Cash in Hand		20	
					2,325
	£8,325				£8,325

Dr — Profit & Loss Appropriation Account for Six Months to 31st December, 19— — Cr

		£	£				£
Interest on Capital				Balance	b/d		4,830·00
Flower		275·00					
Rose		175·00					
			450·00				
Bonus–Rose			657·00				
Share of Profits							
Flower		1,861·50					
Rose		1,861·50					
			3,723·00				
		£	4,830·00			£	4,830·00

BALANCE SHEET OF THE PARTNERSHIP AS AT 1ST JULY, 19—

	£	£			£	£
Capital Accounts:			*Fixed Assets*			
Flower	11,000		Freehold Premises		10,600	
Rose	7,000		Machinery & Tools		4,100	
		18,000				14,700
Current Accounts:			*Current Assets*			
Flower	40		Stock of Materials		1,300	
Rose	55		Stock of Goods		2,400	
		95	Sundry Debtors	£2,600		
Current Liabilities			*Less* Provision	235		
Sundry Creditors		3,610			2,365	
			Rates & Insurance prepaid		90	
			Cash at Bank		800	
			Cash in Hand		50	
						7,005
		£21,705				£21,705

Partners' Salaries

In the illustration above, Rose was paid a percentage of the profits for managing the business. Where one partner contributes more of his time and skill to the management of the partnership business than the other partners, it is usual to allow him a salary or a bonus calculated on profits. This salary may be paid to the managing partner in cash at regular intervals, or credited to his current account at the close of the financial year. In both cases the Partnership Salaries Account is debited, the credit entries being made in the Cash Book if the salary is paid at regular intervals, or in the partner's current account at the end of the year. The Partnership Salaries Account is closed at the end of the trading period by transfer to the Profit & Loss Appropriation Account.

Interest on Capital and on Drawings

On Capital

Where unequal amounts of capital have been contributed by the partners, and the partnership agreement provides for interest on capital, an Interest on Capital Account is debited and the partners' current accounts credited with the interest. The Interest on Capital Account is closed at the end of the trading period by transfer to the Appropriation Account.

On Drawings

If it is customary for the partners to draw out unequal sums during the year in anticipation of profits, the partnership agreement may provide for interest to be charged on drawings. The partners' current accounts are debited with the interest charged and an Interest on Drawings Account credited. The latter account is transferred to the Appropriation Account at the end of the financial period.

New Partner-Retirement-Change of Profit Sharing Ratios

The question of the value of the goodwill of the business arises when a new partner is admitted; when one retires or dies; and when agreement is made to change the ratio in which the partners share profits and losses.

When a person joins an established partnership, his right to a proportionate share of the goodwill of the business diminishes the share of the other partners, and it is fair that the new member should pay for the benefit he receives. If the money paid by the incoming partner for goodwill goes to the old partners personally, in proportion as they share profits and losses, and is not retained in the business as working capital, no entries in the books of the partnership are necessary.

Another way of dealing with goodwill on the admission of a new partner is to raise an account for the full value of the goodwill, and credit the old partners' capital accounts in the proportions in which profits and losses are shared.

ILLUSTRATION 16.3

E. Swan and A. Lark are in partnership, sharing profits and losses equally. Their Balance Sheet at 31st December, 1964 was as follows.

BALANCE SHEET AS AT 31ST DECEMBER, 1964

	£	£		£	£
Capital Accounts:			*Fixed Assets*		
E. Swan	4,200		Freehold Premises	3,000	
A. Lark	3,600		Furniture	250	
		7,800			3,250
Current Liabilities			*Current Assets*		
Sundry Creditors		260	Stock	2,810	
			Debtors	930	
			Cash at Bank	1,050	
			Cash in Hand	20	
					4,810
		£8,060			£8,060

It is agreed to admit N. Sparrow into the partnership, giving him one third of the profits. He is to bring in as capital £3,000. It is further agreed that the goodwill be valued at £1,200 and an account opened to record this amount. Show by means of Journal entries how this agreement is carried out, and prepare a Balance Sheet for the new firm.

Journal

			Dr	Cr
1964			£	£
Dec 31	Goodwill Dr		1,200	
	E. Swan—Capital Account			600
	A. Lark—Capital Account			600
	Being creation of Goodwill as agreed on admission of N. Sparrow			
Dec 31	Cash Dr		3,000	
	N. Sparrow's Capital Account			3,000
	Being capital brought in			

BALANCE SHEET AS AT 31ST DECEMBER, 1964

	£	£		£	£
Capital Accounts:			Goodwill		1,200
A. Lark	4,200		*Fixed Assets*		
E. Swan	4,800		Freehold Premises	3,000	
N. Sparrow	3,000		Furniture	250	
		12,000			3,250
Current Liabilities			*Current Assets*		
Sundry Creditors		260	Stock	2,810	
			Debtors	930	
			Cash in Bank	4,050	
			Cash in Hand	20	
					7,810
		£12,260			£12,260

ILLUSTRATION 16.4

On 1st April, 1962, AB and XY were in partnership sharing profits and losses AB $\frac{5}{8}$ and XY $\frac{3}{8}$.

From the following Trial Balance extracted on 31st March, 1963 and the notes attached prepare the Trading and Profit & Loss Accounts of the partnership for the year ended 31st March, 1963 and a Balance Sheet as on that date.

	£	£
Capital Accounts (1st April, 1962)		
AB		2,500
XY		1,500
Current Accounts:		
AB	3,300	
XY	2,500	
Stock (1st April, 1962)	5,240	
Sundry Debtors	3,720	
Sundry Creditors		5,062
Provision for Bad Debts (1st April, 1962)		250
Office Wages & Salaries	4,090	
Discounts	120	204
Rent & Rates	940	
Furniture & Fittings	800	
Bank Interest	29	
Delivery Expenses	1,210	
Light & Heat	190	
Petty Cash in Hand	30	
Bank Overdraft		813
Sales		61,895
Sales Returns	145	
Purchases	49,640	
Carriage on Purchases	270	
	£72,224	£72,224

Notes:

(1) Stock at 31st March, 1963 was valued at £5,890.
(2) Furniture and fittings are to be depreciated by 5%.
(3) Interest accrued on bank overdraft amounts to £11.
(4) It was decided to write £70 off debtors as bad debts, and to reduce the provision for bad debts to £200.
(5) It was agreed to allow AB £90 and XY £130 for expenses incurred on behalf of the business during the trading period.
(6) It had been agreed during the year that as from 1st October, 1962 profits and losses should be divided equally (it is assumed that profit accrues at an even rate month by month).

G.C.E. 'O' level

(For other accounts see page 191.)

TRADING AND PROFIT & LOSS ACCOUNT FOR THE YEAR ENDED 31ST MARCH, 1963

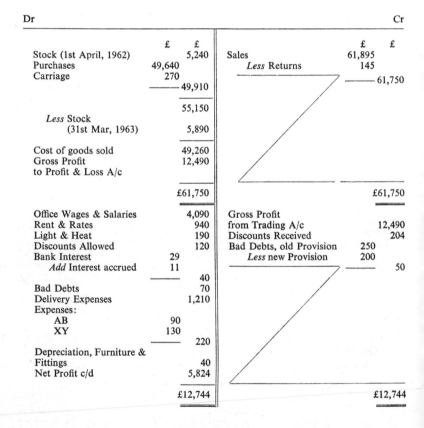

Dr					Cr
	£	£		£	£
Stock (1st April, 1962)		5,240	Sales	61,895	
Purchases	49,640		*Less* Returns	145	
Carriage	270				61,750
		49,910			
		55,150			
Less Stock (31st Mar, 1963)		5,890			
Cost of goods sold		49,260			
Gross Profit to Profit & Loss A/c		12,490			
		£61,750			£61,750
Office Wages & Salaries		4,090	Gross Profit		
Rent & Rates		940	from Trading A/c		12,490
Light & Heat		190	Discounts Received		204
Discounts Allowed		120	Bad Debts, old Provision	250	
Bank Interest	29		*Less* new Provision	200	
Add Interest accrued	11				50
		40			
Bad Debts		70			
Delivery Expenses		1,210			
Expenses:					
AB	90				
XY	130				
		220			
Depreciation, Furniture & Fittings		40			
Net Profit c/d		5,824			
		£12,744			£12,744

Dr	Profit & Loss Appropriation Account						Cr
		£	£			£	£
	AB	1,820		Net Profit	b/d		5,824
	XY	1,092					
	Profit for first 6 months		2,912				
	AB	1,456					
	XY	1,456					
	Profit for second 6 months		2,912				
		£	5,824			£	5,824

BALANCE SHEET AS AT 31ST MARCH, 1963

	£	£		£	£	£
Capital Accounts:			*Fixed Assets*			
AB	2,500		Furniture & Fittings		800	
XY	1,500		*Less* Depreciation		40	
		4,000				760
Current Accounts:			*Current Assets*			
AB	66		Stock		5,890	
XY	178		Debtors	3,720		
		244	*Less* Bad Debts	70		
				3,650		
Current Liabilities						
Bank Overdraft		813	*Less* Provision	200		
Sundry Creditors	5,062				3,450	
Accrued Charge	11		Cash		30	
		5,886				9,370
		£10,130				£10,130

ILLUSTRATION 16.5

A, B, and C were in partnership as estate agents and valuers sharing profits and losses in the ratio 3:2:1.

On 31st December, 1961 the Balance Sheet of the firm was as follows.

BALANCE SHEET

	£	£	£		£
Amounts Due to Clients			3,500	Cash in Hand and Balance at Bank	650
Sundry Creditors			500	Bank Account—Clients	3,500
Current Accounts:				Sundry Debtors	250
A—Cr bal		1,000		Office Furniture & Fittings	300
B—Cr bal		1,500		Freehold Premises at Cost	4,300
			2,500	Freehold Land at Cost	7,000
Capital Accounts:					
A		4,000			
B		4,000			
C	2,000				
Less Dr bal on current A/c	500				
		1,500			
			9,500		
			£16,000		£16,000

(1) On 31st December, 1961, C is to retire and Z is to become a partner in his place under the following arrangements:
(*a*) Prior to C's retirement, freehold premises are to be revalued at £5,900, freehold land at £9,000, and goodwill capitalized at £6,000.
(*b*) The credit balances of the Current Accounts of A and B are to be transferred to their Capital Accounts, and both A and B are to introduce sufficient cash to make their capitals equal to £10,000 each.
(*c*) Z is to bring in £5,000 as his capital.
(*d*) Cash is to be paid out to C for his share of the business.
(*e*) Under the terms of the new partnership each partner is to be entitled to 5% per annum interest on capital and the same rate is to be charged on drawings. Profits and losses are to be shared between A, B and Z in the proportions 3:3:2 respectively.

Show in columnar form the Capital Accounts of A, B, and C recording the above arrangements and prepare the Balance Sheet of the firm after the above arrangements were completed and the amount due to C duly paid.

(2) On 31st December, 1962 the net profit of the firm *before* allowing for interest on capital and on drawings was £8,560. During the year A withdrew £1,600 at the end of each half year, B withdrew £720 at the end of each quarter, and Z withdrew £160 at the end of each month. Prepare the Appropriation Account of the partnership for the year ended 31st December, 1962.

Associated Examining Board, G.C.E. 'A' level

Students will not find this a difficult exercise if they proceed slowly step by step. The amount by which the particular assets are appreciated in value and the goodwill will be divided between A, B, and C in the proportion in which they share profits and losses, namely 3:2:1, and credited to their respective Capital Accounts.

(*a*)

Freehold premises	£1,600
Freehold land	2,000
Goodwill	6,000
	9,600

A gets three sixths	=	£4,800
B „ two sixths	=	3,200
C „ one sixth	=	1,600

(*b*) After the Current Accounts of A and B are transferred to their Capital Accounts, A must introduce £200 cash and B £1,300, in order to bring their capitals up to £10,000 each.

Dr — Capital Accounts — Cr

			A	*B*	*C*				*A*	*B*	*C*
1961			£	£	£	1961			£	£	£
Dec 31	Current A/c				500	Dec 31	Balances	b/d	4,000	4,000	2,000
31	Balances	c/d	10,000	10,000	3,100	„ 31	Revaluation of Assets		4,800	3,200	1,600
						„ 31	Current A/cs		1,000	1,500	
						„ 31	Cash		200	1,300	
		£	10,000	10,000	3,600			£	10,000	10,000	3,600
1961						1961					
Dec 31	Cash				3,100	Dec 31	Balances	b/d	10,000	10,000	3,100

BALANCE SHEET AS AT 31ST DECEMBER, 1961

	£	£		£
Amounts Due to Clients		3,500	Cash in Hand and Balance at Bank	4,050
Sundry Creditors		500	Bank Account—Clients	3,500
Capital Accounts:			Sundry Debtors	250
A	10,000		Office Furniture & Fittings	300
B	10,000		Freehold Premises (at revaluation)	5,900
Z	5,000		Freehold Land (" ")	9,000
		25,000	Goodwill	6,000
		£29,000		£29,000

(*e*) Interest on capital for the year 1962 will be 5% on £10,000 for A and B, which equals £500 each, and 5% on £500 for Z, equalling £250.

The interest on drawings will be:

A £1,600 for ½ year at 5% per annum = £40

B £720 for ¾ year
" " ½ year
" " ¼ year = £720 for 1½ years at 5% per annum = £54

C £160 for 11 months
" " 10 "
" " 9 "
" " 8 "
" " 7 "
" " 6 "
" " 5 "
" " 4 "
" " 3 "
" " 2 "
" " 1 " = £160 for 5½ years at 5% per annum = £44

Dr — Profit & Loss Appropriation Account — Cr

		£	£				£	£
1962 Dec 31	Interest on Capital:			1962 Dec 31	Balance from Profit & Loss A/c	b/d		8,560
	A	500			Interest on Drawings:			
	B	500			A		40	
	Z	250	1,250		B		54	
	Net Divisible Profit:				C		44	138
	A	2,793						
	B	2,793						
	Z	1,862	7,448					
		£	8,698				£	8,698

In the following exercises, VAT is to be ignored.

EXERCISE 16.1

Fowler and Fox are in partnership. On 1st January, 1961 Fowler's capital was £10,000 and Fox's £6,000. Current account balances were Fowler (debit balance) £12 and Fox (credit balance) £24. Each partner is entitled to 6% per annum interest on capital. No interest is allowed on current account balances or charged on drawings. Fox is entitled, as manager, to a bonus of 20% of the remainder of the profits calculated after charging interest on capital, the residue being divided equally between the partners.

The net trading profit for the year ended 31st December, 1961 was £5,665 before allowing for interest on capital and Fox's bonus.

During the year drawings were:

Fowler—1st February £1,000 and 1st September £1,300
Fox —1st March £1,100 and 1st September £2,000.

Show:
(1) the Profit & Loss Appropriation Account, and
(2) the Capital and Current Accounts of the partners for the year ended 31st December, 1961.

G.C.E. 'O' level, Principles of Accounts

EXERCISE 16.2

W. Exton and E. Wain are in partnership. Their assets and liabilities on 1st January, 1960, and 31st December, 1960 were as follows.

	1st Jan	*31st Dec*
	£	£
Petty Cash	20	20
Cash at Bank	168	—
Bank Overdraft	—	154
Stock	1,670	1,995
Debtors	632	984
Creditors: Trade	1,114	909
Expense	46	29
Freehold Premises	9,000	9,000
Machinery & Plant	5,250	4,725
Furniture & Fittings	420	478

The fixed capital accounts of the partners are equal and on 1st January, 1960 there were no balances on their current accounts. Partners are allowed interest on capital at the rate of 5% per annum and the remainder of profits or losses is divided, Wain three fifths and Exton two fifths.

During the year 1960 Exton had withdrawn cash £1,225 and stock £25; Wain had withdrawn cash £1,870.

Prepare a statement to show the net trading profit or loss of the firm for the year 1960 and show how this is divided between the partners.

G.C.E. 'O' level

EXERCISE 16.3

G. Reader and A. Storey are in partnership sharing profits and losses as to two thirds and one third respectively. On 1st January, 19—, the total capital of the firm was £5,000, held by the partners in equal shares, and on 1st July each partner paid into the business bank account £500 as additional capital. During the year each partner drew from the business £80 at the end of each quarter. On 31st December the credit balance of the Profit & Loss Account was £840. Show the Ledger accounts of the partners as they would appear after the books had been balanced on 31st December, 19—.

R.S.A.

EXERCISE 16.4

The following balances appeared in the books of Moon and Starr, trading as partners, on 31st March, 1961. Profits and losses are shared in proportion to capitals.

		£
Freehold Premises		7,000
Machinery & Plant		5,500
Stock of Materials		1,050
Stock of Finished Goods		1,950
Cash at Bank		520
Cash in Hand		30
Sundry Debtors		1,890
Sundry Creditors		2,740
Provision for Bad Debts		80
Rates prepaid		40
Current Accounts; credit balances:	Moon	105
	Starr	55
Capital Accounts:	Moon	9,000
	Starr	6,000

On 31st March, 1961 they agreed to admit F. Way as a partner and to revalue some of the assets.

Way is to bring in cash £2,800 and a motor van valued at £1,200.

Freehold premises are to be revalued at £9,500 and machinery and plant at £4,500. The provision for bad debts is to be increased to £120 and this is to be adjusted through the Current Accounts of Moon and Starr. No other agreement was made.

Draft the opening Balance Sheet of the new firm and state how profits and losses would be shared.

G.C.E. 'O' level

EXERCISE 16.5

C. South and E. Rivers agree to set up in partnership as wholesale and retail traders in china and glass. On 2nd January, 19—, C. South pays £2,000 into a partnership bank account; E. Rivers has no cash, but transfers a freehold shop and warehouse valued at £1,800 and stock valued at £1,200 to the partnership.

You are required to record the foregoing items and the following transactions in the proper books of account. Use a two-column cash book; ignore VAT.

Jan	9	Drew and cashed cheque for £100 for office purposes
,,	10	Paid A. Andrews £150 by cheque, for additions to the buildings
,,	10	Cash sales (not banked), £22·50
,,	10	Received on credit, from Stoke Workers Ltd: 2 doz dinner services at £10·50 each and 1½ doz tea sets at £4 each Nine tea sets were faulty and were returned

EXERCISE 16.6

The following balances were extracted from the books of M and N respectively at 31st December, 1957.

	M	N
	£	£
Freehold Premises ..	2,000	1,750
Machinery & Tools	1,500	1,400
Delivery Vans	—	350
Stock of Materials ..	500	400
Stock of Finished Goods ..	800	600
Cash at Bank	600	—
Cash in Hand	40	25
Bank Overdraft	—	575
Sundry Creditors ..	1,380	965
Rates & Insurance prepaid	40	—
Provision for Bad Debts ..	—	40
Sundry Debtors	900	480

M and N agreed to combine and trade as partners from 1st January, 1958 on the following terms.

(1) N was to pay off the amount of his bank overdraft out of his private funds.
(2) Profits and losses were to be shared in proportion to the amount of capital brought in by each partner.

Draft the opening Balance Sheet of the new firm at 1st January, 1958 and state the ratio in which the profits and losses are to be shared.

G.C.E. 'O' level

EXERCISE 16.7

On 1st January, 1959 A.B. and X.Y. decided to amalgamate their businesses and form a partnership. At that date A.B.'s capital amounted to £8,000 and X.Y.'s to £6,000, but before amalgamation A.B. was allowed to withdraw £1,000 of his capital and certain of X.Y.'s fixed assets were reduced in value by £500.

The new business is to be managed by A.B., who is entitled to the first £500 of each year's profits after charging interest on each partner's capital at the rate of 5% per annum. Remaining profits and losses are to be shared: A.B. three fifths and X.Y. two fifths.

(1) At the end of the first year of trading the net trading profit before charging interest on capital was £4,325.
Partners' drawings for the year were A.B. £2,500 and X.Y. £1,300.
Show the Profit & Loss Appropriation Account, the partners' Current Accounts and the partners' Capital Accounts for the year to 31st December, 1959.
(2) If no agreement had been made regarding the sharing of profits and losses, how would profits and losses be shared?

G.C.E. 'O' level

EXERCISE 16.8

A and B are in partnership sharing profits and losses in the proportions of A one third and B two thirds.

A's capital is £6,000 and B's £10,000. Each partner is entitled to 5% per annum interest on capital before division of profits.

From the above information and the following details relating to the year 1958, prepare the Balance Sheet of A and B at 31st December, 1958.

		£
Net Profit (before charging interest on capital)		5,750
Drawings: A		2,100
B		3,500
Current Account balances at 1st January, 1958: A, debit		28
B, credit		45
Petty Cash		40
Cash at Bank		1,020
Stock		3,500
Debtors		5,200
Provision for Bad Debts		260
Freehold Premises		7,500
Furniture & Equipment at 1st January, 1958		760
Depreciation on Furniture & Equipment		38
Creditors		2,900
Wages Due		95
Motor Vans at 1st January, 1958		1,600
Depreciation on Motor Vans		160

G.C.E. 'O' level

EXERCISE 16.9

M. T. Groom and L. Tarrant are in partnership, sharing profits and losses equally. Their respective capitals are £4,000 and £2,400. Groom drew £80 a month and Tarrant £60 a month on account of profits. At 31st December the net trading profit for the year amounted to £4,400. Show the Capital Account and Current Account for each partner as at 31st December.

EXERCISE 16.10

G.H. and E.F. are in partnership as wholesale warehousemen. They share profits and losses equally and the credit balances of their capital accounts are equal. On 31st December, 1957 the following balances appeared in their books in addition to those of the partners' capital accounts:

		£
Bank Loan on Security of Warehouse		6,000
Sundry Creditors		10,000
Provision for Items Outstanding:		
Salaries	£500	
Insurance	60	
		560
Rates paid in advance		190
Provision for Bad Debts		300
Freehold Warehouse		10,000
Fittings, Fixtures & Furniture		750
Delivery Vans		1,250
Cash in Hand		100
Cash at Bank		400
Sundry Debtors		6,000
G.H. Current Account	Dr	460
E.F. Current Account	Dr	450
Profit & Loss Account to 31st December, 1957	Cr	1,740
Stock at 31st December, 1957		12,000

(1) Prepare the firm's balance sheet at 31st December, 1957.
(2) Calculate the percentage of net profit on the capital invested by each partner.
(3) Calculate the percentage of net profit on the capital employed in the business.

G.C.E. 'O' level

EXERCISE 16.11

How would you deal with the following matters in the books of account of M.N. & Co., a partnership?

(1) Partner M. transfers to the firm private premises owned by him, and valued at £3,000, for the exclusive use of the firm as offices.
(2) Partner N. takes goods from the firm for his own use, valued at £30.
(3) M.'s capital is £4,000 and N.'s capital £2,000. Each partner is entitled to 5% per annum interest on capital, the remainder of the profits being shared equally. After closing the accounts for the year ended 31st December, 1959 it is discovered that interest on capital has been omitted from the accounts.

G.C.E. 'O' level

EXERCISE 16.12

Hare and Hound are in partnership. Hare's capital is £10,000 and Hound's £8,000. Hound is entitled to 10% of the net trading profit as a management bonus. Thereafter each partner is entitled to 5% per annum interest on capital. The remainder of the profit or loss is divided equally.

(1) On 1st December, 1963 the balances on the following accounts in the firm's Ledger were:

	£
Furniture & Fittings (debit balance, 1/1/63)	680
Premises (debit balance 1/1/63)	8,500
Rent Receivable (credit balance)	120
Repairs (debit balance)	176

During the month of December the following transactions took place relating to these accounts.

1963

Dec 1 Purchased additional shop fittings £200 from Shop Supplies Ltd.

" 4 Received cheque £30 for rent of premises sub-let for month ended 30th November, 1963.

" 14 Received invoice from Contractors Ltd for repairs and extensions to premises £1,400. It was decided that £1,200 of this should be capitalized.

" 31 Wrote 5% depreciation off old furniture and fittings and 10% off new fittings.

(*a*) Enter the balances at 1st December, 1963 in the four accounts named above and make the entries which arise in these accounts from the transactions given.

(*b*) Balance these accounts as at the close of the financial year ended 31st December, 1963.

Note: One month's rent receivable £30 is outstanding.

(2) The firm's net trading profit for the year ended 31st December, 1963 was £5,940 (before allowing for Hound's bonus and interest on partners' capital). During the half year Hare had withdrawn £2,700 and Hound £3,000.

Prepare the Profit & Loss Appropriation Account of the partnership for the year ended 31st December, 1963, and show the Current Accounts of the partners as they would appear when balanced at the end of the year.

Note: On 1st January, 1963 Hare's Current Account showed a credit balance of £27 and Hound's a debit balance of £14.

G.C.E. 'O' level

Dissolution of Partnerships

The following are grounds for the dissolution of a partnership in the absence of an agreement to the contrary:

(1) if entered into for a fixed term, by the expiration of the term,
(2) if entered into for a single adventure or undertaking, by the termination of that adventure or undertaking,
(3) if entered into for an undefined time, by any partner giving notice to the other or others of his intention to dissolve the partnership, in which case the partnership is dissolved from the date mentioned in the notice as the date of dissolution, or, if no date is mentioned, as from the date of the communication of the notice, unless the articles provide for some other date,
(4) by the death of any partner,
(5) by the bankruptcy of any partner,
(6) at the option of the other partners, if any partner suffers his share in the partnership property to be judicially charged for his separate debt.,
(7) by the happening of any event which makes it unlawful for the business of the firm to be carried on in partnership.

PROCEDURE FOR CLOSING PARTNERSHIP BOOKS ON DISSOLUTION

(1) Open a Realization Account.
(2) Transfer all assets except cash to the Realization Account at book value.
(3) Credit Cash and debit Realization Account with any expenses of realization.
(4) Pay creditors, debiting their accounts and crediting Cash Account. Debit creditors' accounts with any discount received and credit Realization Account.
(5) Debit Cash and credit Realization Account with the amount realized on sale of assets.
(6) Transfer balance of Realization Account to the debit or credit of partners' capital accounts.
(8) Pay off partners' loans, as distinct from capital. The balance of the Cash Book will be equal to the amount due to the partners on Capital Account. Credit Cash and debit the partners' capital accounts to close the accounts.

Partnership Act, 1890, Section 44

This section governs the distribution of assets upon dissolution. Losses, for example, are to be borne: firstly, out of profits; secondly, out of Capital; and thirdly, by the partners personally. The assets of the firm are to be applied: firstly, in paying outside creditors;

secondly in repaying advances; and thirdly, in repaying Capital. Any residue is distributed to the partners in the proportions in which profits and losses are shared.

ILLUSTRATION 16.6

L. Lee and J. Clyde are in partnership, sharing profits in the ratio ¾ and ¼. They decide to dissolve the partnership, and, at the date of dissolution (31st March, 1965) their Balance Sheet is as follows.

BALANCE SHEET AS AT 31ST MARCH, 1965

	£	£		£	£
Capital Accounts:			*Fixed Assets*		
L. Lee	3,000		Freehold Premises		2,400
J. Clyde	2,600		*Current Assets*		
	——	5,600	Stock	2,800	
Current Liabilities			Sundry Debtors	2,200	
Sundry Creditors		3,000	Bank	1,000	
			Cash	200	
				——	6,200
		£8,600			£8,600

The dissolution was complete by 30th June, 1965. The assets were sold for £9,000. Close the books.

Dr — Realization Account — Cr

Date			£	£	Date			£
1965					1965			
Mar 31	Sundry Assets			7,400	June 30	Cash		9,000
	Capital A/cs							
	L. Lee		1,200					
	J. Clyde		400					
			——	1,600				
	Profit on sale of assets							
				£ 9,000				£ 9,000

Dr — Sundry Creditors — Cr

Date			£	Date			£
1965				1965			
June 30	Cash	CB	3,000	Mar 31	Balance	b/d	3,000

Dr — *Cash Book* — Cr

Date			£	Date			£
1965				1965			
Mar 31	Balance	b/d	1,200	June 30	Creditors		3,000
June 30	Realization		9,000	,, 30	Capital A/cs		
					L. Lee		4,200
					J. Clyde		3,000
			£ 10,200				£ 10,200

Dr L. Lee's Capital Account Cr

1965			£	1965			£
June 30	Cash	CB	4,200	Mar 31	Balance	b/d	3,000
				June 30	Realization		1,200
		£	4,200			£	4,200

Dr J. Clyde's Capital Account Cr

1965			£	1965			£
June 30	Cash		3,000	Mar 31	Balance	b/d	2,600
				June 30	Profit on Realization		400
		£	3,000			£	3,000

Had there been a loss on realization, the Realization Account would have been credited and the partners' capital accounts debited with the loss.

WORKED EXERCISE 16.7

A and B, trading in partnership, decide, as on March 31st, 19—, to dissolve partnership and to liquidate their business.

Their Balance Sheet as on that date was as follows.

BALANCE SHEET AS AT 31ST MARCH, 19—

	£		£
Capital Account—A	2,000	Cash	1,800
Capital Account—B	1,500	Sundry Debtors	2,800
Sundry Creditors	2,750	Other Assets	850
		Goodwill	800
	£6,250		£6,250

Profits and losses are shared equally.

The debtors realized £2,700, other assets £950, and the goodwill of the business was sold for £400. The expenses of liquidation amounted to £100.

Prepare the necessary accounts to show the result of the realization as it would appear in the books of the firm, and the position of the two partners as regards the disposal of the balance of cash remaining after satisfying the firm's liabilities.

R.S.A.

Dr Realization Account C

			£			£	£
	Sundry Debtors		2,800	Cash (Debtors)			2,700
	Assets		850	„ (Other Assets)			950
	Goodwill		800	„ (Goodwill)			400
	Cash (Expense of Dissolution)		100	Capital A/cs			
				A		250	
				B		250	
				Loss on realization			500
		£	4,550			£	4,550

Dr *Cash Book* Cr

Date	Particulars		£	Date	Particulars	£	£
19—				19—			
Mar 31	Balance	b/d	1,800		Realization (Expenses on Dissolution)		100
	Realization (Debtors)		2,700		Sunday Creditors		2,750
	Realization (Other Assets)		950		Capital A/cs		
	Realization (Goodwill)		400		A	1,750	
					B	1,250	
							3,000
			£ 5,850				£ 5,850

Dr Sundry Debtors Cr

Date	Particulars		£	Date	Particulars		£
19— Mar 31	Balance	b/d	2,800	19— Mar 31	Realization A/c		2,800

Dr Sundry Assets Cr

Date	Particulars		£	Date	Particulars		£
19— Mar 31	Balance	b/d	850	19— Mar 31	Realization A/c		850

Dr Goodwill Cr

Date	Particulars		£	Date	Particulars		£
19— Mar 31	Balance	b/d	800	19— Mar 31	Realization A/c		800

Dr Sundry Creditors Cr

Date	Particulars		£	Date	Particulars		£
19— Mar 31	Cash		2,750	19— Mar 31	Balance	b/d	2,750

Dr A's Capital Account Cr

Date	Particulars		£	Date	Particulars		£
19—	Realization A/c (Loss on Dissolution)		250	19— Mar 31	Balance	b/d	2,000
	Cash		1,750				
			£ 2,000				£ 2,000

Dr B's Capital Account Cr

Date	Particulars		£	Date	Particulars		£
19—	Realization A/c (Loss on Dissolution)		250	19— Mar 31	Balance	b/d	1,500
	Cash		1,250				
			£ 1,500				£ 1,500

POSITION ON DISSOLUTION WHEN ONE PARTNER IS INSOLVENT

In the celebrated case of *Garner v Murray*, it was held that the deficiency of an insolvent partner must be borne by the solvent partners *in proportion to their capitals.*

ILLUSTRATION 16.8

Assume that the following was the position of A, B, and C, in partnership after realization of assets and payment of creditors. Profits are shared in proportion $\frac{1}{2}$, $\frac{1}{3}$, $\frac{1}{6}$ respectively.

STATEMENT OF AFFAIRS OF A, B, AND C

	£		£
A's capital	1,500	Cash	1,610
B's capital	500	C's capital	210
		Deficiency	180
	£2,000		£2,000

C is insolvent and unable to contribute to the assets of the business. Show the accounts after the books have been closed.

(C's debt is divided between A and B in the proportion of A's and B's capitals £1,500: £500, that is, $\frac{3}{4}:\frac{1}{4}$.)

Dr *Cash Book* Cr

			£				£
	Balance		1,610		A		1,230
					B		350
		£	1,610			£	1,610

Dr Deficiency Cr

			£				£
	Balance		180		A $\frac{1}{2}$		90
					B $\frac{1}{3}$		60
					C $\frac{1}{6}$		30
		£	180			£	180

Dr A's Capital Account Cr

			£				£
	Deficiency		90		Balance	b/d	1,500
	C's Deficiency		180				
	Cash		1,230				
		£	1,500			£	1,500

Dr **B's Capital Account** Cr

		£			£
Deficiency		60	Balance	b/d	500
C's Deficiency		60			
Cash		380			
	£	500		£	500

Dr **C's Capital Account** C

		£			£
Balance	b/d	210	A ¾		180
Share of Deficiency		30	B ¼		60
	£	240		£	240

EXERCISE 16.13

The partnership of X, Y, and Z came to an end on 25th April. X's capital was £6,600; Y's, £4,400; while Z had overdrawn to the extent of £350. Profits and losses were shared in the proportions of 3, 2, and 1. The assets were: cash at bank, £425; bills receivable, £950; debtors, £6,730; plant, £3,500; stock, £3,500. The liabilities were: bills payable, £805; bank overdraft, £2,000; creditors, £1,650, Z is insolvent, but his partners recover £90 from his separate estate. The assets realized the following sums: bills receivable, £925; debtors, £6,500; plant, £3,000; stock, £3,300. The expenses of winding up amounted to £185. Draw up the final accounts, and show what each partner will receive.

EXERCISE 16.14

The partnership A, B, and C came to an end on 31st December. The capital of A was £5,000, and of B £4,000, while C's account was overdrawn to the extent of £500, and he had no outside means. Profits and losses were shared in the proportions of A ½, B ⅓, and C ⅙. Their assets amounted to £8,870, and their liabilities to £370. The business was sold for £10,000. Show the partners' accounts after the sale had been effected.

EXERCISE 16.15

X and Y are trading in partnership, sharing profits equally; interest on capital is allowed at 5%. The books are kept on a 'single entry' basis, and statements drawn up on 31st December, 1947 and 1948 respectively provide the following information:

Assets	*1947*	*1948*
	£	£
Fixtures & Fittings	350	420
Stock	4,369	4,670
Debtors	1,127	1,043
Cash	630	518
	£6,476	£6,651

Liabilities	*1947*	*1948*
	£	£
Capital A/cs:		
X	4,000	4,000
Y	1,800	2,000
Current A/cs:		
X	318	?
Y	27	?
Sundry Creditors	331	347
	£6,476	£

Day books are kept and these show that the net purchases during the year 1948 amounted to £9,130 and sales to £12,337. Examination of the Cash Book shows that X's drawings amounted to £960 and Y's to £720, and that the £200 additional capital was paid in by Y on 30th June.

Ascertain the expenses for the year, the net profit (before charging partners' interest) and the balances of the current accounts as on 31st December, 1948.

London Chamber of Commerce

EXERCISE 16.16

James and Johns trading as partners and sharing profits and losses in the ratio of 3:2 decide to admit Marks as a partner as from 1st January, 1962. Goodwill stands in the books of the existing partnership at £1,000 but on the admission of Marks this is to be revalued on the basis of two years' purchase of the average net profits for the last three years.

The balances standing at the credit of the existing capital accounts on 1st January, 1962, were James £10,000 and Johns £6,000. Marks is to bring in £4,000 cash as capital and is to have one quarter share of profits or losses, James and Johns sharing the remainder in the same proportion as previously.

Profits for the three years prior to the admission of Marks were 1959—£2,900; 1960—£3,240; 1961—£3,460.

(1) Show the Capital Accounts of the partners recording the above arrangements.

(2) State what proportion of profits would be received by James and Johns respectively in the new partnership.

Associated Examining Board, G.C.E. 'A' level

EXERCISE 16.17

M. Langley and S. Knowles are the two partners of the firm Maximotors, and deal in parts for motor vehicles. They share profits and losses in proportion to their Capital Accounts; S. Knowles is paid a salary of £800 per annum as Sales Manager. On 31st December, 1970, the following details were available from the books of account of the partnership:

	Dr	Cr
	£	£
Premises	5,000	
Fixtures & Fittings...	1,000	
Provision for bad debts		200
Carriage inwards	150	
Returns inwards and outwards	276	317
Purchases and Sales	6,455	10,517

	£	£
Discounts allowed and received	200	148
Stock in hand, 1st January, 1970	4,940	
Debtors and Creditors	2,400	2,070
Salary, S. Knowles	800	
Office salaries	2,260	
Insurance and Rates	725	
Power Bills	119	
Bank Balance	677	
Current Account Balances (1st January, 1970):		
M. Langley		1,250
S. Knowles		1,500
Capital Accounts:		
M. Langley		3,000
S. Knowles		6,000
Totals ...	£25,002	£25,002

The following further information is available:

(*a*) Value of stock on 31st December, 1970 is £6,500.

(*b*) Premises, Fixtures and Fittings are to be depreciated by 10%.

(*c*) An electricity bill of £60 is due and has not been paid on 31st December.

Prepare Trading Account, Profit and Loss Account and Appropriation Account for the year ended 31st December, 1970, and a Balance Sheet as at 31st December, 1970.

G.C.E. 'O' Level

17

Total or Control Accounts and Sectional Balancing

THE Trial Balances which we have compiled in the course of working through exercises have consisted of relatively few items, not more than twenty or thirty entries at the most. Amongst these there may have been three or four debtors' accounts and one or two creditors' accounts. But even so, getting the Trial Balance to agree has occasionally given trouble. Imagine how much more difficult the task of agreeing the Trial Balance would be if there were tens of thousands of debtors' accounts and thousands of creditors' accounts, as there are in many large department stores. Imagine, too, how laborious the process would be if the personal accounts had to be totalled every time the store wished to know how much money was outstanding on the debtors' Ledger. A business with large numbers of personal accounts will not only have separate Sales Ledger and Bought Ledger departments, but in each department the respective Ledgers will be divided into sections which can be separately balanced by means of total or control accounts.

Assume that the Sales Ledger of a certain business undertaking is divided into three sections. All the credit customers' accounts with surnames beginning with any letter ranging between A and F are in one Ledger, those between G and R in another Ledger, and S to Z in a third. We shall concentrate on the section A to F; the method employed will be exactly the same for the other two sections. When postings are made in the individual personal accounts, we shall post them in total to the Sales Ledger Control Account (A–F). It is very simple. For example, supposing during May, 1964 the following entries appeared in the Sales Day Book.

19—			£
May	1	J. Able	10·22
„	3	T. Bostock	19·27
„	10	L. Dedman	5·50
„	12	C. Ford	14·50
„	16	S. Conn	12·00
„	20	C. Blackman	30·50
„	25	R. Corker	2·00
„	30	A. Bedell	7·00
			100·99

These would have been posted to the personal accounts in the Sales Ledger, thus:

Sales Ledger (A–F)

Dr J. Able Cr

19—			£	
May 1	Sales	SDB	10·22	

Dr T. Bostock Cr

19—			£	
May 3	Sales	SDB	19·27	

Dr L. Dedman Cr

19—			£	
May 10	Sales	SDB	5·50	

Dr C. Ford Cr

19—			£	
May 12	Sales	SDB	14·50	

Dr S. Conn Cr

19—			£	
May 16	Sales	SDB	12·00	

Dr C. Blackman Cr

19—			£	
May 20	Sales	SDB	30·50	

Dr R. Corker Cr

19—			£	
May 25	Sales	SDB	2·00	

Dr A. Bedell Cr

19—			£	
May 30	Sales	SDB	7·00	

and the total posted to the credit of Sales Account in the ordinary way.

General Ledger

Dr Sales Account Cr

							£
				May 31	Sundries	SDB	100·99

In addition, we now post the total (figures taken from the Sales Day Book) to the debit of the Sales Ledger Control Account (A–F).

Dr Sales Ledger Control Account (A–F) (in General Ledger) Cr

19—			£				
May	Sales		100·99				

If, during May, L. Dedman and C. Ford paid their accounts, the Cash Book would have been debited and the personal accounts credited in the ordinary way, thus:

Dr *Cash Book* Cr

19—			£				£
May 15	L. Dedman		5·50				
„ 20	C. Ford		14·50				

Dr L. Dedman Cr

19—			£	19—			£
May 10	Sales		5·50	May 15	Cash		5·50

Dr C. Ford Cr

19—			£	19—			£
May 12	Sales		14·50	May 20	Cash		14·50

and, *in addition*, the total cash paid in respect of debtors' accounts (figure taken from Cash Book) is posted to the credit of the Control Account.

Dr Sales Ledger Control Account (A–F) (in General Ledger) Cr

19—			£	19—			£
May	Sales		100·99	May	Cash		20·00

The balance on the Sales Ledger Control Account (A–F) equals the total of all the personal account balances for this section of the Sales Ledger. Entries made separately to the personal accounts are posted in total to the Control Account. Supposing, for example, cash discounts allowed to customers during the month amounted to £10, then the individual customers' accounts would have been credited with these discounts, and the Control Account credited in a similar way with the total sum. *We repeat that what is done to the individual accounts must be done in total to the Control Account.* If any balances are written off to Bad Debts, the relevant personal accounts are credited and the Bad Debts Account debited. We are concerned only with the personal accounts, and so the Control Account will be credited with the total sum written off to Bad Debts Account. What we are doing, in effect, is looking upon the Sales Ledger (A–F) as one single debtor's account. If the student is in any doubt about which side of the Control Account an entry should be made, let him ask himself on which side he made the entries in the customers' personal accounts; the entry is made on the same side in the Control or Total Account.

ILLUSTRATION 17.1

The following is the Sales Ledger Control Account appearing in the General Ledger of a business as at the end of February.

		£			£
Feb 1	Balance b/d	9,172·15	Feb 28	Cash	4,518·77
,, 28	Sales	4,321·25		Discounts	209·86
	Carriage	43·06		Returns	57·50
				Balance c/d	8,750·33
		£13,536·46			£13,536·46
Mar 1	Balance b/d	8,750·33			

Explain the meaning of each of the items appearing in this account and state from which books the several entries are posted.

Feb 1 *To Balance b/d*
The total of the balances on customers' accounts brought down.

Feb 28 *To Sales*
The total sum debited to customers' accounts during February in respect of goods supplied. Posted from the Sales Day Book.

Feb 28 *To Carriage*
The total sum debited to customers' accounts during February in respect of carriage. Posted from Journal or columnar Day Book.

Feb 28 *By Cash*
The total payments made by credit customers during February. Posted from the Cash Book.

Feb 28 *By Discounts*
The total of discounts allowed to customers during February. Posted from the Cash Book.

Feb 28 *By Returns*
The total value of goods returned by credit customers during February. Posted from Sales Returns (or Returns Inwards) Book.

Mar 1 *To Balance b/d*
This figure represents the total owing by credit customers at this date. If the ledger clerk were to total the balances on debtors' personal accounts it should come to this figure.

Purchases Ledger Control Account

In a department store there are likely to be fewer accounts in the Purchases or Bought Ledger than in the Sales Ledger, and less need, therefore, to divide the Ledger into sections. The Purchases Ledger Control Account would be kept in a similar way to the Sales Ledger Control Account. Amounts credited to suppliers' personal accounts in respect of goods supplied would be credited in total to the Purchases Control Account. Payments made to creditors would be debited to their respective personal accounts and in total to the debit of the Purchases Ledger Control Account.

ILLUSTRATION 17.2

In order to locate the difference on the Trial Balance of King and Cross at 30th June, 1958, it was decided to prepare Purchases and Sales Ledger Total (or Control) Accounts.

From the following details, prepare these accounts to show where an error may have been made.

1957		£
July 1	Purchases Ledger Balances	5,982
„ 1	Sales Ledger Balances	9,872
	Totals for year ending 30th June, 1958:	
	Purchases Journal	77,281
	Sales Journal	99,831
	Returns Outwards Journal	1,324
	Returns Inwards Journal	2,278
	Cheques paid to Suppliers	73,050
	Discounts Allowed	2,910
	Discounts Received	1,067
	Petty Cash paid to Suppliers	39
	Cheques and Cash received from Customers	92,980
	Bad Debts Written Off	198
	Customers' Cheques dishonoured	15
	Balances on the Sales Ledger set off against Cr balances in the Purchases Ledger	518

The list of balances taken from the Purchases Ledger shows a total of £7,265 and that from the Sales Ledger a total of £10,829.

Dr — Purchases Ledger Control Account — Cr

1957			£	1957			£
July 1 to June 30 1958	Returns		1,324	July 1 to June 30 1958	Balance	b/d	5,982
	Bank		73,050		Purchases		77,281
	Discounts		1,067				
	Petty Cash		39				
	Sales Ledger		518				
	Balance	c/d	7,265				
		£	83,263			£	83,263
				1958 July 1	Balance	b/d	£7,265

Dr — Sales Ledger Control Account — Cr

1957			£	1957			£
July 1	Balance	b/d	9,872	July 1	Returns		2,278
1957				to	Discounts		2,910
July 1	Sales		99,831	June 30	Cash & Bank		92,980
to	Bank			1958	Bad Debts		198
June 30	(Cheques				Purchases Ledger		518
1958	Dishonoured)		15		Balance	c/d	10,834
		£	109,718			£	109,718
1958							
July 1	Balance		10,834				

The error is in the Sales Ledger; possibly an account £5 balance was overlooked when the ledger clerk listed the balances.

ILLUSTRATION 17.3

The book-keeper employed by South keeps a Purchases Ledger Control Account, and at the balancing date, the net total of the balances extracted from the Purchases Ledger, which was £3,204, did not agree with the balance shown by the Control Account. The following errors were discovered after checking, and after adjustment had been made for them, the books balanced. The corrected net total of the Purchases Ledger balances then agreed with the amended balance of the Control Account.

(1) The Purchases Day Book had been overcast by £100.
(2) £10 received from North (a supplier), in respect of a previous overpayment, had been posted to an account in the Sales Ledger for a different person of the same name, and as such had been transferred to North's account in the Purchases Ledger. No entry had been made in the Control Account as regards this transfer.
(3) A debit balance on West's account of £50 represented a payment to him for goods supplied, the invoice for which had not been entered in the Purchases Day Book.
(4) Credit balances in the Purchases Ledger amounting to £240 and a debit balance of £4 had been omitted from the extracted list of balances.
(5) £85 owing to East had been settled in contra, and the entries had been made in the respective Ledgers, but no entry had been made in the Control Account as regards same.

Give the Journal entries necessary to correct these errors and set out the Purchases Ledger Control Account showing the balance before the correction of the errors and the subsequent adjustments.

A.C.C.A. Intermediate, 1964

(1) This means that the Purchases Ledger Control Account was credited and the Purchases Account debited with £100 in excess of the correct figure. The personal accounts are unaffected. The Journal entry to correct this would be as follows.

Journal

			Dr	Cr
			£	£
	Purchases Ledger Control Account Dr		100	
	Purchases A/c			100
	Correction of error: Purchases Book overcast by £100			

(2) It often helps to make little T accounts on a piece of scrap paper to see more clearly what occurred, e.g. assume £100 was paid to North in respect of a debt of £90.

Bought Ledger
North (Supplier)

100	90

The £10 received from North (Supplier) was wrongly posted to a person of the same name in the Sales Ledger.

Sales Ledger
North

	10

North's account in the Sales Ledger must be debited with £10 and North's account in the Bought Ledger credited with a similar sum. Whatever entries are made in the personal accounts must be repeated in the Control Accounts. The Journal entry will be:

Journal

			Dr	Cr
			£	£
Sales Ledger Control A/c	Dr		10	
Purchases Ledger Control A/c				10
Correction of error: cash transferred from Sales to Purchases Ledger				

(3) In this case West's account has not been credited and the Purchases Account not debited with the £50. The personal account must be credited, and therefore the Purchases Control Account must also be credited. The debit entry will appear in the Purchases Account.

Journal

			Dr	Cr
			£	£
Purchases Account	Dr		50	
Purchases Ledger Control A/c				50
Invoice not entered in Day Book				

(4) These omissions do not affect the Purchases Ledger Control Account and so no Journal entry is necessary.

(5) Using T accounts again,

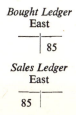

Bought Ledger
East

	85

Sales Ledger
East

85	

This means that the £85 owing by East in the Sales Ledger was set off against the £85 owed to East in the Bought Ledger. East's account in the Sales Ledger was credited with £85, and his account in the Bought Ledger debited with £85. Similar entries must be made in the Control Accounts, viz.

Journal

			Dr	Cr
			£	£
	Purchases Ledger Control Account	Dr	85	
	Sales Ledger Control A/c			85
	Contra item not recorded in Control Accounts			

Before we prepare the Purchases Ledger Control Account, we must calculate the total sum outstanding on the Purchases Ledger. We are told that the extracted balances totalled £3,204. We must add the £240 omitted when the balances were listed and deduct the debit balance of £4 which was also omitted. There was also an invoice of £50 which was not posted. If we make the necessary additions and subtractions, we shall get a figure representing the total sum owing to suppliers of £3,490.

We can now prepare the Purchases Ledger Control Account.

Dr Purchases Ledger Control Account Cr

			£				£
	Purchases		100		Balance	b/d	3,615
	East (contra)		85		North		10
	Balance	c/d	3,490		Purchases		50
		£	3,675			£	3,675
					Balance	b/d	3,490

The Question of Double Entry

The value of keeping total or control accounts has been amply demonstrated, but so far all entries in the control accounts have been made on one side of the account only. A principle of double entry book-keeping, namely, that for every debit entry there must be a corresponding credit entry and vice versa, has thus been violated. There are three possible ways of overcoming this difficulty:

(1) to treat the control account as a memorandum statement and not part of the double entry system at all,

(2) to treat the personal accounts in the Sales Ledger and Bought Ledger as memorandum records and the control accounts in the General Ledger as the essential parts of the double entry system, the personal accounts merely supplying the details of what is contained in the control accounts,

(3) to observe the double entry principle by opening two control, or adjustment, accounts, as they are sometimes called, and keeping one in the Sales Ledger and the other in the General Ledger. The control account kept with the Sales Ledger would show the totals on opposite sides to the postings in the personal accounts.

Dr Adjustment Account (A–F) (in Sales Ledger) Cr

		£				£
Cash		6,500		Sales		10,000
Discounts		70				
Bad Debts		120				
Balance	c/d	3,310				
	£	10,000			£	10,000
				Balance	b/d	3,310

Each section of the Sales Ledger is then completely self-balancing, the total of the personal account balances in the debit column of the Trial Balance agreeing with the credit balance taken from the Adjustment Account in the Sales Ledger.

The corresponding entries appear in the Adjustment Account in the General Ledger on opposite sides of the account. This way there is a credit entry for every debit entry and vice versa.

Dr Adjustment Account (A–F) (in General Ledger) Cr

		£				£
Sales		10,000		Cash		6,500
				Discounts		70
				Bad Debts		120
				Balance	c/d	3,310
	£	10,000			£	10,000
Balance	£	3,310				

The debit and credit entries, which appear respectively in the two Adjustment Accounts, should be passed through the Journal, viz.

Journal			Dr	Cr
			£	£
Adjustment Account (General Ledger)	Dr		10,000	
Adjustment A/c (Sales Ledger)				10,000
Being sales to customers				

SPECIAL RULINGS IN THE BOOKS OF ORIGINAL ENTRY

When the Sales Ledger is divided into sections, it is desirable to introduce additional analysis columns in the books of original entry in order to facilitate postings to the control accounts.

Cash Book (Debit side only)

Date	Particulars	Fol.	Discounts			Details	Bank	Sales Ledger			General Ledger
			A–F	G–R	S–Z	£	£	A–F	G–R	S–Z	

If cash and discount is made as one entry to the personal account in the Sales Ledger, e.g. 'Cash and Discount', the analysis columns for discounts can be dispensed with,

Date	Particulars	Fol.	Total	Sales Ledger		
				A–F	G–R	S–Z

and so on with the other books of original entry.

ADVANTAGES OF CONTROL ACCOUNTS

(1) Errors are localized, and therefore more quickly traced.
(2) Interim Balance Sheets can be quickly prepared.
(3) Responsibility for any errors can be fixed.
(4) Risk of fraud is diminished.
(5) If adjustment accounts are kept in the General Ledger, the General Ledger is completely self-balancing and the Balance Sheet can be prepared without reference to the Bought and Sold Ledgers.

Bills Receivable and Bills Payable

These terms may appear in the Sales Ledger and the Bought Ledger control accounts.

Bills Receivable

When a customer pays an account by a Bill of Exchange (B/E), as distinct from a cheque which is a Bill of Exchange drawn on a banker and payable on demand, the cash will not normally be received until the B/E matures at some date in the future. Note that we send the B/E to our customer for him to accept it and return it to us. Upon receipt of the accepted B/E the following entries will be made in the ledger:

Credit the customers' account with the amount of the B/E, viz.

A. Customer

19— Feb 1	Sales		£ 100·00	19— Mar 1	Bills receivable		£ 100·00

and debit Bills Receivable Account:

Bills Receivable

19— Mar 1	A. Customer		£ 100·00				

It will be seen that one form of asset, namely a debt, has been exchanged for another asset—a B/E.) When the B/E is paid, the Bank Account will be debited and Bills Receivable Account credited.

Bills Payable

If we pay a supplier with a B/E, he will make out the bill and send it to us for acceptance. We will then write 'accepted' across the face of the document, sign it and return it to him. As no money is immediately payable, no entry is made in the Cash Book. Instead we debit the Supplier's Account:

A. Supplier

19— May 2	Bills Payable		£ 300·00	19— Apr 1	Purchases		£ 300·00

and credit Bills Payable Account:

Bills Payable

				19— May 2	A. Supplier		£ 300·00

and we now become liable on the B/E instead of being liable to the supplier. When the B/E matures and has to be paid, we credit our Bank Account and Debit Bills Payable Account. Thus, 'Bills Receivable' will appear on the credit side of the Sales Ledger Control Account and 'Bills Payable' on the debit side of the Purchases Ledger Control Account for these are the sides to which entries are made in the respective personal accounts.

EXERCISE 17.1

From the information below prepare the Purchases Ledger Control Account as it would appear in the General Ledger of Messrs Shaw & Sons as at 31st December, 19—.

	£
Credit balances, 1st December	6,328·08
Cash Paid	10,129·18
Discount Received	809·07
Purchases	18,327·59
Returns	429·88
Bills Payable	5,817·61
Cash Received	21·31
Credit Balances Transferred to Sales Ledger	61·19

EXERCISE 17.2

Prepare, as at 31st December, the necessary Control Account for the Sales Ledger from the following.

			£
Dec	1	Balances Brought Down	6,751
,,	31	Goods Sold on Credit During Month	15,760
		Bills Accepted by Customers	1,234
		Discount Allowed Customers	987
		Cash Received from Customers	13,458
		Goods Returned by Customers	864

EXERCISE 17.3

Show the necessary Control Account arising out of the following figures.

	£
Sundry Debtors, 1st January, 19—	10,000
Credit sales	30,000
Discount Allowed to Debtors	2,000
Cash Received from Debtors	21,000
Bills Accepted by Debtors	5,000
Bad Debts Written Off	500
Sales Returns	1,000

EXERCISE 17.4

A firm keeps a Purchases Ledger which is checked by means of a Control Account. For the month of May, 1962 the following figures are available for the Control Account.

	£
Credit Balance at 1st May, 1962 (agreeing with total balances in Purchases Ledger)	4,609
Purchases	5,402
Purchases Returns	110
Cash Paid	4,875
Discount Received	257
Transfers of Debit Balances in Sales Ledger to Purchases Ledger	80

(1) Construct the Control Account for May, 1962.
(2) State the source from which each of the above figures would be ascertained.
(3) State what the balance of the Control Account represents.

University of London, G.C.E. 'O' level, 1962

Where a firm has a large number of personal accounts, some customers' accounts may have credit balances, e.g. when goods are returned after the account has been settled, and the value of the returned goods has been credited to the customer's account. Similarly, goods may be returned to a supplier after the account has been paid, and there is then a debit balance on the supplier's account. In the control accounts, some undertakings show these credit and debit balances separately. The following worked exercise shows the student who is faced with a control account problem of this kind how the entries are made. Note that the Sales Ledger Control Account must be debited with £110 and this balance carried down to the credit side for the following period before balancing the Control Account. And the Purchases Control Account must be credited with £89 and this figure brought down to the debit side for the following period before the Control Account is balanced.

ILLUSTRATION 17.4

The following figures were taken from the books of A.B.C. Ltd.

		£
Jan 1	Balance on Sales Ledger—Dr..	11,232
	,, ,, ,, ,, —Cr	147
	,, ,, Purchases Ledger—Cr	7,328
	,, ,, ,, ,, —Dr	118
Dec 31	Sales to Customers on Credit	10,845
	Purchases on Credit from Suppliers	6,325
	Allowances Made to Customers	187
	Goods Returned to Suppliers	123
	Cash Received from Customers	9,645
	Bad Debts Written Off	85
	Discounts Allowed to Customers	496
	Discounts Allowed by Suppliers	412
	Cash Paid to Suppliers	6,142
	Cash Repaid to Customers	25
	Transfers from Sales Ledger to the Debit of Purchases Ledger	598
	Transfers from Purchases Ledger to the Credit of .. Sales Ledger	214
	Legal and Other Expenses Charged to Customers	35
	Balances on Sales Ledger—Cr	110
	,, ,, Purchases Ledger—Dr	89

Draw up the necessary Purchases and Sales Ledger Control Accounts and bring down the balances on 31st December.

Dr Sales Ledger Control Account (General Ledger) **Cr**

			£				£
Jan 1	Balance	b/d	11,232	Jan 1	Balance	b/d	147
Dec 31	Sales		10,845	Dec 31	Allowances		187
„ 31	Cash Repaid		25	„ 31	Cash		9,645
„ 31	Legal Expenses		35	„ 31	Bad Debts		85
31	Balance	c/d	110	„ 31	Discounts		496
				„ 31	Purchases Ledger		598
				„ 31	Purchases Ledger		214
				31	Balance	c/d	10,875
		£	22,247			£	22,247
Jan 1	Balance	b/d	10,875	Jan 1	Balance	b/d	110

Dr Purchases Ledger Control Account (General Ledger) **Cr**

			£				£
Jan 1	Balance	To b/d	118	Jan 1	Balance	b/d	7,328
Dec 31	Returns		123	Dec 31	Purchases		6,325
„ 31	Discounts		412	„ 31	Balance	c/d	89
„ 31	Cash		6,142				
„ 31	Sales Ledger		598				
„ 31	Sales Ledger		214				
„ 31	Balance	c/d	6,135				
		£	13,742			£	13,742
Jan 1	Balance	b/d	89	Jan 1	Balance	b/d	6,135

EXERCISE 17.5

(1) What accounts would you expect to find in a Sales Ledger?
(2) J.K. checks his Sales Ledger monthly by means of a Control Account. Name the sources from which J.K. is likely to ascertain the figures to prepare this Control Account.
(3) What should the balance of the Control Account represent and with what amount should it agree?

G.C.E. 'O' level, Principles of Accounts

EXERCISE 17.6

James Packer carries on a factoring business. The following balances appeared in his books on 30th June, 1963.

	£
Travellers' Commission & Expenses	7,484
Telephone & Postage	442
Trade Subscriptions	52
Stock-in-Trade at 1st July, 1962	10,744
Sales Ledger Control	14,430

	£
Sales	153,721
Salaries	5,216
Rent Paid	1,140
Purchases	126,533
Purchase Ledger Control	6,179
Printing, Stationery & Advertising	789
Petty Cash in Hand	16
Office Furniture & Equipment	1,620
Lighting & Heating	406
Insurance	252
General Trade Expenses	1,523
Drawings—James Packer	3,527
Discount Allowed	385
Discount Received	726
Cash at Bank	4,232
Capital A/c—Balance at 1st July, 1962	18,407
Bad Debts Written Off	242

You are given the following additional information.

(1) Items owing by James Packer at 30th June, 1963, were: rent £380; travellers' commission and expenses £615; lighting and heating £56.
(2) The valuation of the stock-in-trade on 30th June, 1963 was £9,556.
(3) Provision is to be made for accountancy charges £231 and in respect of doubtful debts £290.
(4) Office furniture and equipment is to be depreciated by 10 per cent.

You are instructed to prepare:
(*a*) Trading and Profit & Loss Accounts for the year ended 30th June, 1963, so as to show the information contained therein in the most useful and practical manner,
(*b*) a Balance Sheet as on 30th June, 1963.

A.C.C.A.

EXERCISE 17.7

J. Cox keeps five Sales Ledgers (A–D, E–H, I–L, M–R, S–Z), and two Purchases Ledgers (A–L, M–Z).

On 1st May, 1963 the balance on Sales Ledger A–D Control Account was £4,608 and on Purchases Ledger M–Z Control Account £7,018, both balances agreeing with the total balances on the accounts in the respective Ledgers.

(1) From the following details which relate to Sales Ledger A–D and Purchases Ledger M–Z for the month of May, 1963 construct Control Accounts for each Ledger.

	£
Sales	5,119
Sales Returns	107
Purchases	6,843
Purchases Returns	212
Cash Received from Debtors	4,127
Cash Paid to Creditors	6,309
Discount Allowed to Debtors	208
Discount Received from Creditors	285
Cash Refunded to Debtors	13

	£
Interest Charged by Creditors	19
Carriage Charged to Debtors	86
Bad Debts Written Off during May	65
Bad Debt Recovered (written off in January, 1963) (included in Cash from Debtors)	18
Debit Balances in A–D Sales Ledger transferred to A–L Purchases Ledger	201
Credit Balances in M–Z Purchases Ledger transferred to S–Z Sales Ledger	174
Debit Balances in Purchases Ledger M–Z at 31st May	29

(2) The following Ledgers showed a 'difference'.
Sales Ledger I–L: debit balance of Control Account £4,818; total of debtors balances £5,430.
Purchases Ledger A–L: credit balance of Control Account £6,298; total of creditors' balances £6,226.

On investigation the following errors were disclosed.

(*a*) A page of Sales Book I–L had been carried forward as £2,107 instead of £2,701.

(*b*) The A–L column of the Purchases Returns Book had been totalled as £801 instead of £791.

(*c*) A Sales Return had been posted to F. Kay's account as £24 instead of £42.

(*d*) A posting of Discount Received £17 on a payment to W. Carr had been omitted from Carr's account.

(*e*) A debit balance of £102 on T. Little's account in Sales Ledger I–L had been transferred, through the Journal, to T. Little's account in Purchases Ledger A–L. In posting from the Journal the amount had been entered in Little's (Purchases Ledger) account as £201.

State what corrections you would make to rectify these errors and calculate the amount of the rectified balances.

G.C.E. 'A' level

EXERCISE 17.8

(i) Explain the meaning and purpose of Control Accounts.
(ii) From the following information prepare the General Ledger Control Account as it would appear in the Sales Ledger.

	£
1 March 1970:	
Total Debtors—Balance	3,365
Credit Balances	125
During March 1970:	
Sales on Credit	7,894
Returns Inwards	321
Allowances to customers	86
Carriage charges to customers	28
Cheques received from Debtors	7,099
Cheques sent to Debtors	24
Discounts allowed	304
Cheques from Debtors returned marked 'refer to drawer' ...	29
31 March 1970:	
Credit Balances	78

G.C.E. 'O' Level

EXERCISE 17.9

The following items relating to the month of May, 1971, are those appearing among others in the books of a trader:—

	£
Stock in hand: 1 May, 1971	1,000
Stock in hand: 31 May, 1971	1,240
Amounts owing by debtors 1 May, 1971	820
Amounts owing by debtors 31 May, 1971	560
Cash sales	1,700
Cheques received from debtors	1,076
Discount allowed to debtors	20
Goods returned by debtors	40
Purchases on credit	1,900
Purchases for cash	80
Expenses	250

(i) Show, by means of a Sundry Debtors Total or Control account, the amount of the trader's credit sales for the month of May, 1971.

(ii) Calculate the trader's gross profit and net profit for the month of May, 1971.

G.C.E. 'O' Level

18

Correction of Errors-Suspense Accounts

HOWEVER careful the book-keeper is, errors will occasionally occur. An entry in one of the day books may, for example, be posted to the wrong personal account; or an error may be made in totalling a day book, with the result that an incorrect amount is posted to the Sales or Purchases Account; or again, an entry may be posted to the debit side of an account instead of to the credit side, and vice versa. In the early stages of his book-keeping studies, the student must resist the temptation to cross out the offending entry or, worse still, to erase it with an ink rubber. When errors are made, they must be corrected through the Journal by cancelling the incorrect entry and giving effect to the right one.

Let us take a simple example. An entry in the Sales Day Book for 16th May, 1964 for T. Langford £100 is posted wrongly to the debit of T. Langton's account. When the error is discovered, T. Langton's account must be credited with £100 and T. Langford's account debited.

Journal

				Dr	Cr
				£	£
May 20	T. Langford	Dr		100	
	T. Langton				100
	Being correction of error in posting				

ILLUSTRATION 18.1

Show by means of Journal entries how the following errors would be corrected in the books of C. Careless.

(1) Machinery valued at £500 purchased on credit from Excel Engineering Company had been debited to the Purchases Account.

(2) When paying J. Johnson, a creditor, Careless had deducted £5 as cash discount. Johnson had disallowed this discount.

(3) Depreciation of £200 on motor vehicles had been credited to Fixtures & Fittings Account.

R.S.A. Elementary

Journal

		Dr	Cr
		£	£
Machinery Account	Dr	500	
Purchases Account			500
Being correction of error; wrong account debited			
Discounts Received	Dr	5	
J. Johnson			5
Being cash discount disallowed			
Fixtures & Fittings Account	Dr	200	
Motor Vehicles			200
Being correction of error in depreciating F & F A/c instead of Motor Vehicles			

ILLUSTRATION 18.2

Although the Trial Balance of A.B. agreed, the audit of his books of account revealed the following errors.

£15 paid for advertising charges had been debited to the personal account of the advertising contractor.

£60 paid for the purchase of an additional typewriter had been debited to the Purchases Account.

State (1) why these errors were not revealed by the Trial Balance, (2) the effect of their *correction* on the balance of the net profit at the end of the trading period.

G.C.E. 'O' level

(1) These are errors of principle, errors which are not revealed by the Trial Balance. The double entry has been made in both cases; the errors are due to the wrong accounts having been debited. Advertising Charges Account is a nominal account which, in the ordinary way, would be closed by transfer to the Profit & Loss Account and charged against income. Owing to the mistake of debiting the personal account of the advertising contractor, this sum of £15 has not been charged against income, and the Profit & Loss Account shows a net profit of £15 in excess of the true figure.

(2) A real account has been wrongly treated as a nominal account, with the result that the Profit & Loss Account shows net profit £60 less than the true figure. The net profit, because of these two errors, has been understated by £45 in the Profit & Loss Account.

The student should make Journal entries to show how these errors would be corrected in the books of account.

Suspense Accounts

When the Trial Balance does not agree, it is necessary, as a preliminary step, to ensure that the Trial Balance itself is correct, by checking that all the Ledger balances have been recorded on the right sides and that the figures have been correctly copied. Dividing the difference of the two sides of the Trial Balance by two and looking for a corresponding item in the list of balances is sometimes helpful in locating a balance which has been put on the wrong side. It is, of course, desirable that the Trial Balance should agree before preparation of the final accounts is begun. But this is not always possible. The process of finding the errors may take too long, and delay in getting out the trading figures will diminish their value. Where the errors cannot be readily found, it is usual to open a Suspense Account, and to debit or credit the Account with the difference in the Trial Balance so that the Trial Balance then agrees. Thereafter, as the errors are discovered, Journal entries are made to correct these, the double entry being completed by debiting or crediting the Suspense Account. A small difference in the Trial Balance may conceal substantial errors in the Ledger and one should not, therefore, be complacent if only a trifling difference is revealed by the Trial Balance.

ILLUSTRATION 18.3

It should be noticed that when an entry is posted to the wrong side of an account the correction involves a figure twice the amount of the original entry.

On March 2nd a sum of £30 received from T. Sims, a credit customer, is posted wrongly to the debit side of his account, viz.:

Dr Cash Account Cr

19—			£				
Mar 2	T. Sims		30				

Dr T. Sims Cr

19—			£				
Mar 2	Cash		30				

If the error had not been found when the final accounts were prepared and a Suspense Account had been opened, this account would have been credited with £60, the amount by which the two sides of the trial balance were in disagreement.

Dr Suspense Account Cr

19—			£	19—			£
Dec 31	T. Sims		60	Dec 31	Difference—Trial Balance		60

When discovered, the error would have been corrected by crediting T. Sims' Account with £60 and debiting the Suspense Account.

Dr		T. Sims			Cr
19—		£	19—		£
Mar 2	Cash	30	Dec 31	Suspense A/c	60

ILLUSTRATION 18.4

After ascertaining the net profit for the year 19— the Trial Balance of J. Edge's Ledger was as follows.

	£	£
Capital (1st January, 19—)		775·11
Drawings	1,800·00	
Profit & Loss A/c (Cr bal.)		1,960·44
Bank A/c (Cr bal.)		223·80
Petty Cash	20·00	
Stock (31st December, 19—)	1,895·50	
Sundry Debtors	497·16	
Sundry Creditors		1,627·42
Insurance prepaid	11·24	
Heat & Light (amount due)		17·42
Furniture & Equipment	350·00	
Suspense Account	30·29	
	£4,604·19	£4,604·19

The 'difference' in the Trial Balance was eventually found to be due to the following errors.

(1) Interest on the bank overdraft £12·33 had been entered in the Cash Book but had not been posted to a Ledger account.
(2) Insurance prepaid had been correctly credited in the Insurance Account as £11·46 but had been brought down as £11·24.
(3) A purchase of goods £8·89 by a customer, J. Everson, had been correctly entered in the sales record but had been posted to the personal account as £9·88.
(4) A page of the Purchases Book was undercast by £10.
(5) The Discounts received for October £67·41 had been posted to the Discounts Received Account as £76·14

Show *by means of Journal entries* the necessary corrections for the above errors and prepare Edge's Balance Sheet as it should have been at 31st December, 19— if all the errors had been corrected before preparing the final accounts.

We shall show the Suspense Account although this is not asked for in the question.

Journal

	Dr	Cr
	£	£
Bank Interest Account Dr	12·33	
Suspense Account		12·33
Being correction of error: double entry not completed		
Insurance Account Dr	0·22	
Suspense Account		0·22
Being correction of error: balance brought down wrongly		
Suspense Account Dr	0·99	
J. Everson		0·99
Being correction of error: wrong figure posted to debit of personal A/c		
Purchases Account Dr	10·00	
Suspense Account		10·00
Being correction of error: Purchases Book undercast		
Discounts Received Dr	8·73	
Suspense Account		8·73
Being correction of error: incorrect figure posted to Discounts Recd A/c		

Dr Suspense Account Cr

			£				£
19—				19—			
Dec 31.	Difference in Trial Balance		30·29	Dec 31	Interest		12·33
31	J. Everson		·99	„ 31	Insurance		0·22
				„ 31	Purchases		10·00
				„ 31	Disc. Recd		8·73
		£	31·28			£	31·28

BALANCE SHEET AS AT 31ST DECEMBER, 1960

	£	£		£	£
Capital		775·11	*Fixed Assets*		
			Furniture & Equipment		350·00
Profit & Loss	1,929·38				
Less Drawings	1,800·00		*Current Assets*		
		129·38	Stock	1,895·50	
Current Liabilities			Debtors	496·17	
			Insurance prepaid	11·46	
Bank Overdraft	238·80		Petty Cash	20·00	
Sundry Creditors	1,627·42				
Accrued Charges	17·42				2,423·13
		1,868·64			
	£	2,773·13		£	2,773·13

POINTS TO NOTE

(1) In opening a Suspense Account, one entry only is made; the double entry is completed when the errors are located and corrected through the Journal.

(2) After all the errors have been discovered and the corrections made, the balance on the Suspense Account is extinguished.

(3) The Suspense Account has uses other than those described. For example, if a payment of £10 is received, with no enclosure to show who sent it, the money is paid into the bank, the Cash Book debited, and the Suspense Account credited with this payment, viz.

Dr *Cash Book* Cr

	Suspense A/c		£ 10				

Dr Suspense Account Cr

					Cash		£ 10

Upon discovery of the identity of the sender, the Suspense Account is debited and the personal account of the customer credited with the payment.

EXERCISE 18.1

A book-keeper made the following errors in writing up his business accounts for May, 19—.

(1) A sum of £18·52½ received from a debtor was debited in the Cash Book and also debited to the debtor's account.
(2) Discount allowed £31·12 was not posted to the Discount Allowed Account.
(3) An allowance £10·25 received from a creditor was credited to the account of the creditor.
(4) A payment of £36 for rates was debited in error to the Rent Account.

(*a*) State exactly what effect *each* of the above errors would have on the agreement of the Trial Balance.
(*b*) What entries would be necessary to correct each of the above errors?

EXERCISE 18.2

When the Trial Balance of Oxford and Co. was prepared, it was found that the total of the credit side exceeded that of the debit side by £1,061, and a Suspense Account was opened with this amount.

On checking the records, it was found that:

(1) a debit balance of £520 on Rent Account had been entered on the credit side of the Trial Balance,
(2) the Sales Account was overcast by £10,
(3) an invoice for £60 in respect of goods purchased from J. Williams had been credited to the account of J. Williamson,
(4) the purchase of a motor truck for £647 had been correctly entered in the Cash Book but had been posted to the Motor Truck Account as £674,
(5) a balance of £38 due from C. Cambridge had been omitted from the Trial Balance,
(6) goods to the value of £40 returned by D. Durham were not entered in the Returns Inwards Book but had been included in the stock on hand.

Write up the Suspense Account showing how it would be affected, if at all, by these errors.

R.S·A. II (Intermediate), 1959

EXERCISE 18.3

The final accounts prepared by a trader for the year ended 30th April, 1971 showed a gross profit of £8,961 and a net profit of £3,562.

It has now been discovered that a number of errors had been made:

(*a*) At the stocktaking on 30th April, 1971, one item of £80 had been entered on the stock list twice; another item was shown as 64 articles at £6·50 each instead of 64 articles at £0·65 each.
(*b*) No adjustment had been made in respect of rent payable by the trader, £86 for April 1971, which remained unpaid at 30th April, 1971.
(*c*) In calculating the profit, no account had been taken of goods to the value of £156 taken from the business by the proprietor for his own use.
(*d*) The cost of a new typewriter, £84, purchased on 1st May, 1970 for use in the office had been debited to Purchases Account. In consequence of this, the necessary provision for depreciation on this typewriter (£16) had been omitted from the profit calculation.
(*e*) An invoice for £191 in respect of goods received by the business on 27th April had not been entered in the books; the goods had, however, been included in the closing stock valuation.

You are asked:

(i) to explain briefly what effect each of these errors had had on the calculation of gross profit and/or net profit;
(ii) to show your calculation of the correct gross profit and net profit for the year.

G.C.E. 'O' Level

19
Manufacturing Accounts

So far we have been mainly concerned with the accounts of traders who carry on business as wholesalers or retailers, and who perform the important service of holding stocks of goods so that shopkeepers, and consumers generally, can replenish their own stocks easily and quickly whenever the need to do so arises. The gross profit which such traders make is the difference between what the goods actually cost them to buy and what they receive for them when they are sold. We have now to turn our attention to the accounting methods of a business organization which includes manufacturing, as well as selling, among its activities, and where the gross profit is the difference between what the goods cost to make and what they fetch when sold.

Generally speaking, a manufacturer is engaged in converting raw materials into finished goods. To do this, he has to buy raw materials, labour, power, etc., and since these activities are best kept separate from the trading aspects of the business, the manufacturer divides his Trading Account into two parts. Only the first part of the Trading Account, which is usually termed the Manufacturing Account, need concern us here; the second part of the Trading Account is prepared in a similar way to other Trading Accounts.

All the costs of actually making the goods will appear in the Manufacturing Account, but it is usual to divide these costs into those which are directly identified with production, e.g. raw materials and productive wages, termed 'prime' costs, and those expenses, such as rent and rates of factory, light and heat, insurance, etc., which are incurred in carrying on production generally, and which are not related directly to any particular units of production. These latter costs plus the prime costs make up the factory or 'works' cost.

$$\left.\begin{array}{r} \text{Prime cost} = \left\{\begin{array}{l} \text{Direct materials} \\ \text{Direct labour costs} \\ \text{Direct expenses} \end{array}\right. \\ \\ \text{Factory overheads} \end{array}\right\} = \begin{array}{c} \text{Production} \\ \text{or} \\ \text{Factory or} \\ \text{Works cost} \end{array}$$

Examples

(1) Direct materials—raw materials, cost of carriage inwards on raw materials

(2) Direct labour cost—machine operator's wages (because traceable to a unit of manufacture)
(3) Indirect labour cost—foreman's wages (because cost is not traceable to a unit of manufacture and so is part of factory overheads)
(4) Direct expenses—royalties payable to an inventor and charged on each unit produced; hire of special plant for a specific job.

Work in Progress or Partly finished Goods

In any manufacturing undertaking there will invariably be some work at the end of the financial period which is partly finished. These items are dealt with in a similar way to stock; the work in progress at the beginning of the financial year is likely to be completed during the year and so is added to the total works cost, and the work in progress at the end of the year, which is likely to be finished the following year, is deducted from the total of works cost. The latter will appear in the Balance Sheet for the end of the period with the other current assets.

Notes

(1) If the work in progress is valued at prime cost, the adjustment should be made to the prime cost figure instead of to the works cost figure.
(2) The manufacturing account is concerned with the production cost of goods *completed* in the year under review, regardless of when the work started—hence the reason for including work in progress at the beginning of the period and excluding work in progress at the end of the period.

ILLUSTRATION 19.1

F. Wayman is a manufacturer. From the following information prepare his Manufacturing Account and Trading Account for the year ended 31st December 1961. (For accounts see opposite.)

	£
Sales ..	34,690
Stocks (1st January, 1961)	
Raw Materials ..	510
Work in Progress ..	810
Finished Goods ..	3,120
Purchases of Raw Materials ..	5,298
Stocks (31st December, 1961)	
Raw Materials ..	490
Work in Progress ..	670
Finished Goods ..	2,980
Factory Wages Paid ..	14,340
,, ,, Due at 31st December, 1961 ..	150

	£
Factory & Machinery Maintenance	520
Depreciation on Plant & Machinery	1,140
Factory Power	490
Factory Salaries	1,830
Factory Expenses:	
Rent, Rates & Insurance	570
Lighting & Heating	72

G.C.E. 'O' level

MANUFACTURING AND TRADING ACCOUNT FOR THE YEAR ENDED 31ST DECEMBER, 1961

Dr	£	£		Cr £
Raw Materials (1st Jan)		510	Transfer to Trading A/c	
Purchases		5,298	Cost of Goods Produced	24,570
		5,808		
Less Stock (31st Dec)		490		
Cost of Raw Materials Consumed		5,318		
Factory Wages	14,340			
Add wages accrued	150			
		14,490		
Prime Costs		19,808		
Factory Power		490		
Factory Salaries		1,830		
Rent, Rates & Insurance		570		
Lighting & Heating		72		
Factory & Machinery Maintenance		520		
Depreciation on Plant & Machinery		1,140		
		24,430		
Add Work in Progress (1st Jan)		810		
		25,240		
Less Work in Progress (31st Dec)		670		
Works Cost of Production	£	24,570		£ 24,570
Stocks of Finished Goods (1st Jan)		3,120	Sales	34,690
Cost of Finished Goods Produced		24,570		
		27,690		
Less Stock of Finished Goods (31st Dec)		2,980		
Cost of Sales		24,710		
Gross Profit to Profit & Loss A/c		9,980		
	£	34,690		£ 34,690

Items of Expenditure which Sometimes Give Trouble

Without an intimate knowledge of the industry for which the accounts are being prepared, it is not always easy to decide to which account, Manufacturing or Profit & Loss, certain items should be debited.

One such item is 'Wages'. Where manufacturing wages are kept separate, as in the illustration above, there is no problem. But if this particular expense is not qualified, and is simply shown as Wages, it should, in the absence of any additional information, be debited to Profit & Loss Account. Similarly, some salaries may be chargeable to Manufacturing Account, but should be put in that account only if identified as manufacturing salaries. Charges for packing materials may give trouble. If a manufacturer is making soft drinks, the bottles in which the liquid is contained are clearly part of the manufacturing costs, and so is the paper or cellophane in which the bottles are sold to consumers. On the other hand, the cost of packing cases used to send the bottles of soft drinks to retailers is a distribution expense which should go in the Profit & Loss Account.

Factory power is clearly a manufacturing expense, but is it part of the prime costs? If there is a recognizable relationship between the amount of factory power consumed and the number of units of product actually made, there is something to be said for including it with the other items of prime cost, viz. raw materials and productive wages. If this relationship is obscure, it is better to include factory power with the other manufacturing costs.

ILLUSTRATION 19.2

B. Williams is a small manufacturer of scents and essences which are sold in bottles. The finished goods are dispatched in packing cases to customers.

From the following information prepare his Manufacturing, Trading and Profit & Loss Accounts for the year ended 31st December, 1960.

The accounts are to be prepared in such a way as to show clearly:

(1) the cost of goods manufactured, and
(2) the cost of goods sold.

	£
Stocks (1st January, 1960)	
Raw Materials ..	715
Bottles ..	275
Finished Goods ..	1,665
Packing Cases ..	190
Purchases	
Raw Materials ..	4,260
Bottles ..	2,110
Packing Cases ..	650
Sales ..	18,790
Manufacturing Wages ..	5,615
,, Expenses ..	745
Salaries: Factory ..	1,600
Office ..	1,310
Office Expenses ..	220
Delivery Expenses ..	340
Selling Expenses ..	630
Stocks (31st December, 1960)	
Raw Materials ..	835

	£
Bottles	290
Finished Goods	1,715
Packing Cases	185

G.C.E. 'O' level

MANUFACTURING, TRADING, AND PROFIT & LOSS ACCOUNT
FOR THE YEAR ENDED 31ST DECEMBER, 1960

Dr	£	£		£ Cr
Raw Materials:			Transfer to Trading A/c	
Stock (1st Jan)		715	Cost of Goods Manufactured	14,195
Purchases		4,260		
		4,975		
Less Stock (31st Dec)		835		
Cost of Raw Materials Consumed		4,140		
Bottles:				
Stock (1st Jan)	275			
Purchases	2,110			
	2,385			
Less Stock (31st Dec)	290			
Cost of Bottles Used		2,095		
Manufacturing Wages		5,615		
Prime Costs		11,850		
Manufacturing Expenses		745		
Salaries (Factory)		1,600		
Cost of Goods Manufactured	£	14,195		£ 14,195
Stock of Finished Goods (1st Jan)		1,665	Sales	18,790
Cost of Finished Goods		14,195		
		15,860		
Less Stock (31st Dec)		1,715		
Cost of Goods Sold		14,145		
Gross Profit to P & L A/c		4,645		
	£	18,790		£ 18,790

	£	£	£		£
Administration:					
Office Salaries		1,310		Gross Profit from Trading A/c	4,645
Office Expenses		220			
			1,530		
Selling:					
Delivery Expenses		340			
Selling Expenses		630			
Packing Cases:					
Stock 1/1/60	190				
Add Purchases	650				
	840				
Less Stock 31/12/60	185				
		655	1,625		
Net Profit to Capital A/c			1,490		
		£	4,645		£ 4,645

Goods Charged to the Selling Department at a Profit

A manufacturer who has his own wholesale and retail outlets may require the manufacturing unit to show a profit. He will therefore charge the goods to the selling department at a price above the works cost. The profit on manufacturing is then credited to the Profit & Loss Account or the Profit & Loss Appropriation Account.

ILLUSTRATION 19.3

Goods which cost £5,000 to manufacture are charged to the Trading Account at £5,500. Show how this profit on manufacture is dealt with in the Manufacturing, Trading, and Profit & Loss Accounts.

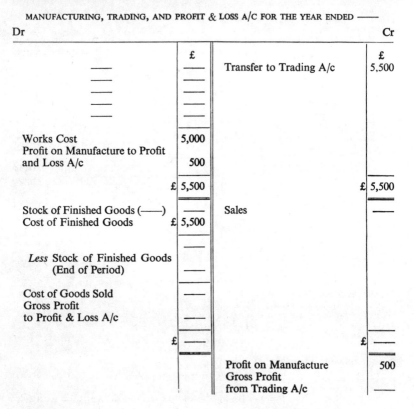

MANUFACTURING, TRADING, AND PROFIT & LOSS A/C FOR THE YEAR ENDED ——

Dr	£		Cr £
——	——	Transfer to Trading A/c	5,500
——	——		
——	——		
——	——		
——	——		
Works Cost	5,000		
Profit on Manufacture to Profit and Loss A/c	500		
£	5,500	£	5,500
Stock of Finished Goods (——)	——	Sales	——
Cost of Finished Goods £	5,500		
	——		
Less Stock of Finished Goods (End of Period)	——		
Cost of Goods Sold	——		
Gross Profit to Profit & Loss A/c	——		
£	——	£	——
		Profit on Manufacture	500
		Gross Profit from Trading A/c	——

EXERCISE 19.1

X.Y. is a manufacturer. From the following details prepare:
(1) X.Y.'s Manufacturing Account,
(2) X.Y.'s Trading Account,
for the year ended 31st December, 1963.

The accounts should be prepared in such a way as to show clearly:

(*a*) the cost of goods manufactured during the year, and
(*b*) the cost of goods sold during the year.

	£
Stocks at 1st January, 1963 (valued at cost)	
Raw Materials	760
Finished Goods	2,890
Stocks at 31st December, 1963 (valued at cost)	
Raw Materials	640
Finished Goods	2,950
Purchases of Raw Materials	3,890
Carriage on Raw Materials	110
Sales of Finished Goods	29,780
Factory Wages	8,670
Factory Expenses	7,220

G.C.E. 'O' level

EXERCISE 19.2

The following items were extracted from the books of F. Tasker, a manufacturer, for the year ended 31st December, 1961.

	£
Stocks (1st January, 1961)	
Raw Materials	3,650
Finished Goods	3,450
Purchases of Raw Materials	21,740
Sales	57,120
Carriage on Purchases	720
Depreciation of Machinery (chargeable to Manufacturing Account)	1,315
Factory Wages	13,980
Factory Expenses	384
Factory Power	1,260
Light & Heat (four fifths Factory)	780
Salaries (£3,000 chargeable to Factory)	6,100
Rent & Rates (three fourths Factory)	556
Insurance (three fourths Factory)	84

On 31st December, 1961 valuations of stocks in hand were raw materials £3,550; finished goods £2,980. Factory wages due amounted to £195.

(1) Prepare Tasker's Manufacturing Account and Trading Account for the year.
(2) Calculate Tasker's ratio of gross profit to turnover.

G.C.E. 'O' level

EXERCISE 19.3

The following information is extracted from the books of a small manufacturer at 31st December, 1959.

You are required to prepare Trading and Profit & Loss Accounts for year ended 31st December, 1959, and a Balance Sheet at that date.

	£
Cost of Production of Goods Manufactured during the year	142,400
Stocks: Finished Goods (1st January, 1959)	12,670
" " (31st December, 1959)	11,990
Raw Materials (31st December, 1959)	5,650

	£
Sales	196,000
General and Administrative Expenses	3,820
Carriage on Sales	890
Advertising	6,200
Travellers' Salaries & Expenses	15,670
Office and Administrative Wages & Salaries	9,430
Sundry Debtors	16,940
Sundry Creditors	17,033
Capital (1st January, 1959)	47,000
Drawings	12,000
Machinery & Plant (31st December, 1959)	23,200
Furniture & Fittings (31st December, 1959)	1,840
Depreciation	3,960
Provision for Bad Debts (Credit balance)	847
Cash at Bank and in Hand	6,210

You are required to set out your accounts in such a way as to show clearly:
(1) the cost of goods sold,
(2) the total of general and administrative charges,
(3) the total of selling charges,
(4) the totals of current assets and of fixed assets.

G.C.E. O' level

EXERCISE 19.4

Prepare Manufacturing and Trading Accounts for the year ending 31st December 19— from the following balances.

	£
Stock of Raw Materials, 1st January, 19—	2,237
Raw Materials Purchased	29,314
Carriage on Purchases	276
Stock of Raw Materials, 31st December, 19—	3,072
Manufacturing Wages	21,984
Manufacturing Power	9,431
Work in Progress, 1st January, 19—	586
Work in Progress, 31st December, 19—	317
Stock of Finished Goods, 1st January, 19—	5,341
Sales	103,127
Purchases of Finished Goods	873
Stock of Finished Goods, 31st December, 19—	6,095
Manufacturing Expenses	892

G.C.E. 'O' level

EXERCISE 19.5

The following information was extracted from the accounts of A. Wheeler Ltd, manufacturers, as at 30th June, 1971. Prepare their Manufacturing, Trading and Profit and Loss Accounts for the year ended 30th June, 1971. Show clearly *within* these accounts, the cost of materials used, prime cost, factory cost of goods completed, and the cost of goods sold.

	£
Stocks at 1st July, 1970:	
Raw Materials at cost	6,500
Finished Goods (at factory cost)	5,700
Purchases for year to 30th June, 1971:	
Raw Materials	132,000
Other Factory Materials (indirect)	3,900

	£
Direct Wages	41,340
Factory Fuel and Power	4,100
Heating and lighting of which amount $\frac{3}{4}$ is chargeable to Factory, $\frac{1}{4}$ to office	1,600
Fire Insurance, of which amount $\frac{3}{4}$ is chargeable to Factory, $\frac{1}{4}$ to office	1,620
Rent and Rates of Factory	4,500
Rent and Rates of Office	1,500
Factory Salaries	7,000
Sundry expenses and Advertising	4,800
Office salaries	4,000
Provision for bad debts	220
Depreciation:	
Factory machinery	6,000
Office furniture	700
Sales	247,000

On 30th June, 1971, the following valuations were made of stocks:

	£
Raw Materials at cost	8,500
Finished goods (at factory cost)	5,900

In addition you are given the following information:

Prepayments at 30th June, 1971—Fire Insurance: Factory—£200; Office—£30.

The provision for bad debts to be increased to £320.

G.C.E. 'O' Level

EXERCISE 19.6

J. Wynne and T. Pickford are partners in a manufacturing business. They make one product in two grades ('standard' and 'super'). The trial balance extracted from their books on 31st March, 1970 was as follows:

	£	£
Trade debtors	6,560	
Trade creditors		10,223
Bank balance	2,326	
Petty cash	44	
Freehold premises	9,275	
Plant and machinery	12,552	
Machinery repairs	484	
Sales:		
'super'		35,217
'standard'		62,799
Purchases of raw materials	49,722	
Carriage outwards	826	
Stocks at 1st April, 1969:		
Raw materials	6,167	
'super'	7,291	
'standard'	9,114	
Advertising	2,626	
Office salaries	3,594	
Sundry office expenses	1,158	
Power, light and heating (factory)	1,540	
J. Wynne capital		16,000

	£	£
T. Pickford capital		16,000
J. Wynne current account	2,520	
T. Pickford current account	2,964	
Manufacturing wages...	19,422	
Office equipment	680	
Sundry manufacturing expenses	1,374	
	£140,239	£140,239

You are asked to prepare:

(i) Manufacturing Accounts and Trading Accounts to show the gross profit made on each grade of the product in the year ended 31st March, 1970:

(ii) Profit and Loss Account for the year ended 31st March, 1970 to show the net profit or loss made by the business as a whole in the year ended 31st March, 1970;

(iii) Balance Sheet as at 31st March, 1970.

The following matters should be taken into account:

(*a*) Of the cost of raw materials consumed, £32,550 related to the production of the 'standard' grade and the remainder to the 'super' grade. **All** other expenses of manufacturing are to be apportioned: 'super' one-third, 'standard' two-thirds.

(*b*) Provide for depreciation: on plant and machinery, 12½% of book value; on office equipment, 15% of book value.

(*c*) Allow for expenses in arrears: repairs to machinery, £95; factory power, lighting and heating, £320.

(*d*) Stock values at 31st March, 1970 were: raw materials £5,889, 'super' £5,292, 'standard' £7,901.

(*e*) The partners share profits and losses equally.

G.C.E. 'O' Level

EXERCISE 19.7

At the end of their accounting year on 30th April, 1971, the balances in a firm's ledger included these items:

	£
Raw materials purchased	42,650
Manufacturing wages	11,530
Other manufacturing expenses (power etc.)	7,650
Sales	84,270
Stock of raw materials, 1st May, 1970	6,060
Stock of finished goods, 1st May, 1970	11,220
Selling and distribution expenses	8,910
Financial and administration expenses	7,620
Plant and machinery	14,100
Office equipment...	2,600
Vehicles (used for distributing goods to customers)	3,600

Depreciation for the year ended 30th April, 1971 has not yet been entered in the books; it is to be calculated as follows: plant and machinery 20%, office equipment 15%, vehicles 30% (all on the book values given above).

At 30th April, 1971, stock values were: raw materials £6,710, finished goods £9,720.

You are asked to prepare the following accounts for the year ended 30th April, 1971:

(i) Manufacturing Account, showing cost of raw materials consumed and factory cost of goods produced;
(ii) Trading Account, showing cost of goods sold and gross profit or gross loss;
(iii) Profit and Loss Account, showing net profit or net loss.

G.C.E. 'O' Level

20

Some Practical Matters-P.A.Y.E., Graduated Pension Contributions, and National Insurance

WE have commented earlier on the difficulty which sometimes arises in deciding to which of the final accounts wages should be transferred. The wages paid to a machine operator in a manufacturing undertaking are clearly part of the prime costs of manufacture, and therefore belong to the Manufacturing Account. But what should a student do when both wages and salaries appear in a trader's Trial Balance? Should wages be transferred to the Trading Account and salaries to the Profit & Loss Account? Students are sometimes advised, in these cases, to transfer wages to the Trading Account, on the ground that wages are presumed to be part of the costs of putting the goods into a saleable condition. In the absence of any further information, this might be the best course to follow. If, however, the only distinction between wages and salaries is that the former are paid weekly while the latter are paid monthly, it is illogical to separate them in the final accounts, and both should be transferred to the Profit & Loss Account.

Deductions from Wages, etc., which an Employer is under a Statutory Duty to Make

Whatever form an employee's remuneration takes, whether it is a wage, a salary, a fee, or commission, his employer is required by law to deduct income tax, and pay it over to the Inland Revenue. This system of deducting income tax is known as P.A.Y.E. (pay as you earn), and it imposes on an employer a duty to act as a collecting 'agent' of income tax for the Inland Revenue, and to keep proper financial records to show that the correct deductions have been made.

In addition to income tax, an employer is required to deduct graduated contributions under the National Insurance Act, 1959, which are collected through the P.A.Y.E. system along with income tax. These latter contributions are in addition to the flat-rate national insurance contributions which are paid by means of stamped cards or other approved methods.

P.A.Y.E.

The terms contained in employment contracts vary greatly, and it is impossible to cover all the problems which arise in operating the P.A.Y.E. system. For more details, students are referred to the booklets issued free to employers by the Board of Inland Revenue.

An employer must deduct Income Tax from the pay of his employees whether or not he has been directed to do so by the Inland Revenue. To make the proper deductions, the employer must have certain information. He must, for example, know each employee's tax code number.

TAX CODE NUMBERS

Every employee is required each year to complete a 'Return of Income and Claim for Allowances' form, giving all the sources of his income and the amount from each source for the income tax year just ended, e.g. 5th April, 1974, and any claims to allowances additional to those to which taxpayers generally are entitled. In due course he receives from H.M. Inspector of Taxes a 'Notice of Coding', giving his allowances to be set against pay and the code number corresponding with this entitlement. His employer is advised of this number and must deduct tax at the appropriate rate for the code number; the amount to deduct each week or month is found from tables supplied by the Inland Revenue.

UNIFIED TAX SYSTEM

On 6th April, 1973, the unified tax system replaced the former separate assessments for income tax and surtax.

Whereas under the old system surtax was charged separately, under the unified tax system both are deducted from earnings under P.A.Y.E. and so the collection of the tax has been greatly speeded up; previously surtax payers did not pay surtax until some nine months after the end of the tax year. This reform is intended to simplify assessment and collection, rather than to change the amount of tax payable.

TAX CREDIT SYSTEM

Proposals have been put forward by the Government for a tax-credit system which will replace P.A.Y.E. and to a large extent the Social Security system. Under the tax credit system the main tax-free allowances and family allowances will be replaced by cash credits. If such a system is implemented employers will still be liable to collect tax from employees whose earnings were bigger than their tax credits. Persons not earning enough to use up their tax credits would be paid the balance in cash. It is thought that such a system is unlikely to start before 1980.

The Wages Book

The details of each employee's weekly gross pay, or monthly gross pay, and the various deductions in respect of P.A.Y.E., etc. are recorded in the Wages Book. This book is not part of the double entry book-keeping system.

THE BOOK-KEEPING ENTRIES NECESSARY TO RECORD WAGES AND THE VARIOUS STATUTORY DEDUCTIONS

The wages clerk will draw a cheque for the *net* wages to be paid, but before going to the bank to cash it, he will carefully work out how he wants the cash paid to him by the bank, that is, how many £5 notes, £1 notes, 50p coins, 10p coins, 5p coins etc. he will need, in order to pay to each employee the exact amount due without having to change money.

Let us suppose that the total net wages and the statutory deductions as shown by the Wages Book are for a particular week, as follows.

	£
Net wages	85·43
Income tax	5·10
Graduated pension contributions ..	1·63
National insurance	7·26

(The graduated pension contributions and the flat rate national insurance payments include the employer's share.)

Dr *Cash Book* Cr

				£
			Wages Payable	85·43

Dr Wages Payable Account Cr

		£			£
	Bank	85·43		Wages	99·42
	N.I. Stamps	7·26			
	P.A.Y.E.	5·10			
	Grad. Pen. Cs	1·63			

Dr Wages Account Cr

	Wages Payable		£ 99·42				

Dr P.A.Y.E. & Graduated Pension Contributions Cr

					Wages (P.A.Y.E.)		£ 5·10
					Wages (Grad. Pen. Cs)		1·63

Dr National Insurance (Employers and Employees) Cr

					Wages (N.I.)		£ 7·26

POINTS TO NOTICE

(1) The debit entries in the Wages Account equal the total gross wages plus the employer's share of the graduated pension and flat-rate national insurance contributions.

(2) The corresponding credit entries in respect of income tax and graduated pension contributions appear in the P.A.Y.E. & Graduated Pensions Contribution Account. When this money is paid over to the Inland Revenue each month, the Cash Book will be credited and the P.A.Y.E. Account debited.

(3) Any other deductions which the employee may have authorized his employer to make, such as welfare or sports club contributions, are dealt with in the same way as income tax. The Wages Account is debited with the total sum of such deductions and the Welfare Fund or Sports Club Account credited.

EXERCISE 20.1

After the profit and loss account of a firm of wholesalers had been prepared for the year ending 30th April, 1971, the balances remaining in the books included:

Bank Account (credit balance £869)
Travellers' Commission Account (credit balance £86)
Rent Payable Account (debit balance £60)
Income Tax (P.A.Y.E.) Account (credit balance £35)

You are asked to explain carefully and concisely what you think *each* of these balances signifies.

G.C.E. 'O' Level

21

Receipts & Payments Accounts- Income & Expenditure Accounts

THE present chapter deals with the book-keeping operations of non-trading organizations. A large variety of associations come within this category, e.g. clubs for fostering and promoting every conceivable kind of interest and activity, professional associations, trade unions, charities, firms established on a commercial basis to provide specialist services such as accountants, solicitors, etc. The provision of services rather than goods is a common purpose of the non-trading organization whose accounting methods we are about to explore.

Receipts & Payments Accounts

A small club, owning little or no property, may keep a Receipts & Payments Account. Since this is merely a summary of the Cash Book, the preparation of the Receipts & Payments Account is made easier if the Cash Book is kept in columnar form.

NEWTON TENNIS CLUB

RECEIPTS AND PAYMENTS ACCOUNT FOR THE YEAR ENDED 30TH APRIL, 1964

Dr		Cr	
	£		£
Receipts		*Payments*	
Balance b/fwd	100·00	Wages	700·00
Subscriptions	1,120·00	Rent	270·00
Profits on Dance	14·00	Postage	20·00
		Printing	40·50
		Sub. to County Association	10·50
		Balance in Hand	193·00
£	1,234·00	£	1,234·00

THE DISADVANTAGES OF A RECEIPTS & PAYMENTS ACCOUNT

(1) The account shows merely the receipt and payment of money; the financial results of the year's activities, i.e. the excess of income over expenditure or expenditure over income are not shown. Subscriptions in arrear and paid the following year and subscriptions paid in advance are all included under receipts.

(2) Expenses which relate to more than one period are not apportioned.

(3) Information about outstanding liabilities, or subscriptions due but not paid, are not given.

(4) Capital expenditure is entered under payments as though the services derived from these assets were used up completely during the accounting period.

(5) Being merely a summary of the Cash Book, the Receipts & Payments Account does not form part of a double entry system.

Income & Expenditure Accounts

For the majority of non-trading organizations, a Receipts & Payments Account is quite unsuitable. Most of these associations will want to know by what amount their income for the year has exceeded their expenditure, or vice versa. All revenue and expenditure which relates to a period other than the one for which the accounts are being prepared must therefore be excluded from the final accounts. There is nothing new about this. We do this when we prepare a Profit & Loss Account for a trading concern. Similarly, capital receipts and expenditure must not appear in the account of income and expenditure. When we produce an account of this kind, it is called an Income & Expenditure Account, and is similar in form to an ordinary Profit & Loss Account; it is part of the double entry system. Any surplus or deficiency is transferred finally to the Accumulated Fund Account, which is equivalent to the Capital Account in the case of a firm. A Balance Sheet, prepared at the same time as the Income & Expenditure Account, shows what the association owns, and what it owes, at the year's end.

ILLUSTRATION 21.1

On 1st April, 1963, the assets of the Acme Youth Centre were: cash in hand and balance at bank £46; furniture and fittings £150; games equipment £64; tools and hobbies equipment £41; subscriptions in arrear £3; insurance prepaid £2. There were no liabilities.

For the year ended 31st March, 1964 the treasurer produced the following summary of receipts and payments.

Receipts	£	*Payments*	£
Subscriptions	52	Light & Heat	27
Donations	50	Expenses of Annual Fête	31
Sale of Tickets for Annual Fête	59	New Tools	9
Sale of Dance Tickets	67	New Games Equipment	6
		Expenses of Dances	27
		Cleaners' Wages	52
		Printing & Stationery	5
		Repairs & Renewals	14
		Insurance	12

Prepare an Income & Expenditure Account for the year ended 31st March, 1964 and a Balance Sheet as at that date, taking into account the following adjustments.

(1) Subscriptions received included the amount in arrear for the previous year. £2 was in arrear for the year of account.
(2) Repairs and renewals outstanding £3.
(3) Annual insurance premiums £12 were paid to 30th June, 1964.
(4) 10% depreciation is to be written off the balance at 31st March, 1964 of furniture and fittings, games equipment, and tools and hobbies equipment.

G.C.E. 'O' level

ACME YOUTH CENTRE

INCOME & EXPENDITURE ACCOUNT FOR THE YEAR ENDED 31ST MARCH, 1964

Dr					Cr
	£	£		£	£
Light & Heat		27	Subscriptions	52	
Cleaners' Wages		52	*Less* Arrears Paid	3	
Printing & Stationery		5			
Repairs & Renewals	14			49	
Add accrued charges	3		*Add* Subs Due	2	
		17			51
Insurance		11	Donations		50
Depreciation:			Sale of Tickets for Annual		
Fixtures & Fittings	15		Fête	59	
Games & Equipment	7		*Less* Expenses	31	
Tools & Hobbies	5				28
		27	Sale of Dance Tickets	67	
Excess of Income Over			*Less* Expenses	27	
Expenditure to Accumulated Fund					40
		30			
		£ 169			£ 169

BALANCE SHEET AS AT 31ST MARCH, 1964

	£	£		£	£	£
Accumulated Fund	306		Furniture & Fittings	150		
Excess of Income Over Expenditure			*Less* Depreciation	15		
	30				135	
		336	Games & Equipment	70		
Repairs & Renewals accrued		3	*Less* Depreciation	7		
					63	
			Tools & Hobbies	50		
			Less Depreciation	5		
					45	
						243
			Insurance Prepaid		3	
			Subscriptions Due		2	
			Cash at Bank and in Hand		91	
						96
		£ 339				£ 339

Notes:

(1) In calculating the cash and balance at bank on 31st March, 1964 the balance at 1st April, 1963 must be added to the difference between the receipts and payments summary.
(2) The Insurance Account would appear in the Ledger as follows.

Dr Insurance Account Cr

		£			£
Insurance in Advance		2	Income & Expenditure A/c		11
Cash		12	Insurance in Advance	c/d	3
	£	14		£	14
Insurance in Advance	b/d	3			

(The annual premium has increased from £8 to £12 in the last year.)

EXERCISE 21.1 (Ignore VAT.)

F. J. Tutor, M.A., is the proprietor of a private preparatory school. The following details relate to the school year 1960–1.

	£
Stationery Account	
Stock (1st September, 1960)	280
Purchases	250
Sales	390
Stock (31st August, 1961)	200
School Meals Account	
Sales	1,610
Purchases of Provisions	1,225
Wages of School Meals Staff	350
Tuck Shop Account	
Sales of Confectionery	380
Cost of Confectionery Sold	304
Wages and Salaries: Teaching Staff	2,750
Office Staff	500
Cleaners	295
Tuition Fees Received	6,050
,, ,, Outstanding	25
Rates & Insurance	160
Advertising	220
Office Expenses	65

Prepare:

(1) accounts to show the profit or loss on (*a*) stationery, (*b*) school meals, (*c*) tuck shop.

(2) the Profit & Loss Account of the school for the year ended 31st August, 1961, taking into account the profits or losses on stationery, school meals and tuck shop and the following adjustments:
  (*a*) rates for the half year 1st April, 1961 to 30th September, 1961 amounted to £60 and are included in the above amount,
  (*b*) furniture and equipment valued at £1,600 on 1st September, 1960 is to be depreciated by 10%.

University of London, G.C.E. 'O' level

EXERCISE 21.2

The assets and liabilities of the Brightside Social Club on 1st April 1960 were cash in hand £12; cash at bank £134; bar stocks £310; furniture and fittings £560; subscriptions due for year to 31st March, 1960 £14.

On 31st March, 1961 the official cash record showed:

	£
Cash Withdrawn from Bank	800
Wages Paid: Cleaners	375
Barman	350
Postage and Sundry Expenses	62

the bank paying-in slips showed:

Subscriptions Received (this included the amount due at 1st April, 1960)	380
Receipts from Dances and Socials	126
Receipts from Bar	3,650

cheque book counterfoils showed:

Rent	280
Rates & Insurance	105
Lighting & Heating	73
Expenses of Dances and Socials	82
Cash for Office Use	800
Purchases of Stocks for Bar	2,732

The annual subscription to the club was £2 and 10 members were in arrears for one year's subscription.

Insurance £12 was prepaid.

It was decided to depreciate furniture and fittings by 10%.

Stock in the bar at 31st March, 1961 was valued at £285.

Prepare the Revenue & Expenditure Account of the club for the year ended 31st March, 1961 and a Balance Sheet on that date.

N.B. In preparing the account, show the profit made on the bar and on dances and socials.

Calculations must be shown in the accounts or immediately below them.

University of London, G.C.E. 'O' level

EXERCISE 21.3

(1) (*a*) What is a Receipts & Payments Account?
(*b*) What advantages has an Income & Expenditure Account over such an account?

(2) Draw up a columnar Cash Book suitable for a small tennis club which prepares only Receipts & Payments Accounts.

EXERCISE 21.4

The following is a summary of the Cash Book of Benworth Social Club for the year to 31st December, 1958.

Cash Book

		£		£
Balance at bank, 1st January, 1958		360	Restaurant and Bar Supplies	6,000
Members' Subscriptions:			Wages	2,120
For 1958	£2,660		Printing, Stationery, and Postage	140
For 1959	100		General Expenses	1,830
		2,760	Balance at Bank, 31st December, 1958	1,030
Restaurant and Bar Takings		8,000		
		£11,120		£11,120

Additional information is obtained as follows.

	31st Dec 1957	*31st Dec 1958*
	£	£
Freehold Premises	5,000	5,000
Furniture	3,620	3,620
Stock of Restaurant and Bar Supplies	618	548
Creditors for Restaurant and Bar Supplies	450	490

You are required to prepare:

(1) a Trading Account for the Restaurant and Bar for 1958,
(2) an Income & Expenditure Account for the year 1958,
(3) a Balance Sheet on 31st December, 1958.

Note: Ignore depreciation.

R.S.A. Intermediate, 1959

EXERCISE 21.5

At 1st January, 1959 D. Dickinson valued his stock in hand at £3,925. For the ensuing year he made the following estimates: sales, £12,500; returns inwards, £500; carriage inwards, £275; manufacturing wages, £2,200; and purchases, £5,500. Dickinson's gross profit ratio on all his sales was 17½ per cent.

(1) Prepare Dickinson's Estimated Trading Account, showing the value of his stock at 31st December, 1959.
(2) To what amount must Dickinson limit his revenue expenditure to ensure at least a 10 per cent return on his capital of £6,000?

R.S.A. I

EXERCISE 21.6

The following figures were taken from the records of the Riverside Club for the year 1961.

Prepare:

(1) the Receipts & Payments Account, and
(2) the Income & Expenditure Account of the club for the year ended 31st December, 1961.

	£
Receipts	
Members' Subscriptions	690
Sale of Refreshments	2,021
Sundry Receipts	140
Payments	
Suppliers of Refreshments	1,434
Wages	650
Rent, Rates & Insurance	250
Repairs & Renewals	213
Purchase of New Furniture for lounge	205
Sundry Expenses	126

Notes:	£
All receipts and payments were passed through the club's bank account.	
Members' subscriptions in arrear at 1st January, 1961, and paid during 1961	60
Members' subscriptions in arrear at 31st December, 1961	35
Cash at bank, 1st January, 1961	131

Rates paid in advance at 31st December, 1961	
Depreciation on club furniture and fixtures for the year 1961 was estimated to be	72
Purchases of refreshments during the year	1,540
Stocks of refreshments at 1st January, 1961	138
" " " " 31st December, 1961	156

N.B. Necessary calculations must be shown clearly either above or below the accounts.

University of London, G.C.E. 'O' level

EXERCISE 21.7

W. Appleby started business on 1st April, 1959. On that date he purchased premises on a 60 year lease for £7,200, and machinery for £6,000.

Appleby decided to close his books each year at 31st December, to write off each year 10% per annum on the original cost of machinery, and an appropriate amount from the leasehold premises.

On 1st August, 1960 he purchased another machine for £192 and decided to write this off in the same way as previously.

Show the Ledger accounts relating to Machinery, Depreciation and Leasehold Premises for the years 1959, 1960 and 1961.

Note: Depreciation on machinery is charged to Manufacturing Account.

Associated Examining Board, G.C.E. 'O' level

EXERCISE 21.8

The following statement is prepared by the treasurer of the Firbank Social Club for the year ended 31st December, 1961.

Receipts and Payments—1st January to 31st December, 1961

Receipts	£	*Payments*	£
Balance at Bank (1st January)	108	Payments for Liquor	753
Liquor Sales	1,140	Postage, Stationery and Telephone	49
Members' Subscriptions	680	Steward's Wages	450
Sale of Old Furniture	17	Lighting & Heating	96
Entrance Fees	40	Rates (1/4/61 to 31/9/61)	47
		Rates (1/10/61 to 31/3/62)	52
		Rent	200
		New Furniture	95
		Cleaning and Sundries	69
		Balance at Bank—31st December	174
	£1,985		£1,985

The treasurer has kept receipted bills and vouchers and a subscription list for members. From these the following facts are ascertained.

(*a*) Payments £47 were made during 1961 for liquor supplies delivered before 1st January, 1961.

(*b*) On 31st December, 1961 outstanding accounts for liquor supplies amounted to £39.

(*c*) Rates amounting to £23 were paid in 1960 in respect of the period 1st January to 31st March, 1961.

(*d*) £7 of the telephone charges is applicable to the year 1960 and £9 was owing on 31st December, 1961.

(*e*) The amount received for members' subscriptions included £60 in respect of the year 1960.

(*f*) At 31st December, 1961 members' subscriptions outstanding for 1961 amounted to £30.

(*g*) There was an outstanding account for lighting and heating £10 at 31st December, 1961.

The club steward has kept liquor records, and it is ascertained that the stock on 1st January, 1961 was worth £190 and on 31st December, 1961 £175.

On 31st December, 1961 the club secretary had a stock of unused stamps and stationery valued at £4. He estimated that the furniture, fixtures and equipment of the club were worth £500 as compared to £460 on 1st January, 1961.

Prepare:

(1) an account to show the profit or loss on the club bar for the year 1961 (it is agreed that two fifths of the steward's wages are chargeable to the bar),

(2) the Income & Expenditure Account of the club (including the profit or loss on the bar) for the year ended 31st December, 1961,

(3) the Balance Sheet of the club as on 31st December, 1961.

Associated Examining Board, G.C.E. 'A' level

EXERCISE 21.9

A club treasurer keeps the club's accounts by double entry. The following were the balances in the books at 30th April, 1971, omitting only the General Fund Account (the club's 'Capital Account'). You are asked to arrange them in the form of a trial balance, including the General Fund Account as the balancing figure:

	£
Donations received	18
Stock of refreshments, 1st May, 1970	275
Rent and Rates	620
Bank balance (overdrawn)	117
Purchases of refreshments	893
Sundry creditors for refreshments	131
Members' subscriptions	559
Sale of Dance tickets	524
Equipment	396
Sale of refreshments	1,053
Secretary's expenses (postage, etc.)	127
Cash in hand	22
Dance expenses	421

G.C.E. 'O' Level

22

Incomplete Records

In single entry book-keeping only one aspect of an exchange is recorded, either the giving of a benefit or the receipt of one. A trader who keeps only a Cash Book, but fails to post the entries recorded therein to appropriate Ledger accounts, is employing single entry book-keeping. Similar incomplete records are kept if, in addition to a Cash Book, a trader opens personal accounts for customers and suppliers but keeps no accounts for purchases and sales.

Single entry book-keeping, in all its varied forms, suffers from most of the following disadvantages and is therefore a thoroughly unsatisfactory way of keeping financial records:

(1) no check on the accuracy of entries,
(2) no safeguard against fraud,
(3) no classified information,
(4) usually no real and no nominal accounts are kept, and so assets have to be valued each time profits are calculated and the nature of losses and gains is often unknown,
(5) no Trial Balance can be extracted, and final results are consequently unreliable,
(6) for taxation purposes, or as a basis for the sale or valuation of a business, single entry records are generally unacceptable.

Despite these weighty objections to single entry book-keeping, it is still used in many small businesses, and the task of the accountant is then to calculate the firm's profits for a given trading period from whatever records the owner keeps. A similar calculation is sometimes necessary when proper books of account are kept but records are inadvertently lost or destroyed. The steps by which the accountant proceeds to make his computations have now to be examined.

Statement of Affairs

We have already seen that generally net profit is equal to the increase in the net value of a firm's assets over the period for which the final accounts are prepared. This has been fully demonstrated in earlier exercises, and provides a clue to calculating the net profit of a business which employs single entry book-keeping. If we prepare a Balance Sheet—or a Statement of Affairs, as we prefer to call it, when compiled from incomplete records—showing the net worth of the business at the beginning of the period, and we produce a Statement of Affairs for the end of the period, any increase or decrease in the net worth of the business will represent the net profit or net loss for that period.

In calculating the net profit by this method, money which has been taken out of the business during the trading period must be added to the difference shown, or, if there is a loss, deducted. This is so because if the money had been left in the business, and not taken out, the net worth of the business would have been greater at the end of the period by the amount withdrawn.

Fresh capital introduced during the trading year must be deducted from the net profit. The reason for this is plain. If a firm makes no profit and no loss one year (due allowance being made for depreciation of assets, etc.), its net worth will be the same at the end of the year as it was at the beginning. But if additional capital is brought in during the year, the net worth of the business will be greater at the end by a sum equal to the new capital introduced.

ILLUSTRATION 22.1

A and B are partners in business, keeping their books on a single entry system. Profits are shared equally, and a Balance Sheet was drawn up as on 1st January as follows.

	£	£		£
Creditors		918	Motor Vans	2,300
Capital Accounts:			Fixtures & Fittings	660
A	8,233		Stock	7,240
B	5,996		Debtors	4,119
		14,229	Cash	828
		£15,147		£15,147

As on 31st December the following assets were valued as follows: stock £7,312; debtors £4,361; cash £932. Creditors amounted to £1,104.

Purchases during the year amounted to £12,662 and sales to £17,108. Examination of the Cash Book disclosed that A's drawings during the year had amounted to £900 and B's to £750, and a new motor van had been bought for £550.

It is agreed that as on 31st December the motor vans are to be valued at £2,400 and the fixtures and fittings at £620.

Ascertain:

(1) the gross profit,
(2) the net profit for the year.
(3) Show the partners' Capital Accounts at the end of the year.
(4) Prepare a Balance Sheet as at 31st December.

Dr TRADING ACCOUNT FOR THE YEAR ENDED 31ST DECEMBER, 19— Cr

		£		£
	Stock (1/1/19—)	7,240	Sales	17,108
	Purchases	12,662		
		19,902		
	Less Stock (31/12/19—)	7,312		
		12,590		
(1)	Gross Profit	4,518		
		£ 17,108		£ 17,108

The net worth of the business on 1st January was £14,229. To find the net profit for the year, we must draw up a Statement of Affairs for 31st December, 19—, in order to see by what amount the net worth of the business has increased during the year.

STATEMENT OF AFFAIRS AT 31ST DECEMBER, 19—

	£	£		£	£
Capital:			*Fixed Assets*		
A	8,304		Motor Vans	2,850	
B	6,217		*Less* Depreciation	450	
		14,521			2,400
			Fixtures & Fittings	660	
			Less Depreciation	40	
					620
Current Liabilities			*Current Assets*		
Creditors		1,104	Stock	7,312	
			Debtors	4,361	
			Cash	932	
					12,605
		£ 15,625			£ 15,625

STATEMENT OF PROFIT

		£	£
	Net Worth of Business 31st December, 19—		14,521
	Net Worth of Business 1st January, 19—		14,229
			292
	Add Drawings of Partners: A	900	
	B	750	
			1,650
(2)	Net Profit for the Year		£ 1,942

Dr Capital Account—A Cr

			£			£
(3)	Drawings		900	Balance	b/d	8,233
	Balance	c/d	8,304	Profit		971
		£	9,204		£	9,204
				Balance	b/d	8,304

Dr Capital Account—B Cr

			£			£
(3)	Drawings		750	Balance		5,996
	Balance	c/d	6,217	Profit		971
		£	6,967		£	6,967
				Balance	b/d	6,217

(4) The Balance Sheet for 31st December would be the same as the Statement of Affairs shown above.

EXERCISE 22.1

S.J. started business on 1st January, 1957 with a balance at the bank of £2,000, of which he had borrowed £500 from R.T. At the end of the year some of the records kept by S.J. were lost but at 31st December, 1957 a valuation showed the following assets and liabilities.

	£
Fittings	600
Van	450
Stock-in-Trade	850
Sundry Debtors	270
Cash at Bank	600
Sundry Creditors	620

The loan from R.T. was outstanding and interest at 5% per annum was to be charged on this loan. During the year S.J. had drawn £8 per week in anticipation of profits.

From the above information draw up a statement showing the profit or loss for the year ended 31st December, 1957 and a Balance Sheet at that date.

G.C.E. 'O' level

Conversion from Single to Double Entry

Having prepared a Statement of Affairs on the date the conversion is to be made, we have only to enter the various items in the Journal in the form of opening entries and post these to the Ledger.

STATEMENT OF AFFAIRS AT 1ST JANUARY, 1965

	£	£			£	£
Capital		12,262	*Fixed Assets*			
			Leasehold Premises		10,000	
			Furniture & Fittings		700	
						10,700
Creditors:			*Current Assets*			
Thames Trading Co.		427	Stock		1,750	
			Debtors:			
			L. Smith	£10		
			B. Jones	17		
					27	
			Cash at Bank		192	
			Cash in Hand		20	
						1,989
		£ 12,689				£ 12,689

Journal

				Dr	Cr
1965				£	£
Jan 1	Leasehold Premises	Dr		10,000	
	Furniture & Fittings			700	
	Stock			1,750	
	Debtors:				
	L. Smith			10	
	B. Jones			17	
	Creditors:				
	Thames Trading Co				427
	Cash at Bank			192	
	Cash in Hand			20	
	Capital				12,262
	Being assets, liabilities and capital at this date				
				£ 12,689	12,689

POINTS TO NOTE

(1) In preparing the list of debtors and creditors, account must be taken of any bad debts.

(2) Accrued expenses, such as rent and rates, must be entered.

EXERCISE 22.2

T. Ford commenced business on the 1st April, 1964 with £4,000 capital. He has not kept proper records of his transactions, but it is found that on 31st March, 1965 he has the following assets and liabilities.

	£
Fixtures & Fittings	720
Sundry Debtors	840
Sundry Creditors	580
Stock-in-Trade	1,396
Cash at Bank	1,944
Cash in Hand	48

His drawings during the year amounted to £200. Make out a Statement of Affairs and show what profit or loss has been made during the year.

The Preparation of Accounts from Incomplete Records

The computation of net profit by the methods discussed above has a very limited usefulness. In the first place, these figures would not provide a basis for a proper income tax assessment, and, for another thing, the trader needs more information than is disclosed by a comparison of two Statements of Affairs. It is often necessary, therefore, to prepare, from the accounting records available, a Trading and Profit & Loss Account and a Balance Sheet. This can be done by:

(1) preparing a summary of receipts and payments during the financial year, and
(2) valuing the assets and liabilities at the end of the financial year.

From this information, Ledger accounts can be opened and the transactions, as totals, e.g. total debtors, recorded in double entry form.

ILLUSTRATION 22.2

The following is a summary of the receipts and payments of H. Field, a trader for 1964.

Receipts and Payments Summary

Receipts	£	*Payments*		£
Balance, 1st January, 1964	420	Payments to Trade Creditors		8,120
Cash Sales	7,400	New Fixtures & Fittings Purchased		380
Receipts in Respect of Credit Sales	3,225	Rent		500
		Printing & Stationery		150
		General Expenses		621
		Wages		1,000
		Balance	c/d	274
	£11,045			£11,045
Balance, 1st January, 1965 b/d	274			

Field's assets and liabilities at 31st December, 1963 and at 31st December, 1964 were as follows:

	31st December 1963	*31st December 1964*
	£	£
Stock-in-Trade	980	1,120
Fixtures & Fittings	400	780
Trade Creditors	760	600
Trade Debtors	250	380
Creditors for General Expenses	40	90
Cash	420	274

During 1964 discounts allowed amounted to £50, discounts received £210, and one debt of £30 was written off as bad.

First Step

Prepare total accounts for Trade Creditors and Trade Debtors. This will give us the year's credit purchases and credit sales.

Dr — Creditors — Cr

		£		£
Bank		8,120	Balance, 31st December, 1963	760
Discounts Received		210	Purchases	8,170
Balance	c/d	600		
		£ 8,930		£ 8,930
			Balance, 31st December, 1964	600

Dr — Debtors — Cr

	£		£
Balance, 31st December, 1963	250	Bank	3,225
Credit Sales	3,435	Discounts Allowed	50
		Bad Debt	30
		Balance, 31st December, 1964	380
	£ 3,685		£ 3,685
Balance 31st December, 1964	380		

The credit purchases (£8,170) and credit sales (£3,435) are the two amounts which are inserted respectively to make the accounts balance.

Second Step

Prepare the other accounts as follows.

Dr Creditors (General Expenses) Cr

		£			£
Bank		621	Balance, 31st December, 1963		40
Balance, 31st December, 1964		90	General Expenses for 1964		671
	£	711		£	711
			Balance, 31st December, 1964		90

Dr General Expenses Cr

		£	
Creditors		671	

Dr Rent Cr

		£	
Cash		500	

Dr Fixtures & Fittings Cr

		£	
Balance, 31st December, 1963		400	
Cash		380	

Dr Purchases Cr

		£	
Creditors		8,170	

Dr		Sales		Cr
				£
		Credit		3,435
		Cash		7,400

Dr		Wages		Cr
		£		
Cash		1,000		

Dr		Printing & Stationery		Cr
		£		
Cash		150		

Dr		Discounts Allowed		Cr
		£		
Debtors		50		

Dr		Discounts Received		Cr
				£
		Creditors		210

Dr		Bad Debts		Cr
		£		
Debtors		30		

Dr		Stock-in-Trade		Cr
		£		
Balance, 31st December, 1963		980		

Dr		Capital Account		Cr
				£
		Balance, 31st December, 1963		1,250

This is calculated by totalling the assets and deducting the liabilities at 31st December, 1963, e.g.

Assets	
	£
Bank	420
F & F	400
Stock	980
Debtors	250
	2,050
Less Liabilities	800
	£1,250

Third Step

Prepare a Trial Balance at 31st December, 1964.

	Dr	Cr
	£	£
Capital		1,250
Bank	274	
Trade Creditors		600
Trade Debtors	380	
Other Creditors		90
General Expenses	671	
Rent	500	
Fixtures & Fittings	780	
Purchases	8,170	
Sales		10,835
Wages	1,000	
Printing & Stationery	150	
Discounts	50	210
Bad Debts	30	
Stock-in-Trade	980	
£	12,985	12,985

Stock at 31st December, 1964 was £1,120.

Supposing we are required to depreciate fixtures and fittings by £50. The final accounts would be as follows.

TRADING AND PROFIT & LOSS ACCOUNT FOR THE YEAR ENDED 31ST DECEMBER, 1964

Dr			Cr
	£		£
Stock (31/12/63)	980	Sales	10,835
Purchases	8,170		
	9,150		
Less Stock (31/12/64)	1,120		
Cost of Sales	8,030		
Gross Profit c/d	2,805		
	£ 10,835		£ 10,835
Rent	500	Gross Profit b/d	2,805
Wages	1,000	Discounts Received	210
Printing & Stationery	150		
Discounts Allowed	50		
Bad Debts	30		
General Expenses	671		
Depreciation	50		
Net Profit to Capital Account	564		
	£ 3,015		£ 3,015

BALANCE SHEET AS AT 31ST DECEMBER, 1964

	£	£		£	£
			Fixed Assets		
Capital	1,250		Fixtures & Fittings	780	
Add Profit	564		*Less* Depreciation	50	
		1,814			730
Current Liabilities			*Current Assets*		
Trade Creditors	600		Stock	1,120	
Other "	90		Debtors	380	
		690	Bank	274	
					1,774
		£ 2,504			£ 2,504

EXERCISE 22.3

On 1st April, 1958 G. Gerrard purchased a business for £2,360, having assets as follows: goodwill £1,000; fixtures and fittings £400; and stock £960. To pay the price of the business he opened a banking account with £2,500, of which £500 was a loan from C. Cross.

Proper books of account were not kept, but at 31st March, 1959 the assets and liabilities of the business were: goodwill £1,000; fixtures and fittings at cost £550; stock £1,050; debtors £580; creditors £260; and balance at bank £400.

During the year Gerrard had drawn £10 per week and had sold a private investment for £500, paying off the loan out of the proceeds together with interest amounting to £25.

Prepare a Balance Sheet as at 31st March, 1959, and a statement showing how the profit or loss during the year is calculated.

R.S.A. Intermediate, 1959

EXERCISE 22.4

Allen and Newry are partners with capitals of £8,000 and £6,000 respectively They share profits equally.

On 1st April, 1964 they agree to admit Pender as an equal partner on the following terms:

(1) goodwill is to be valued at £3,000, but no goodwill account is to be opened in the books,

(2) Pender is to bring in £9,000 in cash as his capital and his share of goodwill. Allen and Newry are to adjust their capitals by introducing or withdrawing cash so that each partner's capital is equal.

Show the Ledger accounts of the three partners, assuming the agreement to be implemented on 2nd April, 1964.

A.C.A. Intermediate

EXERCISE 22.5

L. Hunter does not keep proper books of account. The following information is available for thc year ended 31st December, 1965:

	1st Jan £ 1965	*31st Dec* £ 1965
Stock-in-Trade	1,368	1,294
Trade Debtors	428	386
Amounts Prepaid	23	29
Bank Overdraft	210	—
Cash in Hand and Balance at Bank	—	147
Motor Vans	520	416
Furniture and Fittings	340	323
Trade Creditors	989	1,037
Expense Creditors	17	14

(a) Prepare a statement to show the profit or loss made by Hunter for the year ended 31st December, 1965, taking account of the following:

(i) £38 of the trade debtors at 31st December, 1965 were considered to be bad debts and in addition it was decided to make a provision of £39 for doubtful debts.

(ii) During the year 1965 Hunter had withdrawn £90 each month from the business.

(iii) During the year Hunter had won a football pool and paid £200 of the proceeds into the business bank account.

(b) With the information given above and the following additional information calculate Hunter's gross profit for the year ended 31st December, 1965:

	£
Receipts from Trade Debtors for the Year	8,122
Payments to Trade Creditors for the Year	6,262

University of London, G.C.E. 'O' level, 1966

EXERCISE 22.6

T. Thame, who does not keep his accounts by double entry, submits to you the following Statements of Affairs showing his position at the end of two successive financial years.

STATEMENT OF AFFAIRS 31ST MARCH 1969

	£		£
Capital	12,560	Premises	6,500
Creditors	798	Furniture and Fittings	988
Bank overdraft	1,266	Stock	4,520
		Debtors	2,583
		Cash	33
	£14,624		£14,624

STATEMENT OF AFFAIRS 31ST MARCH, 1970

	£		£
Capital	12,160	Premises	6,500
Creditors	640	Furniture and Fittings	1,022
Expenses accrued	48	Stock	3,610
		Debtors	1,543
		Cash and Bank	173
	£12,848		£12,848

In addition, T. Thame informs you that:

(1) During the year ended 31st March, 1970 he paid out £2,900 as Expenses, incurred Bad Debts £38 and that his drawings were £2,300.

(2) The difference in the values of the Furniture and Fittings is because new Furniture was bought for £134 and he considered £100 should be written off as Depreciation.

Draw up T. Thames' Capital Account for the year, and prepare a statement to show his apparent gross and net profits (or loss).

G.C.E. 'O' Level

23

Consignment Accounts-Joint Ventures

Consignment Accounts

WHEN a merchant or manufacturer in Great Britain sells his products abroad, he often does so by consigning the goods to an agent living within the particular foreign country. The agent undertakes to sell the goods on behalf of the exporter on a commission basis. If the agent also guarantees payment of the purchase price of goods sold, he usually receives an additional commission and he is then called a 'del credere' agent. The latter arrangement is in the form of an insurance against the risks of making bad debts.

It is important to note that when goods are sent in this way, they remain the property of the sender until sold, the agent merely having custody of them in the meantime. The agent is not a debtor for the goods he holds, and he may return them to the consignor without incurring any liability. Because of the special relationship existing between the consignor and his agent, their transactions require distinct treatment in the books of account. We shall deal first with the steps taken by the consignor when sending goods to his agent abroad.

(1) The bill of lading, under which the goods are shipped, and a pro forma invoice are sent to the agent. The agent needs the former to obtain possession of the goods when they reach port, and he requires the latter for customs purposes and as an indication of the approximate price the consignor hopes to obtain for them.

(2) The consignor opens in his books (*a*) a Consignment Account, which he debits with the cost price of the goods, and (*b*) a Consignment Outwards Account, showing the corresponding credit, viz.

Dr — Consignment to X. Y. & Co. — Cr

		£			
Goods		2,000			

Dr Consignment Outwards Account Cr

				£
			Consignment A/c (X. Y. & Co.)	2,000

(3) The consignor debits the consignment account with all expenses paid by him in connection with the transaction.

(4) As soon as the goods have been sold, the agent sends the consignor an account sales giving full particulars of the sale of the goods, i.e. the amount he has received from the sale of the goods with deductions for expenses he has incurred in connection with the consignment, such as insurance, customs dues, etc., and his commission.

(5) Upon receipt of the account sales, the consignor opens a personal account for the consignee (the agent), debiting this account with the *gross* proceeds. This personal account is not opened until the account sales is received because the agent becomes a debtor of the consignor only after the goods have been sold. The corresponding credit entry (*gross*) is made in the Consignment Account.

(6) The expenses incurred by the agent, plus his commission are credited to the agent's personal account and debited to the Consignment Account.

(7) The agent's remittance will close his personal account.

(8) The Consignment Account, which is in effect a special profit and loss account, is closed by transfer of the balance to the general Profit & Loss Account. This balance shows the profit or loss made on the particular venture.

(9) The Consignment Outwards Account is closed at the end of the financial year by transfer to the Purchases Account.

POINTS TO NOTE

(1) The personal account of the consignee is debited with the gross amount of the account sales.

(2) The balance of unsold stock on consignment is carried down at the end of the accounting period to the beginning of the next.

(3) The valuation of the unsold stock must include a proper proportion of the expenses incurred in getting the goods to the agent.

ILLUSTRATION 23.1

X. Y. & Co. Ltd of Cardiff consign 100 machines, valued at £40 each at cost, to L. Vickers & Co. Ltd of Montreal on 1st September, 1964. X. Y. & Co. Ltd pay the following expenses: freight £300, insurance £100. Upon arrival of the goods in Montreal, L. Vickers pay customs duties £800, and landing charges £40.

On 10th December, 1964 X. Y. & Co. Ltd receive an account sales from L. Vickers & Co. Ltd, showing the sale of 80 machines, as follows.

Marks	No. of machines		Weight	Per machine	£
	80	Machines	—	£60	4,800
◇		Charges:			
		Customs Duties	£800		
		Landing Charges	40		
		Commission	240		1,080
				£	3,720

L. Vickers & Co. Ltd enclose a draft for £3,720.
Enter the above transactions in the books of account of X. Y. & Co. Ltd.

Dr Consignment Account to L. Vickers & Co. Ltd Cr

			£				£
1964				1964			
Sep 1	Goods		4,000	Dec 10	L. Vickers & Co. Ltd		4,800
	Bank:			„ 31	Stock	c/d	1,048
	Freight		300				
	Insurance		100				
Dec 10	L. Vickers & Co. Ltd:						
	Duty		800				
	Landing Charges		40				
	Commission		240				
„ 31	Profit & Loss (Net Profit)		368				
		£	5,848			£	5,848
Jan 1	Stock	b/d	1,048				

Dr Consignments Outwards Cr

			£				£
1964				1964			
Dec 31	Purchases A/c		4,000	Sep 1	Consignment A/c		4,000

Dr L. Vickers & Co. Ltd Cr

1964		£	1964		£
Dec 10	Consignment A/c	4,800	Dec 10	Duty	800
			„ 10	Landing Charges	40
			„ 10	Commission	240
			„ 10	Draft	3,720
		£ 4,800			£ 4,800

The value of unsold stock at 31st December, 1964 is calculated as follows:

Cost price of machines unsold (20 machines @ £40) £800
(This is ⅙ of the total consignment.)

The expenses incurred in getting the goods to Montreal were:

	£
Freight	300
Insurance	100
Duty	800
Landing Charges	40
	£1,240
One fifth of these equals	248
Unsold Stock	£1,048

CONSIGNMENTS INWARDS

So far we have considered the records kept by the consignor. We have now to look at the entries which are made in the books of the consignee.

(1) No entry is made when the goods are received except in memorandum books.
(2) The personal account of the consignor is debited with any expenses; the Cash Account is credited.
(3) On the sale of the goods, the Cash Account is debited and the consignor's personal account is credited.
(4) The consignor's account is debited with the amount of the commission and the Commission Account credited. The balance on this latter account is eventually closed by transfer to the Profit & Loss Account.
(5) When a cheque or bill of exchange is sent to the consignor, the Cash Account (or Bills Payable Account) is credited and the consignor's account debited.

In the books of L. Vickers & Co. the entries would appear as follows.

Dr X. Y. & Co. Ltd Cr

	£			£
Cash:			Cash, (Sale of 80 machines)	4,800
Duty	800			
Landing Charges	40			
Commission A/c	240			
Remittance to X. Y. & Co.	3,720			
	£ 4,800			£ 4,800

Dr Commission Account Cr

				£
			X. Y. & Co. Ltd	240

EXERCISE 23.1

A received from B on consignment 600 barrels of flour at £4 per barrel. He paid freight £100, insurance £20, storage £20. He sold 300 barrels at £5·20, and the remainder at £5, and charged B a commission of 2¼% on such sales. You are required to show how such transactions would appear in the books of A.

C.I.S. Final

Joint Ventures

A joint venture is an agreement entered into by two or more persons, limited to a definite business speculation, which agreement is discharged when the profits or losses arising therefrom are distributed or apportioned. It is really a partnership agreement for a specific piece of business, and if, therefore, a dispute arises between the parties which is not covered in their agreement, the provisions of the Partnership Act, 1890 apply. For example, if nothing is said in the agreement about the respective amounts each person is to contribute to the venture, then it will be assumed that each contributes the same capital sum. Similarly, in the absence of any provision for the division of the profits afterwards, equality will again be assumed.

If one accountant acts for both parties to the venture, his task is merely that of keeping the accounts of the partnership. But if the parties keep their own records, the book-keeping is a little more complicated. In this chapter we shall assume that each of the parties keeps his own financial records of the venture, following ordinary double entry principles. Later, each party renders a complete statement of these transactions to the other parties, and these are combined into a Joint Venture Account, which is similar to an ordinary Profit & Loss Account. The profits are then shared in accordance with the agreement, and a final settlement made by the parties to the venture.

ILLUSTRATION 23.2

Mr T. Melton entered into a joint venture with Mr S. Mowbray on 1st May, 1964. The agreement provided as follows.

(1) Mr Mowbray was to supply two thirds of the capital required, whilst Mr Melton did the work.
(2) Profits were to be shared equally.
(3) On 10th May Mowbray gave Melton £2,000, his share of the capital. On 14th May Melton bought timber for the joint account from E. Frome £3,000; on 16th May he paid carriage £22 and sundry expenses £27. He sold the timber as follows:

May 19th to L. Bridport £608,
May 23rd to T. Mallett £2,492, and the remainder on
May 25th to A. Fowey £400.

Show these transactions as they would appear (*a*) in Melton's books of account, and (*b*) in Mowbray's books.

In Melton's Books

Dr — Joint Venture with S. Mowbray — Cr

19—		£	19—			£
May 14	E. Frome	3,000·00	May 19	L. Bridport		608·00
,, 16	Cash (Carriage)	22·00	,, 23	T. Mallett		2,492·00
,, 16	Cash (Expenses)	27·00	,, 25	A. Fowey		400·00
31	Profit Transferred:					
	S. Mowbray	225·50				
	Profit & Loss A/c	225·50				
	£	3,500·00			£	3,500·00

Dr — S. Mowbray — Cr

					£
			May 10	Bank	2,000·00
			,, 31	Joint A/c (Profit)	225·50

Dr — E. Frome — Cr

					£
			May 14	Joint Venture with S. Mowbray	3,000·00

Dr — L. Bridport — Cr

19—		£			
May 19	To Joint A/c	608·00			

Dr **T. Mallett** Cr

19—			£				
May 23	Joint A/c		2,492·00				

Dr **A. Fowey** Cr

19—			£				
May 25	Joint A/c		400·00				

Dr *Cash Book* Cr

19—			£	19—			£
May 10	S. Mowbray		2,000·00	May 16	Carriage		22·00
				" 16	Expenses		27·00

Half the profit (£225·50) is credited to S. Mowbray's Account, and T. Melton's own Profit & Loss Account is credited with his share. The personal accounts will be settled in due course, bringing the joint venture to a close.

In Mowbray's Books

Dr *Cash Book* Cr

				19—			£
				May 10	T. Melton (Joint Venture)		2,000·00

Dr **Joint Venture with T. Melton** Cr

19—			£				
May 10	Cash		2,000·00				
	Profit & Loss A/c		225·50				

Eventually T. Melton will send a cheque to S. Mowbray for £2,225·50 to clear this account.

EXERCISE 23.2

Thomas Chipping and Leslie Norton entered into a joint venture for the sale of motor-cycles abroad.

Chipping paid the following costs and charges.

	£
80 Motor-cycles	8,000
Freight	1,400
Insurance	800
Sundries	150

It was agreed between the parties that any profit or loss on the venture should be divided in the proportion of $\frac{2}{3}$ Chipping and $\frac{1}{3}$ Norton, and that Chipping should receive a commission of 5% on the amount for which the goods were sold. Norton handed to Chipping a cheque for £5,000. Later, an account sales from the agents abroad, X & Co. Ltd, was received, showing that the goods were sold for £13,500 and that the agent's charges amounted to £630 and commission 5%. X & Co. Ltd sent a sight draft in settlement.

Make the entries recording the above in Chipping's books, and set out the Joint Venture Account and Norton's personal account.

EXERCISE 23.3

Richard Day and Raymond Knight engaged in a joint venture. Richard Day financed and managed the affair, and received an extra 10% of the net profit for his trouble. The transactions were as follows: goods purchased £5,000, carriage £25, insurance £150, freight £250. The net proceeds amounted to £6,425. Make out the proper account in the Ledger.

EXERCISE 23.4

On 1st November, 1963 L.S., a London trader, consigned goods to his agent R.T. in New Zealand. The cost of the goods was £2,600. L.S. paid freight and insurance £230. He drew a bill of exchange at 4 months on R.T. for £2,000 which he discounted on 15th November, 1963, for £1,985.

By 31st March, 1964, when L.S. made up his annual accounts, he had received an account sales showing that goods costing £2,000 had realized £2,800. R.T. had paid duty and landing charges £134 on the whole consignment and had charged a commission of 5% on sales.

Show the accounts relating to these transactions in L.S.'s Ledger.

G.C.E. 'A' level

EXERCISE 23.5

R.T., an agent, receives a consignment of goods from Exporters Ltd to be sold on their behalf. The goods were invoiced pro forma at £3,000 and R.T. accepted a bill of exchange at 3 months for £2,500.

R.T. was entitled to a commission of 5% on sales and a del credere commission of 1% on sales. R.T. paid landing, customs and warehouse charges £84.

R.T. sold all the goods on credit for £4,000. Of this amount £3,900 was eventually collected by R.T. and £100 was irrecoverable.

Show the entries for the above in R.T.'s Ledger.

Associated Examining Board, G.C.E. 'A' level, 1965

EXERCISE 23.6

Short and Tall enter into a joint venture to buy, recondition and sell second-hand furniture. Purchases, sales and disbursements are made by both Short and Tall. Profits and losses are to be shared equally.

Short purchased furniture for £120 and paid carriage £7 and repairs £7. He sold this furniture for £180.

Tall purchased furniture for cash £120 on which he paid carriage £6 and £5 for repolishing. Tall also purchased furniture on credit for £60 and paid carriage £2. On paying the invoice for this furniture he received a cash discount of £3. Tall sold all the furniture purchased by him for £240.

Cash was remitted in payment of the balance due between the parties.
You are required:

(1) to show the account relating to the joint venture in (*a*) Short's Ledger, (*b*) Tall's Ledger,
(2) to prepare a pro forma (memorandum) Joint Venture Account to show the profit or loss on the joint venture and how it is divided.

G.C.E. 'A' level

Bills of Exchange

Where goods are sold abroad through agents, bills of exchange often play an important role in financing the transactions. Unlike a cheque, the bill is drawn by the *creditor*, who sends it to the debtor for acceptance, and when he gets the bill back he may either retain it until maturity and then present it through his bank to the bank specified for payment or he may discount it, that is, turn it immediately into cash, again through his own banker. The latter will of course pay a sum less than the face value of the bill depending on the length of time the bill has still to run.

EXAMPLE 23.3

A owes B £100 for goods supplied. In B's books the account will be as follows:

A

	£		£
Goods	100		

B sends A a B/E payable in 3 months time. A accepts and returns the bill to B. Entries now are:

A

	£		£
Goods	100	Bills Receivable	100

Bills Receivable

	£		£
A	100	(Bank	100)

B decides to discount bill—assume he receives £95:

Cash Book

	£		£
Bills Receivable	100	Discount on Bills Account	5

Discount on Bills Account

	£		
Bank	5		

Note that the full amount of the bill is debited to the Cash Book although the full £100 is not received—the amount charged by the bank for discounting the bill is shown as a credit entry and posted to the debit of Discount on Bills Account. A will remain liable on the bill until it is actually paid. If dishonoured B will credit his bank account with the full amount of the bill and debit A's account. B will not be able to charge A with the bank's discount charges, since it was for B's own financial convenience that he discounted the bill in the first place. When bills are discounted in this way a footnote should be added to the accounts to the effect that there is a contingent liability for bills discounted amounting to such and such a figure.

24

Introduction to Company Accounts

The form of business organization with which this chapter deals is the company, a corporate body which exists quite separately from its members (or shareholders) and which is recognized in law as a 'fictitious' person having similar rights and obligations to those of natural persons. It is the company, for example, which owns the assets and not the members. Some of the advantages of such an organization over those already discussed are (1) there is no limit, in the case of the public company, on the number of persons who may be members; (2) the liability of members, except in the case of the unlimited company, is limited; (3) there is, what the lawyers call perpetual succession which means that if all the members die the company still goes on; the members' shares simply pass to other people, namely, the beneficiaries under the wills of the former members. A partnership on the other hand can be a very fragile form of business organization.

Forms of Incorporation

The following chart shows how persons can be incorporated for trading purposes.

FORMS OF INCORPORATION

- (1) *By Royal Charter* e.g. The British South Africa Co.
- (2) *By Statute* Public utilities, railways etc., were incorporated in this way
- (3) *By Registration* Joint-stock companies—by far the most numerous and important—can be of three kinds
  - *Unlimited companies* Shareholders' liability is unlimited
  - *Companies limited by guarantee*
  - *Companies limited by shares*
    - *Public Companies* (min. number 7, maximum unlimited)
    - *Private Companies* (min. 2, max 50, excluding past and present employees)

We are concerned only with the companies limited by shares of which there are two kinds, Private and Public Companies. A private company must restrict the right to transfer its shares; limit the number of members to fifty exclusive of shareholders who are or have been in the employ of the business; and undertake not to invite the public to subscribe for its shares. Since 1967 private companies, as well as public companies, have been obliged to file accounts with their annual returns and some family businesses, in order to preserve secrecy, have re-registered as unlimited companies or disincorporated and become partnerships. A public company must have a minimum of seven members (two in the case of the private company) and can have any number it likes above this figure.

The affairs of the company, whether public or private, are conducted by an elected Board of Directors, who are required to report to members on their stewardship once a year at the Annual General Meeting of the company.

The Company's Capital

The capital of a company incorporated by registration is divided into shares which may be of different kinds, carrying different rights and appealing to different members of the investing public. The commonest types are as follows:

PREFERENCE SHARES

These carry a fixed dividend which is paid out of profits before other shareholders receive a dividend. They are usually cumulative, which means that if there is not enough profit one year to pay the preference shareholders their dividend it is added on to the next year's dividend and so on. They may be preferred as to capital as well, that is, in the event of the company going into liquidation the preference shareholders will get their capital back before the other shareholders. Preference shares may also be redeemable, i.e., the company may have the power to buy them back from shareholders at a later date. There are certain safeguards upon which the law insists when this is done. Preference shareholders usually have very restricted voting rights, for example, they may only be able to vote at an A.G.M. if it is proposed to alter their rights in some way.

ORDINARY SHARES

Ordinary shareholders' dividends fluctuate with the profits. If the company is doing well, and there is no Government restriction on the rate of dividend the company may pay, the dividend could be very high, or, on the other hand, if it has been a poor year, ordinary shareholders may get nothing at all. Such shares normally carry full voting rights but a practice grew up after the second world war of issuing ordinary 'A' shares, shares which gave their holders all the rights of the ordinary shareholders except the right, or a restricted right, to vote at meetings of the company. It will, however, soon be illegal for companies to issue them. The nominal value of ordinary shares may be quite small, e.g., 5p, 25p, or 50p per share.

DEFERRED, MANAGEMENT OR FOUNDERS' SHARES

These are rarely issued nowadays and if issued, details must be given in any prospectus put out by the company. Generally the holders do not receive dividends until the other shareholders have been paid an agreed minimum. Their value often rests on the substantial voting power they confer on their owners.

CAPITAL SHARES

The holders agree to receive further ordinary shares in the company in lieu of dividends.

DIFFERENCE BETWEEN STOCK AND SHARES

The difference between stock and shares is that the latter are definite specified units, for example, 1,000 shares of £1 each, numbered 1 to 1,000; but stock is consolidated into a block, and may be transferred in units of a fixed amount, £1 or £5, or multiples thereof, or even in fractions of a £. It will be clear, therefore, that stock cannot bear distinctive numbers, and also that it must be paid in full. A registered company cannot make an *original* issue of stock; it can arise only by conversion of fully-paid shares into stock.

DEBENTURES

Debentures are loans for a specified period, and the holders as such have no proprietary interest in the company; they are creditors of the company, and interest accrues and is chargeable, whether the company makes profits or not. Debentures registered in the books of the company can be transferred in the same way as shares. Debentures can also be consolidated into one mass and issued as debenture stock. A mortgage debenture is one which gives to the holder as security a mortgage on assets, or an asset, of the company.

SHARES ISSUED AT A DISCOUNT

Formerly, shares in a company could not be issued at a discount; that is to say, if a company's shares were of the nominal value of £1 each, these shares could not be *issued* at a price lower than £1 each. But under a valid and registered contract, the company was permitted to buy property for shares, so that the shares were paid for by a transfer of the property instead of in cash.

Section 57 of the Act of 1948 now provides that a company may issue at a discount shares of a class already issued, provided that:

(1) the issue of the shares at a discount must be authorized by resolution passed in general meeting of the company, and must be sanctioned by the Court,

(2) the resolution must specify the maximum rate of discount at which the shares are to be issued,

(3) not less than one year must, at the date of the issue, have elapsed since the date on which the company was entitled to commence business,

(4) the shares to be issued at a discount must be issued within one month after the date on which the issue is sanctioned by the Court, or within such extended time as the Court may allow.

Every prospectus relating to the issue of the shares, and every Balance Sheet issued subsequently, must contain particulars of the discount allowed on the issue, or so much of that discount as has not been written off at the date of the issue of the document in question; and particulars of the discount allowed, or of the amount not written off, must be stated in the Annual Return.

The book-keeping entries relating to issue of shares at a discount would be similar to the entries on the issue of debentures at a discount. (See Book 2.)

Dividends and Interest

It is worth repeating that the law is strict about a company maintaining its capital and a company's capital can only be reduced with the approval of the Court. It follows, therefore, that dividends can be paid only out of profits. The position is different in the case of debenture holders. They are creditors and receive interest on their loans and this interest may have to be paid out of capital if there is no other way of paying it. Debenture interest is an expense and appears in the Profit & Loss Account; dividends are an appropriation of profit and are shown in a separate appropriation account.

DECLARING DIVIDENDS

The Board of Directors usually has the power to recommend an interim dividend half-way through the financial year if the trading figures justify it and at the end of the year a final dividend for the year. At the Annual General Meeting of the company the shareholders are asked to approve the Board's recommendation and whilst it is possible for a shareholder to propose a lesser dividend than the one recommended, a shareholder may not propose a larger one.

The Final Accounts of Companies

TRADING AND PROFIT & LOSS ACCOUNTS

Although companies must file accounts with their annual returns, they are not required to provide detailed copies of their Trading and Profit & Loss Accounts. The Companies Acts, 1948 and 1967 state what information must be given. The Trading and Profit & Loss Accounts of a company are not very different from those of sole traders and partnerships except that there may be some items not customarily found in the accounts of non-corporate bodies, e.g. directors' remuneration and emoluments, debenture interest. The Companies Act, 1967 abolished the exempt and non-exempt private company and made it obligatory for companies to give more information about their affairs.

Some matters which must now be disclosed in the company's accounts, directors' reports, or in notes attached to the accounts are:

(1) Principal activities of the company.
(2) Significant changes in fixed assets.
(3) Market value of interests in land held as fixed assets if materially different from book values.
(4) Directors' contracts with the company and directors' rights to acquire shares or debentures in the company.
(5) Analysis of turnover/profits or losses before taxation:
  (i) turnover for different classes of business;
  (ii) profit or loss of each class.
(6) Average number of employees per week if 100 or more.
(7) Aggregate wages paid to employees (if 100 or more), including bonuses.
(8) Contributions to political and charitable bodies.
(9) Value of exports where turnover exceeds £50,000 (nil return required if there are no exports).

THE APPROPRIATION ACCOUNT

You are familiar with the appropriation accounts of partnerships, showing how the profit for the year is divided amongst the partners in accordance with the Partnership Agreement. The appropriation account of a company will show how the directors propose to deal with the profits, how much for example, they wish to transfer to reserves, the amounts payable to shareholders if their dividend recommendations are accepted, and the balance of profit to be retained in the business.

APPROPRIATION ACCOUNT FOR THE YEAR ENDED 31ST DECEMBER, 19—

			£			£
General Reserve			2,500	Net Profit	b/d	4,260
Dividends:				Balance from previous year		1,400
5% Cum. Preference Shares		£500				
Recommended Ord. Div.						
12%	1,200					
			1,700			
Balance c/f			1,460			
			£5,660			£5,660
				Balance b/f		£1,460

Reserves and Provisions

Revenue reserves consist of sums which could have been used to pay cash dividends to shareholders but which the directors think it wiser to retain in the business, either to increase the working capital or to provide for some specific contingency. As we have already seen, one of the effects of inflation is to make fixed assets more expensive to replace and sometimes a company will create a Fixed Asset Replacement Reserve to meet this situation. Inflation also produces a need for increased working capital, quite apart from any development plans the company may have, simply because prices are rising, and a General Reserve may thus be needed to counter the effects of inflation. Furthermore there is nearly always a credit balance on the Appropriation Account, consisting of profits which have not been distributed, and this too may be classified as a revenue reserve. On the other hand, the credit balance may have arisen simply because it was inconvenient to pay dividends in fractions of a percentage. Where a General Reserve has been built up out of past appropriations of profit, a part or the whole of such a reserve can be transferred back to the Appropriation Account and be made available to pay cash dividends to shareholders.

CAPITAL RESERVE

This is a term which is used to identify those reserves which are not available for transfer back to the Appropriation Account for distribution to shareholders in the form of cash dividends. They may, however, form part of a capitalization issue, for such issues do not reduce the resources employed in the company. Capital reserves can arise in a number of ways. For example:

(1) When preference shares are redeemed.
(2) When shares are issued at a premium. The difference between the par value of the shares and the sale price is credited to a share premium account.
(3) When the book value of an asset is increased.

The need to distinguish in the Balance Sheet between Capital Reserves and Revenue Reserves was abolished by the Companies Act, 1967, and companies may now classify reserves under headings most appropriate to the kind of business carried on. Reserves which are not legally necessary can be used for any purpose not forbidden by the Companies Acts; they may be used, for example, to pay cash dividends to shareholders or for a capitalization issue, but if a reduction of capital is involved the court must sanction it.

The Companies Acts allow Capital Reserves to be used for certain purposes, provided there is nothing in the Articles of Association which prohibit such a use. For example:

(1) For an issue of bonus shares, i.e. a capitalization issue.
(2) For writing off preliminary expenses.
(3) For writing off expenses and commission paid on the issue of shares or debentures.
(4) For providing any premium payable on redemption of redeemable preference shares or debentures.

PROVISIONS

As we have seen, these consist of amounts which are retained in the business by way of providing for depreciation or the diminution in the value of fixed assets, or for providing for a known liability which cannot be determined at the time with any degree of accuracy. Liabilities differ from provisions inasmuch as the former can be determined with substantial accuracy. Provisions are created to provide for depreciation, bad debts, cash discounts and exceptional expenses, for example, expenses that may arise in connection with litigation in which the company has, or will, become involved.

WORKED EXERCISE 24.1

(*a*) A limited company has an authorized capital of £100,000 divided into 25,000 7 per cent preference shares of £1 each, and 75,000 ordinary shares of £1 each. All the preference shares are issued and fully paid and 60,000 ordinary shares are issued and fully paid.

At 1st January, 1970, there is a 'general reserve' of £25,000 and a credit balance on profit and loss account of £3,000. Creditors are £12,550; fixed assets (at cost) £60,000; provision for depreciation of fixed assets £12,000; current assets £86,000. The net profit for the year ending 31st December, 1970 is £10,200; the preference dividend has been paid; the directors recommend a transfer to general reserve of £2,500 and a dividend of 10 per cent for the year on the ordinary shares.

Prepare the profit and loss appropriation account for the year ended 31st December, 1970 and a balance sheet at that date. (Ignore taxation.)

(*b*) (i) Explain the term 'authorized capital'.

(ii) What do you think is meant by the words 'ordinary shareholders' interest'?

(iii) From the balance sheet you have prepared, what is the amount of the 'ordinary shareholders' interest'?

G.C.E. 'O' Level

APPROPRIATION ACCOUNT FOR THE YEAR ENDED 31ST DECEMBER, 1970

		£			£
General Reserve		2,500	Balance (net profit) b/d		10,200
Preference Dividend		1,750	Balance b/fwd from year previous		3,000
Proposed Dividend on ord. shares 10%		6,000			
Balance	c/d	2,950			
		£13,200			£13,200
			Balance	b/d	2,950

BALANCE SHEET AS AT 31ST DECEMBER, 1970

		£		£	£
Authorized Capital:			Fixed Assets at cost	60,000	
25,000 7% Pref. Shares of £1 ea.		25,000	*Less* Provision for Depreciation	12,000	
75,000 Ord. Shares of £1 ea.		75,000			48,000
		£100,000			
Issued and Paid Up Capital:			Current Assets		86,000
25,000 7% Pref. Shares of £1 ea.		25,000			
60,000 Ord. Shares of £1 ea.		60,000			
Revenue Reserves:	£				
General Reserve	27,500				
Profit & Loss A/c	2,950				
		30,450			
Current Liabilities:	£				
Proposed Ord. Dividend	6,000				
Creditors	12,550				
		18,550			
		£134,000			£134,000

Alternative form of Balance sheet:

BALANCE SHEET AS AT 31ST DECEMBER, 1970

	£	£	£
Fixed Assets at cost		60,000	
Less Provision for depreciation		12,000	48,000
Current Assets		86,000	
Deduct current liabilities:			
Proposed Ordinary Dividend	6,000		
Creditors	12,550	18,550	
		Net Current Assets	67,450
		Total Net Assets	£115,450

	Authorized	Issued and Paid up
Represented by:		
Share Capital:		
7% Pref. Shares of £1 each	25,000	25,000
Ordinary Shares of £1 each	75,000	60,000
	£100,000	£85,000
	£	
Revenue Reserves:		
General Reserve	27,500	
Profit and Loss Account	2,950	30,450
		£115,450

(i) The authorized capital is the amount of capital with which the company was registered on incorporation. The company may issue shares up to this sum. Another term for authorized capital is 'nominal' capital. The authorized capital must always be shown in the Balance Sheet of the company.

(ii) The ordinary shareholders are entitled to the profits which remain after the preference shareholders have been paid their fixed dividend. If these profits are not paid to the ordinary shareholders but put to a reserve they remain part of the ordinary shareholders interest. These reserves may at a subsequent date be transferred back to the Profit and Loss Account and distributed in the form of cash dividends, or they may be converted into bonus* shares. These reserves are then said to be capitalized.

(iii) The amount of the ordinary shareholders' interest consists of:

	£
(i) Capital subscribed	60,000
(ii) Reserves	30,450
(iii) Proposed Ord. Dividend	6,000
	£96,450

* N.B.—The term 'bonus shares' is deemed nowadays to be misleading and the term 'capitalisation issues' is preferred.

EXERCISE 24.1

Explain the meaning of the following pairs of terms so as to show the difference between them:

(*a*)	Authorised Capital;	Paid-up Capital
(*b*)	Preference Shares;	Ordinary Shares
(*c*)	Ordinary Shares;	Debentures.

G.C.E. 'O' Level

EXERCISE 24.2

A limited liability company has an authorized capital of £200,000 divided into 20,000 6 per cent preference shares of £1 each and 180,000 ordinary shares of £1 each. All the preference shares are issued and fully paid: 100,000 ordinary shares are issued with 75p per share paid on each share.

On 31st December, 19–2 the company's revenue reserves were £30,000, current liabilities £7,500, current assets £62,750, fixed assets (at cost) £90,000 and provisions for depreciation on fixed assets £20,250. Make a summarized balance sheet as at 31st December, 19–2, to display this information. Set out the balance sheet in such a way as to show clearly the net value of current assets.

G.C.E. 'O' Level

Reporting

The following is an example of the kind of report the Directors of a small private company might submit to the shareholders prior to the Company's Annual General Meeting.

CAR BODIES (NEWTOWN) LTD

REPORT OF THE DIRECTORS

The Directors have pleasure in submitting their Annual Report together with the Accounts of the Company for the year ended 30th June, 1973.

(1) DIRECTORS

R. T. Makewell, Esq. (Chairman),
F. Milsom, Esq.,
L. Brooke, Esq.

Mr. L. Brooke is due to retire by rotation under the Articles of the Company and being eligible offers himself for re-election.

(2) SUMMARY OF ACCOUNTS

	1973	1972
	£	£
The Profit before Taxation amounts to	19,054	11,938
Less: Taxation	7,779	1,155
Available for distribution	11,275	10,783
Less: Dividends paid and proposed	2,218	*2,523
Profits Retained	9,057	8,260
Reserves brought forward (See 3 below)	16,002	5,731
Reserves carried forward	£25,059	£13,991

(3) DIVIDENDS*

For the year ended 30th June, 1972 it was proposed to pay a dividend of 60% on the Ordinary Shares amounting to £2,413 gross. However, this dividend was restricted by the Treasury under the Counter Inflation (Temporary Provisions) Act, 1972 to 10%, which has been paid. The unpaid balance of this dividend amounting to £2,011 has been credited to Reserves.

Formal consent having been received from the Treasury, an interim dividend of 30% for the year ended 30th June, 1973 amounting to £1,206 gross was declared and paid on 15th March, 1973.

Consent also having been received, the Directors now recommend the payment of a final dividend in respect of the year ended 30th June, 1973 of 24·5%. Under the new taxation system the imputed tax credit available to shareholders when added to the dividend, produces a 'gross' equivalent of 35%.

The final dividend on the 7½% Redeemable Cumulative Preference Shares to the date of redemption amounting to £27 gross was paid during the year.

(4) PRINCIPAL ACTIVITIES

The principal activities of the Company are Motor Vehicle Dealers and repairers.

(5) FIXED ASSETS

Details of the changes in Fixed Assets during the year are shown in Note 5 of the Notes to the Accounts.

(6) EXPORTS

No goods were exported during the year by the Company.

(7) DIRECTORS' SHAREHOLDINGS

The interests of the Directors in the Shares of the Company at 1st July, 1972 and 30th June, 1973 were as follows:

R. T. Makewell	660 Ordinary Shares
F. Milsom	nil
L. Brooke	100 Ordinary Shares

(8) AUDITORS

Messrs. Jones, Smith, Jones & Co., have expressed their willingness to continue in office and a resolution authorising the Directors to fix the remuneration of the Auditors will be submitted to the Annual General Meeting.

On behalf of the Board,

R. T. Makewell,

CHAIRMAN

Bridge Street,
NEWTOWN,
Herts.

CAR BODIES (NEWTOWN) LTD

PROFIT AND LOSS ACCOUNT FOR THE YEAR ENDED 30TH JUNE, 1973

	Note		1973 £	1972 £
Turnover	1		454,793	346,756
Net Profit for the year before Taxation	2		19,054	11,938
Deduct: Taxation	4		7,779	1,155
Net Profit for the year after Taxation			11,275	10,783
Deduct: Dividends—		£		
Paid—7½% Redeemable Cumulative Preference Shares (Gross)		27		
Ord. Shares—Interim at 30% (Gross)		1,206		
Proposed—Ordinary Shares—Final 24·5%		985		
			2,218	2,523

		£	£
Profits Retained for the year		9,057	8,260
Reserves brought forward	13,991		
Add: Adjustment for Proposed Ordinary Dividend of 60% for year ended 30th June, 1972—10% only paid	2,011		
		16,002	5,731
Reserves carried forward		£25,059	£13,991

CAR BODIES (NEWTOWN) LTD

BALANCE SHEET AS AT 30TH JUNE, 1973

	Note	1973 £	1973 £	1972 £	1972 £
FIXED ASSETS	5		2,988		2,713
CURRENT ASSETS					
Stocks and Work in Progress	1	37,046		21,287	
Debtors and Prepayments		33,261		31,960	
Cash at Bank and in Hand		15,053		1,383	
		85,360		54,630	
DEDUCT: CURRENT LIABILITIES					
Short Term Loans	6	21,250		10,397	
Creditors and Accrued Charges		23,354		19,873	
Hire Purchase Creditors		3,284		2,572	
Current Taxation		1,573		—	
Proposed Dividend		985		2,413	
		50,446		35,255	
NET CURRENT ASSETS			34,914		19,375
ADVANCE CORPORATION TAX RECOVERABLE			423		
			£38,325		£22,088

Represented by:	1973 *Authorized* £	1973 *Issued and Fully Paid* £	1972 *Issued and Fully Paid* £
SHARE CAPITAL			
7½% Redeemable Cumulative Pref. Share of £1 each	5,000	—	1,460
Ordinary Shares of £1 each	5,000	4,022	4,022
	£10,000	4,022	5,482
CAPITAL REDEMPTION RESERVE FUND		1,460	1,460
RESERVES		25,059	13,991
DEFERRED TAXATION			
Corporation Tax Payable 1st July, 1974		7,784	1,155
TOTAL CAPITAL EMPLOYED		£38,325	£22,088

NOTES TO THE ACCOUNTS—30TH JUNE, 1973

(1) ACCOUNTING POLICIES

(*a*) *Depreciation of Fixed Assets*

Fixed Assets are written off over their estimated useful lives.

The following rates of depreciation are used:

Plant, Fixtures and Fittings	15% on the reducing balance
Office Equipment	20% on the reducing balance
Motor Vehicles	25% on the reducing balance

(*b*) *Stocks and Work in Progress*

Stocks and Work in Progress have been valued at the lower of cost, net realisable value and replacement price.

(*c*) *Repairs and Renewals*

Repairs and Renewals are charged to revenue in the year in which they are incurred.

(*d*) *Turnover*

Turnover represents the total value of sales and work done at invoice price excluding VAT.

(2) NET PROFIT BEFORE TAXATION	1973	1972
The Net Profit has been arrived at after charging:	£	£
Directors' Emoluments (See Note 3)	10,315	8,390
Auditors' Remuneration	650	650
Short Term Loan Interest	614	736
Long Term Loan Interest	—	145
Depreciation of Fixed Assets	563	510

(3) DIRECTORS' EMOLUMENTS		
Fees	360	360
As Executives	9,955	8,030
	10,315	8,390

(4) TAXATION		
Corporation Tax based upon the profits for the year and provided at the rate of 40% up to 31st March, 1973 and at 50% from that date ...	7,900	1,155
Deemed A.C.T. recoverable	(116)	—
Adjustment in respect of previous years... ...	(5)	—
	£7,779	£1,155

(5) FIXED ASSETS	Plant, Fixtures and Fittings	Office Equipment	Company Vehicles
	£	£	£
Cost			
At beginning of year ...	11,237	1,395	715
Additions...	590	247	—
At end of year	11,827	1,642	715
Depreciation			
At beginning of year ...	8,848	1,161	625
Provision for year	446	94	22
At end of year	9,294	1,255	647
Net Book Values			
30th June, 1973	2,533	387	68
30th June, 1972	2,389	234	90

		1973	1972
(6)	SHORT-TERM LOANS		
	Stocking Loans (Repayable on sale of stock)	£20,874	£10,021
	Loan on Plant and Equipment (Repayable by yearly instalments of £188 and free of interest).	376	376
		£21,250	£10,397
(7)	CAPITAL EXPENDITURE		
	(*a*) Contracted for but not provided ...	Nil	Nil
	(*b*) Authorized by the Directors but not contracted for	Nil	Nil

AUDITORS' REPORT TO THE MEMBERS OF CAR BODIES (NEWTOWN) LTD

We have examined the Accounts set out on pages 3 to 8 and report that in our opinion, they give a true and fair view of the state of the Company's affairs at 30th June, 1973 and of its profit for the year ended on that date and comply with the Companies Acts, 1948 and 1967.

Jones, Smith, Jones & Co.,
Chartered Accountants.

Stock Exchange Regulations

So far we have mentioned some of the provisions of the Companies Acts applicable to registered companies, but if a public company wishes to obtain a Stock Exchange quotation the company must also comply with Stock Exchange regulations. Without such a quotation there would be only a restricted market for such shares and the public would be less inclined to buy them. Most investors in companies want to be able to sell their shares readily in an emergency and the existence of a Stock Exchange allows them to do this by providing a market place where buyers and sellers can come together. These Stock Exchange regulations have since 1948 received some recognition by the legislature, for under Section 51 of the Companies Act, 1948, if a prospectus of a company states that an application is being made for a quotation, any allotment or sale made in pursuance of the prospectus will be void unless application is made before the third day after the first issue of the prospectus and unless the application is granted. The scrutiny of Stock Exchanges is a major safeguard for investors and is a continuing one.

The most important Stock Exchange is situated in the City of London but there are Stock Exchanges in the principal cities of the United Kingdom. In order to establish uniform requirements for official quotations and other matters, these Stock Exchanges have formed the Federation of Stock Exchanges.

Capitalization Issues

When a company decides to capitalize some of its reserves, whether capital or revenue reserves, it transfers the required sum from the reserve accounts to the share capital accounts and issues new shares to this value and distributes them to existing shareholders, usually on a pro rata basis, for example, one new share for every two ordinary shares already held. Let us suppose that the following Balance Sheet showed the position of the company prior to a capitalization issue:

BALANCE SHEET 31ST DECEMBER, 1974

		£
FIXED ASSETS		150,000
NET CURRENT ASSETS		75,000
		£225,000
		Issued and
REPRESENTED BY:	*Authorized*	*Fully Paid*
£1 Ordinary Shares	£200,000	£100,000
Share Premium Account		25,000
General Reserve		90,000
Profit and Loss Account		10,000
		£225,000

Let us further suppose that the company decides to capitalize £100,000 of its reserves (Share Premium Account £25,000 plus £75,000 of the General Reserve). This would allow the company to issue one share for each existing share and the new position would be as follows:

BALANCE SHEET..............................

		£
FIXED ASSETS		150,000
NET CURRENT ASSETS		75,000
		£225,000
		Issued and
REPRESENTED BY:	*Authorized*	*Fully Paid*
£1 Ordinary Shares	£200,000	£200,000
General Reserve		15,000
Profit and Loss Account		10,000
		225,000

A holder of, say 100 £1 ordinary shares in the company would have, following the capitalization issue, 200 £1 ordinary shares but he would not be ostensibly better off. Whereas formerly he was the owner of $\frac{100}{100,000}$ of the net assets of £225,000, his share after the capitalization issue would be $\frac{200}{200,000}$ of the same total net assets. One might expect, therefore, that the market price of the ordinary shares would drop to half their former market price. This would not necessarily be so, for the conversion of reserves into more permanent capital is generally looked upon with favour by the market as a possible sign of company development. The market price might, consequently, settle at a figure in excess of half the former price.

Similarly with dividends, if distributable profits remained the same after the issue the dividends would tend to be half what they were before the issue. If before the issue the dividend was 20%, it would probably be 10% after the capitalization issue. By capitalizing reserves in this way, a company establishes a position more closely resembling the real position, and one advantage of this is that the shareholders will be seen not to be receiving an over-generous share of the profits.

RIGHTS ISSUES

A rights issue is one in which a public company with quoted shares raises additional capital by issuing further shares for cash and offering these to existing shareholders at a price below the current market price. Any shareholder who does not wish to take up his allocation can renounce his right and the shares are then sold and he receives a sum of money equal to the difference between the price at which they were offered to him and the price obtained from their sale.

Company Law Reform

Recent happenings have focused attention on the need for changes in Company Law. Defects in the current law, brought to light by some recent disturbing disclosures in the press, resulted in a Bill being put before Parliament in January, 1974 which sought, amongst other things, to restrain persons who have inside knowledge of a company's affairs from taking advantage of this special knowledge to deal in the company's shares for personal gain. Heavier penalties were also proposed against those companies who are late in filing their annual returns at Companies House. The trend is clearly towards making it obligatory on all companies to make a fuller disclosure of their affairs.

Interest in Company Law reform has been further stimulated by our membership of the European Economic Community. It is widely believed that Company Law will be one of the first areas in which harmonization of the Laws of the nine members will first be seriously attempted. Already there is support for a company structure, common in Germany and Holland, which provides, inter alia, for two Boards—a Supervisory Board on which workers' representatives serve and a lower and subordinate Board responsible for the day-to-day running of the company.

25

Interpretation of Accounts

THE value of keeping books of account on the double entry principle was discussed in an earlier chapter. Among the many advantages that were then listed was the very important one of enabling the proprietor to manage his enterprise more efficiently. Not that good accounting procedures will, of themselves, ensure good management, for management is a complex function requiring the exercise of many and varied skills. But in the exercise of these skills, notably control, the keeping of proper financial records has an important role to play.

Control may be described as the task of directing the affairs of the company so that the plans which have been prepared, and the targets which have been set, are achieved. Just as the motorist, who aims to reach a certain point at a certain time, will head his car in the direction in which he wishes to go, varying the car's speed and its course to meet the changing situations as they arise, and thus finally reaching his destination as planned, so too with the business man; he must control his organization by 'steering' it in the right direction, take steps when necessary to deal with unexpected developments, and thus achieve his predetermined objectives. In this task an ability to interpret the accounts placed before him is a most valuable aid to control. We shall, therefore, examine some specimen final accounts and Balance Sheets with the purpose of seeing what facts, useful in the control of the business, are revealed by the figures shown and what other facts, of similar value, it is possible to deduce from them. We begin with a simple Trading Account.

Dr TRADING ACCOUNT FOR THE YEAR ENDED 31ST DECEMBER, 1964 Cr

1963		£	£		£	£	*1963*
(£150)	Stock (1st January)		210	Sales	10,500		—
	Purchases	7,400		*Less* Returns	250		
	Less Returns	60				10,250	(£8,100)
(£6,500)			7,340				
			7,550				
(£250)	*Less* Closing Stock		440				
	Cost of Goods Sold		7,110				
	Gross Profit transferred						
(£1,700)	to Profit & Loss A/c		3,140				
			£10,250			£10,250	

Turnover or Sales

One of the first figures the manager will look for as soon as he receives the firm's Trading Account will be the figure for sales. Although it is possible for a firm to make larger profits from selling fewer products, this is a rare phenomenon. The sales figure is a measure of the firm's activity, and larger profits usually come from increased sales. Unless he is able to compare the current year's sales with the previous year's sales, the figures may not mean very much, and it is customary, therefore, to add a memorandum column, giving the sales figure for the previous trading period. This may be done for other figures appearing in the Trading Account. If the firm markets a variety of different products, or has a number of separate departments, a Trading Account produced in tabular form, showing sales according to products or departments, will obviously be more useful than one giving only a single total sales figure. In comparing sales figures, allowance must be made for any changes in the selling prices of the products sold. If it is possible also to give the number of actual units of product sold, the effects of price fluctuations can be largely eliminated.

Accounting Ratios

In analysing financial statements much use is made of accounting ratios. The value of such ratios depends upon their relevance to the particular situation and to the sort of questions they ought properly to provoke.

Gross Profit as a Ratio of Sales

In the above Trading Account the gross profit as a ratio of sales = $\frac{£3,140}{£10,250} \times \frac{100}{1} = 30{\cdot}63\%$. This means that out of every £100 worth of sales £30·63 is gross profit, out of which the trader must pay his administrative and selling expenses. Since he will fix selling prices by adding a certain percentage to the cost price (termed 'mark up'), he knows beforehand with reasonable accuracy what his gross profit ought to be. If the mark up varies with different goods or departments, the Trading Account ought to be produced in columnar form so that ratios can be calculated for each product or department.

Any difference between the actual percentage as shown by the Trading Account figures and the expected figures calls for an immediate investigation. There are a number of possibilities to account for a disparity, for example:

(1) goods sold below the marked prices,
(2) pilferage,
(3) mistakes in preparing the inventories of closing and opening stocks.

Suppose that in the Trading Account above, the closing stock had been inflated by £200, then the gross profit would have been £200 more and gross profit as a percentage of sales would have been 32·44%. Conversely, if items had been wrongly omitted from the inventory of closing stock, the percentage would have been lower than the expected 31%.

Since the closing stock of one period is the opening stock of the next, inflation of closing stock will reduce the ratio in the next period. We can see this if we assume that opening stock in the example above had been given as £410 instead of £210. Gross profit would then have been £200 less and the % would have been 28·68% instead of approximately 31%. The convention of prudence should be applied in valuing closing stock.

Rate of Turnover

Rate of turnover is the number of times stocks are sold during the trading period. Thus if a trader holds on average stocks valued at £400 cost, and his turnover for the year is £1,600 at cost, then he turns his stock over four times a year and his rate of turnover is 4. Most traders will endeavour to turn over their stocks as frequently as possible, particularly in those trades where the risks of holding stocks are exceptionally great. It often pays a shopkeeper to reduce his prices if this increases his rate of turnover. Take two traders for example, A and B, both of whom are in the same kind of business and both of whom hold, on average, £500 worth of stock. A makes a profit of 50% on cost and turns over his stock once a year, i.e. gross profit is £250. B, on the other hand, prices his wares to give him a gross profit of 20% on cost but turns over his stock four times a year. His gross profit = £100 × 4 = £400. B earns his smaller profit four times during the year, whereas A earns his larger profit only once. We can look at this another way. A's stock remains on his warehouse shelves on average for 12 months whereas B's stock remains only three months. B's risks are less and his capital more active than those of A.

CALCULATING RATE OF TURNOVER FROM THE TRADING ACCOUNT FIGURES

We begin a Trading Account with the opening stock, to which we add purchases and then take away closing stock to give the cost of the goods sold. If the total value of stocks held by the business varies very little from one month to the next, an arithmetic average of the opening and closing stocks will be sufficient to give us an idea of the value of the stocks normally held. In the Trading Account above there is a big difference between the opening and closing stocks, and it might be better to find out from other records the value of the stock normally held. Had the closing stock been £300 instead of £440, our calculation of rate of turnover could have proceeded as follows.

	£
Opening stock	210
Closing stock	300
	2)510
Average stock at cost	£255

$$\text{Rate of turnover equals } \frac{£7{,}250}{255} = 28{\cdot}4$$

In estimating the rate of turnover of a company from published financial statements the 'sales at cost' figure will probably not be given and then the 'sales at selling prices' would have to be used.

ILLUSTRATION 25.1

M. Lawrence, a sole trader, holds, on average, stocks valued at £80,000 at cost price. In 1973 he turned his stock over six times. His gross profit for the year was £200,000. He hopes in 1974, without changing his selling prices, and by carrying the same quantity of stocks, to turn his stock over eight times. If he achieves this, by how much can he expect to increase his gross profit?

1973 Sales at cost = £80,000 × 6 = £480,000
1974 Sales at cost = £80,000 × 8 = £640,000

$$\text{Estimated Gross profit for 1974} = \frac{640{,}000}{480{,}000} \times £200{,}000$$
$$= £266{,}666{\cdot}67$$
$$\text{Increase in gross profit} = £66{,}666{\cdot}67.$$

The Profit & Loss Account

Net profits, like gross profits, can be expressed as a percentage of sales. Thus if the figure is 12%, it means that of every £100 of sales £12 is net profit. If the ratio of gross profit to sales remains constant but the ratio of net profit to sales declines, then the administrative and selling expenses are increasing disproportionately. If, in any one year, there is exceptional expenditure of a non-recurrent nature, a note of explanation should be appended to the accounts.

Students are sometimes asked to show administrative and selling expenses separately in the Profit & Loss Account. If double columns are used, this is easily done; the details of each can be shown in the first column and the totals in the second.

KEEPING A CHECK ON TRADE DEBTORS

Where credit facilities are provided, steps must be taken to ensure that there is no unnecessary increase in the total amount of capital tied up in book debts. Statements of account must be sent out promptly, and there must be an effective system for chasing slow payers.

One way of calculating the length of credit being given is to divide the average weekly credit sales for a four weekly period into the amount outstanding on the Sales Ledger Control Account. If, for example, in a four weekly period credit sales totalled £10,000, i.e. on average

£2,500 a week and the Sales Ledger Control Account (Total Debtors' Account) shows a figure of £15,000, then the number of weeks' credit being given is £15,000 divided by £2,500 which is six weeks. A table for succeeding periods can be constructed, viz.

Trade Debtors (four weekly periods)

Period	Credit Sales	Total Debtors	No. of weeks' credit
1	£10,000	£15,000	6·0
2	12,000	20,000	6·6
3	16,000	30,000	7·5
4	16,000	32,000	8·0

Here it can be seen that customers are tending to pay their accounts more slowly, and a reason must be sought and remedial action taken.

If the only available figure for credit sales is the one which appears in the published accounts of the business, it is still possible—assuming all the sales are credit sales—to estimate roughly how quickly debts are being collected. We simply divide the annual credit sales by the average amount owing by debtors to find the turnover of debtors for the year. For example, if credit sales for 1974 were £25,000 and sundry debtors shown in the Balance Sheets for 1973 and 1974 were £2,600 and £2,400 respectively, then

$$£25,000 \div \tfrac{1}{2}\,(2,600 + £2,400) = 10$$

and average length of credit $= 12 \div 10 = 1{\cdot}2$ months.

ILLUSTRATION 25.2

During the year 1962 J. W. Hardman made a gross profit of 25% on a turnover of £21,600, and a net profit of 12% on turnover. His rate of turnover of stock for the year was 10.

For the year 1963 Hardman estimates that he can increase his rate of turnover of stock to 14, while carrying the same average stock, by reducing his prices by 5% on selling price and that, if he does this, his ratio of expenses to turnover will be reduced by 2%.

Calculate:

(1) Hardman's gross profit for 1962,
(2) Hardman's expenses for 1962,
(3) Hardman's net profit for 1962;

and then calculate to the nearest £1:

(*a*) Hardman's estimated sales for 1963,
(*b*) Hardman's estimated gross profit for 1963,
(*c*) Hardman's estimated expenses for 1963,
(*d*) Hardman's estimated net profit for 1963.

University of London, G.C.E. 'O' level

1962

(1)	A gross profit of 25% on a turnover of £21,600 is ¼ of £21,600	= £5,400
(2)	Expenses for 1962 = 13% of £21,600 (or gross profit less net profit)	= £2,808
(3)	Net profit 12% of £21,600	= £2 592

1963

(*a*) Hardman's estimated sales = Average stock at cost × rate of stock turnover × change in % gross profit

= £1,620 × 14 × $\frac{5}{4}$ = £28,350

(*b*)	Estimated gross profit 20% of £28,350	= £5,670
(*c*)	Estimated expenses 11% of £28,350	= £3,118
(*d*)	Estimated net profit 9% of £28,350 (or difference between gross profit and expenses)	= £2,551

EXERCISE 25.1

From the following figures you are required to prepare an estimate of A. Trader's stock at 31st May, 1960.

	£
Stock at 1st January, 1960 (at Cost)	4,000
Purchases from 1st January to 31st May, 1960	33,000
Sales from 1st January to 31st May, 1960	42,000
Goods Given Away for Advertising Purposes Valued at Cost	300

A. Trader adds 33⅓% to his cost prices to ascertain selling prices.

University of London, G.C.E. 'O' level

EXERCISE 25.2

In making a comparison between two successive years of trading F. Taylor, a trader, has the following information.

	Year 1 £	*Year 2* £
Turnover	46,000	54,000
Gross Profit	15,180	16,200
Net Profit	5,520	6,750

Present these results in such a way as to make a comparison between the two years and state the conclusions you draw from the comparison.

University of London, G.C.E. 'O' level

EXERCISE 25.3

(1) The following information relates to the accounts of a trader for two successive years.

	Year 1 £	*Year 2* £
Turnover	18,000	22,000
Gross Profit as a Percentage of Turnover	34	35
Net Profit as a Percentage of Turnover	12	11

State, with possible reasons, the conclusions you draw from this information.

(2) Indicate, with reasons, which of the following represent capital expenditure and which represent revenue expenditure:
   (*a*) bank overdraft interest,
   (*b*) purchase of an additional typewriter for the office,
   (*c*) purchase of goods for resale.

Associated Examining Board, G.C.E. 'O' level

Evaluating Performance — Return on Capital Employed

Expressing net profit as a ratio of the value of the resources employed in the business is one of the steps in assessing a company's performance. But what figures for net profit ought we to take? Ought it to be net profit before or after tax? And then with regard to resources employed, ought we to use the figures for total assets or only the figure for total net assets, that is, fixed assets plus current assets less current liabilities? It depends to a large extent upon what we are seeking to do and upon the available information. Whatever method we employ, it is essential, if we wish to discover trends, to be consistent and to use the same method each time.

The figure for net profit before tax is preferred to the figure after tax; a company is seeking to assess performance, and the amount of tax it must pay is beyond its control. To the net profit we must add back any interest paid on loans or debentures, for these are not operating expenses but returns to the persons who advanced this part of the company's capital.

As to resources employed, the argument for using the total net assets figure is that this amount is invested in the business on a long-term basis.

ILLUSTRATION 25.3

We are required from the figures given below to calculate the net profit of the company as a percentage of average capital employed. (These are taken from the actual accounts of a small private company. Only the name has been changed.)

CAR BODIES (NEWTOWN) LTD

	1973	1972
	£	£
Capital employed (assets employed less current liabilities)	38,325	22,088
Net profit for the year before taxation (the company has no loan capital)	19,054	

$$\text{Average net assets employed} = \frac{£38,325 + £22,088}{2} = £30,206$$

$$\text{Net profit for 1973 as a percentage of net assets employed} = \frac{19,054}{30,206} \times 100 = 63\%$$

The net profit in the example just given has been arrived at after charging, among other things, the directors' emoluments. In assessing the performance of a one-man business we would need to take into account the opportunity cost of the proprietor's services, that is, the amount he could have earned managing someone else's business.

The Balance Sheet

A Balance Sheet is a statement which shows, at a point in time, what assets the business owns, what money the business owes, and the value of the owners' interest in the company. Any balances remaining in the Ledger after all the nominal accounts have been closed by transfer to the Trading and Profit & Loss Account will appear in the Balance Sheet, classified according to the kind of asset or liability each balance represents.

The Balance Sheet is a summary, and therefore necessarily condensed, but it must nevertheless contain sufficient detail to give anyone reading it a 'true and fair' view of the company's financial position at the given date.

Fixed assets, e.g. freehold land, plant and machinery, which remain in the business to earn profits, must be grouped together and distinguished from current assets such as stock, sundry debtors, etc., which will be converted into cash. Similarly, on the other side of the statement, liabilities which are short term, i.e. those which will become payable within the next trading period, should be kept separate from the long term liabilities, e.g. long term loans.

In addition to grouping the assets, they should also be properly marshalled, i.e. assets should be put in order of liquidity or illiquidity; it does not matter in most cases which order is adopted, as long as there is an orderly and logical arrangement. If current assets are put first in order of liquidity, e.g. cash, debtors, etc., then on the other side the liabilities should be marshalled according to the order in which they would become payable in the event of the business being dissolved.

The following Balance Sheet, taken from an answer given to an examination question in a previous chapter, shows how the items in a Balance Sheet should be grouped and marshalled.

BALANCE SHEET AT 1ST JULY, 1960

	£	£		£	£	£
Capital Accounts:			*Fixed Assets*			
Flower	11,000		Freehold Premises		10,600	
Rose	7,000		Machinery & Tools		4,100	
		18,000				14,700
Current Accounts:			*Current Assets*			
Flower	40		Stock of Materials		1,300	
Rose	55		Stock of Goods		2,400	
		95	Sundry Debtors	2,600		
Current Liabilities			*Less* Provision	235		
Sundry Creditors		3,610			2,365	
			Rates & Insurance prepaid		90	
			Cash at Bank		800	
			Cash in Hand		50	
						7,005
		£21,705				£21,705

Because a Balance Sheet is a statement expressed in financial terms, there are limitations on the information it reveals. The Balance Sheet will not, for example, tell us very much about customer goodwill or about the quality of the human resources the company can command. Investors and others interested in a company's prospects will be able to deduce little from a study of the company's Balance Sheet. Indeed the Balance Sheet might show what appears to be a very healthy position when, at the same time, the company's order books are practically empty. Moreover a Balance Sheet shows the financial position of a company at a moment in time and the position at that moment may not represent the typical position, especially if the activities of the company are subject to cyclical fluctuations. Furthermore the assets of the company are valued in pounds which had a different value at the time the assets were acquired. In studying a company's Balance Sheet it is helpful to have information from competitors' accounts or information relating to the particular trade as a whole. Such information is often readily available through a company's own trade association.

WORKING CAPITAL

It has already been observed that as a business grows, it may find itself short of liquid resources. Money may be withdrawn by the firm's owners in anticipation of profits or used to buy fixed assets. Profitability and financial stability do not always go together. The owners of a business have a discretion as to how they distribute their resources, and it is important that they distribute them in such a way as to retain sufficient of their assets in a form which will enable them to pay their debts as they become due. Fixed assets are acquired for retention in the business, and are not available for the discharge of debts; if a firm can only remain solvent by selling off some of its fixed assets, its position is indeed grave. The current assets, on the other hand, consist of cash, and other assets which are convertible into cash, and these provide a fund out of which a firm can pay its liabilities, i.e. those debts which must be paid within a short space of time. A firm is financially stable when the total of its current assets exceeds the total of its current liabilities by a safe margin, that is, when it has sufficient working capital. (*Working capital = excess of current assets over current liabilities.*)

A firm which is making substantial profits will not necessarily be adding substantially to its working capital. If all the profits are paid out to the firm's owners, no new capital is acquired, either fixed or current. Nor is working capital increased if all the profits are expended on fixed assets. In a period of prosperity the owners of a business will be greatly tempted to invest their profits in new and more efficient machinery. When the cold winds of a trade recession blow, the machines are idle and the firm may have insufficient current assets to meet its obligations. Over-trading, as this practice is termed, has caused more than one prosperous undertaking to fail.

SHOWING THE WORKING CAPITAL IN THE BALANCE SHEET

If the assets and liabilities are properly grouped in the Balance Sheet, working capital can be calculated quickly and easily. Look again at the Balance Sheet on page 288. You will see that current assets total £85,360 and current liabilities £50,446. The working capital is therefore £34,914. One should not be too dogmatic about what is sufficient working capital; it will depend upon the particular trade and the policies of the particular business firm. The Companies Act, 1948 requires working capital to be shown in the Balance Sheet, or the assets and liabilities arranged in a way which will enable it to be readily calculated. If the current liabilities are shown as a deduction from current assets on the assets side of the Balance Sheet, which is becoming a common practice, the figure for working capital can be seen at a glance.

TURNOVER OF WORKING CAPITAL

It is not enough for a company to have adequate working capital; it is important to ensure that the working capital is effectively employed. One way of measuring this is by calculating the rate of turnover of working capital. This is done by dividing sales by the average working capital. Supposing sales for the year were £70,000 and average working capital was £7,000, then turnover of working capital equals 10. Each £1 of working capital has generated £10 worth of sales. The figure for turnover of working capital needs to be compared with previous years and with the figures of other undertakings in a similar business to give it meaning.

CURRENT RATIOS AND LIQUIDITY RATIOS

The term 'current ratio' is sometimes used to describe the relationship between current assets and current liabilities. If current assets are twice as large as current liabilities, we speak of a 2 to 1 ratio. The current assets, however, include some items which are not available to meet very short term obligations. Stock, for example, may not be sold for some time and pre-payments are not convertible into cash for meeting immediate commitments. A liquidity ratio is similar to a current ratio except that only the very short term obligations, and only those assets which are sufficiently 'liquid' to be available to meet them, are included. The denominator, consisting of the very short term obligations, will include trade creditors, accrued expenses, bills payable, provision for taxation and dividends, and the numerator will include most of the current assets with the exception of stocks, investments held to meet a specific future commitment and pre-payments. In ordinary circumstances the liquidity ratio should not fall below 1 to 1, but it all depends upon the particular type of enterprise. The longer the production cycle the greater the need for working capital.

SHARE CAPITAL AND LOAN CAPITAL

There are two principal ways in which a limited liability company can raise additional long-term capital. One is by issuing shares and the other is by issuing debentures. The latter are loans, usually secured by a charge on the company's assets. If the company issues shares, it pays dividends to shareholders only if there are profits out of which to pay them; but if it issues debentures, the interest on them must be paid whether the company is making profits or not. It follows from this that in periods of bad trade the company with a large proportion of its capital in the form of loan capital will be worse off than the company whose capital consists entirely of share capital.

Where a company has a large part of its capital in debentures and preference shares, so that a relatively small change in profit will lead to a large alteration in the rate of the ordinary dividend, the capital is said to be high geared.

AN OUTSIDER'S VIEW OF THE BALANCE SHEET

It is to be expected that the owners of a business will be interested in the facts disclosed by the Balance Sheet; but there may also be other persons who, though having no connection with the company at the moment, may decide, on the strength of the information provided by the Balance Sheet, to give credit to the business, or to grant loans to it, or to invest money in it by buying its shares. What will these people be looking for when they read a Balance Sheet?

A person who is about to grant credit to a registered company will have a special interest in the realizable value of the fixed assets, for if the company is unable to meet its debts from current assets, it might have to sell its fixed ones. If the company has issued debentures which are secured by a fixed charge, only some of these fixed assets—perhaps none at all—will be available to meet his claims in a crisis. There may, however, be some uncalled capital available, a matter of no small interest to the creditor. Thus, if a company has issued 200,000 £1 ordinary shares of which only 50p per share has been called up, shareholders would be required, in the event of liquidation, to subscribe a further £100,000 if necessary. This uncalled capital may, however, already be the subject of a floating charge.

The same considerations would obtain in the case of a company requesting a bank overdraft or a bank loan. The bank manager would be particularly concerned with the financial stability of the company, and would attach great importance to the amount of working capital the company has.

Different considerations would apply in the case of a person who was thinking of investing money in the company. If he was a cautious man, he would be tempted to buy debentures, in which case he would become not a member of the company but a creditor. However badly the company did, he would still get his interest, and since his debt would probably also be secured by a charge on the company's assets, he would be unlikely to lose all his investment if the company failed. For this absence of risk the price would be a lower return on his investment than he would probably get if he bought shares. If he decided to buy shares, he would, in most instances, have a choice between preference and ordinary shares. The dividend on the former would be fixed, and the shares might give prior rights to repayment of capital in the event of the company being wound up. Moreover, as a preference shareholder he would get his fixed dividend before the other shareholders received any share of the profits. But if the company does well, he could receive a much greater return on his investment by buying ordinary shares.

EXERCISE 25.4

The total net assets of L. Gayler Ltd for the years 1972 and 1973 were respectively £200,000 and £250,000. The company's net profit for 1973 before tax was £80,000. Debenture interest for 1973 totalled £4.000. Analyse the performance of L. Gayler Ltd for the year 1973.

EXERCISE 25.5

Compare the performances of the following companies for the year 1971 in the same industry (in £ thousands):

	Company A	*Company B*	*Company C*
Average Capital employed during 1971 (Total net assets)	£1,099	£2,552	£3,963
Profit before tax plus debenture interest ...	100	307	1,309

EXERCISE 25.6

Calculate for 1971 (i) the current ratio (current assets to current liabilities); (ii) the liquid ratio (liquid assets to current liabilities) for companies *X* and *Y* from the following figures (£000's):

	Company X	*Company Y*
Current Assets	£1,485	£4,961
Current Liabilities	1,282	2,164
Liquid Assets (Debtors, Cash)	1,147	3,135

EXERCISE 25.7

On 1st January, 1963 R. L. Gale's Capital Account showed a credit balance of £450. During the year 1963 sales were £4,850. The cost of goods sold was £3,510 and total operating expenses were £1,150. During the year Gale withdrew £400 for private expenses.

On 31st December, 1963 Gale's Ledger accounts showed:

	£
Stock (31/12/63)	520
Sundry Debtors	210
Furniture & Fittings	180
Motor Van	300
Sundry Creditors	820
Bank Overdraft	150

(1) Ascertain Gale's gross and net profits for the year ended 31st December, 1963, and prepare his Balance Sheet as on that date.

(2) Give your opinion on the state of Gale's business. *G.C.E. 'O' level*

EXERCISE 25.8

A company made a gross profit of £135,000 on a turnover of £540,000 during the six months ended 30th September, 1962. Fixed expenses amounted to £24,000 and variable expenses to £51,000.

It was estimated that for the following six months ending 31st March, 1963 turnover should increase by £60,000 with the same average margin of gross profit as during the previous six months. On this basis it was estimated that there would be a 20% increase in the amount of net profit. It was assumed that fixed expenses would be unchanged.

On 31st March, 1963 turnover for the six months ended on that date was £620,000; gross profit was £161,200; fixed expenses were the same as in the previous six months and variable expenses were £64,660.

Draw up a statement in columnar form for the directors of the company to show clearly how the actual results for the six months ended 31st March, 1963 compared with the estimated results for the same period and the results for the previous six months. Attach to the statement any observations which you think may be helpful in making this comparison.

G.C.E. 'A' level

EXERCISE 25.9

From the details given below you are asked to calculate:

(i) the cost of goods sold;
(ii) the rate per cent of gross profit on turnover;
(iii) the rate of turnover of stock;
(iv) the rate per cent of net profit on turnover.

	£
1st April, 1970: Stock	4,500
31st March, 1971: Stock	3,600
1st April, 1970–31st March, 1971:	
Purchases	31,960
Sales	41,140
Returns outwards	460
Returns inwards	640
Selling, administration and distribution expenses	4,860

G.C.E. 'O' Level

wers to Exercises

1.1 (2) Wholesalers hold and display stocks of goods so that retailers can replace their own stocks easily and quickly. This involves risks—stocks may deteriorate, fashions change, prices fall. The profits of the wholesaler represent his remuneration for providing these services to the retailer and taking the risks. Other services a wholesaler may provide include: financing the retailer by supplying goods on credit, breaking bulk, that is, buying certain goods in large quantities (for example, tea) and redistributing the product in packets of a size convenient for consumers to buy.

(4) See text.

3.1 Fixed assets £100, Current Assets £2,975: Capital £3,000, current liabilities £75.

3.2 (*a*) asset side—stock increases: liabilities side—creditors increase by same amount.

(*b*) asset side—bank balance falls: liabilities side—figure for creditors reduced by same sum.

(*c*) both entries on asset side: value for stock falls, figure for debtors increases.

(*d*) both entries on asset side: fixed assets go up, bank balance goes down by same amount.

(*e*) both entries on asset side: stock increases by £10: figure for debtors falls by £10.

(*f*) on asset side—bank or cash is reduced by sum withdrawn; liabilities side—proprietor's capital reduced.

(*g*) on asset side—bank balance increases; on liabilities side—liabilities (bank) increase.

3.3 (J. Smith)

(*a*) Fixed assets £4,200. Current assets £830: Capital £5,000, Creditors £30.

(*b*) Fixed assets £4,200. Current assets £1,457: Capital £5,027, Creditors £630.

3.4 (T. Bate)
Fixed Assets £10,370. Net current assets £5,630: Capital £16,000.

3.5 (Goddard)
Fixed assets £58,000, net current assets or working capital £1,130; Mr Goddard's equity £29,130.

3.6 Suggested answer: increase in value of assets over year (1970) £1,950 financed by Profits not withdrawn £600, increase in bank overdraft £950, increase in credit given by suppliers £400.

4.1 (Robinson)
(1) Debit (2) Debit (3) Credit (4) Credit (5) Debit (6) Credit (7) Debit.

4.2 Bank £9,800 (dr), F & F £2,950 (dr), Purchases £12,380 (dr), Capital £16,970 (cr), Motor Vehicles £2,700 (dr), James Thistlewaite £2,450 (cr).

4.3 Fixed Assets £20,800. Net current assets £3,500: Capital £24,300.

4.4 (A. Fox)
(*a*) Total current assets £5,090.
(*b*) Working capital £3,630.
(*c*) Fixed assets £16,080; Net current assets £3,445: Capital £17,525; Long-term loan £2,000.

6.1 Balance £3·35 (dr).

6.2 Balance £53·30 (dr).

6.3 Balance £19·37½ (dr).

6.4 Balance £32·81 (dr).

6.5 Balance £10·00 (dr).

6.6 Total of trial balance (Apr. 6th) £891·38. Trial balance total (Apr. 13th) £1,150·68. (£883·30 and £1,137·10 respectively if VAT excluded)

6.7 (Robbins) Trial Balance total £752·00. (£729·90 excluding VAT)

7.1 Totals: Goods £1,179·40. VAT £117·94. Total £1,297·34.

7.2 P.D.B. Goods £416·00. VAT £41·60. Total £457·60.

7.3 (Simpkins) Balance £1,313·25 (cr): L. Simpkins owes T. Atkins £1,313·25 12th June—Returns outwards a/c and VAT Account: 29th June—Purchases a/c and VAT a/c.

7.4 (Johnson) Returns outwards Book. Goods £28·00. VAT £2·80. Total £30·80.

8.1 D.E. (R.V.) Totals of dr and cr sides £300·00.

8.2 See text.

8.3 (Kershaw) SDB totals £810·00, VAT £81·00, total £891. Trial Balance total £891.

8.4 (Wade) Sales a/c (cr) £2,147, £2,321, £2,629. Purchases a/c (dr) £1,324, £1,472, £1,584. Sales returns a/c (dr) £32, £41, £26.

8.5 (1) May 10th—Rose returned goods, May 23rd—Further goods supplied to Rose. May 23rd—Rose paid £95 on account.
(2) Credit limit £300. £95 paid so credit limit was not exceeded.
(3) Rose owes £300, the maximum credit allowed him.

9.1 Balances (dr) Cash a/c: Cash £27·96, Bank £145·75. Trial Balance total £292·25. (Excluding VAT)

9.2 Totals (dr & cr side) £300. (Excluding VAT)

9.3 (Turner) (Excluding VAT)
(1) Balance £587·75 (cr).
(2) (*a*) 10th Jan—Purchases Day Book.
(*b*) 15th Jan—Cash Book.
(*c*) 22nd Jan—Journal.
(3) (1) Crediting machinery a/c or crediting disposal of asset a/c.

9.4 Balances cash £31·70, bank £419·95. (Excluding VAT)

9.5 Balances cash £49·84, bank £748·91. (Excluding VAT)

9.6 See text.

9.7 Total £6·24 (Postage £3·31, Telegrams £0·89, Travelling £1·05, Stationery £0·79, Sundries £0·12, VAT £0·08).

9.8 Total £49·60.

9.9 Draft of Petty Cash Book.

9.10 Balances: Frobisher £228.80 (dr), T.X. Manufacturers £336.60 (cr).

10.1 Journal totals £5,625·63.

10.2 Totals: Journal £10,340·09, PDB £466·40, ROB £30·80, SDB £580·80, RIB £25·30, Trial Balance £11,465·61.

10.3 (*a*) (1) Cash Book (2) PDB (3) RIB (4) PCB (5) Cash Book (6) SDB.
(*b*) (1) Cheque book counterfoil (2) Supplier's invoice (3) own credit note (4) Petty cash voucher (invoice attached) (5) paying-in slip (6) firm's own invoice.

10.4 Plant & Machinery (dr), Scotswood (cr); B.D. a/c (dr), Burke (cr); Dep. a/c (dr), P. & Mchy (cr), Office furniture (cr); office furniture a/c (dr £120·31), Office Furniture a/c (cr £32·00), A. Bright (cr) £88·31; Interest a/c (dr), A. White (cr); Telephone a/c (dr), G.P.O. (cr); Office Stationery (dr), W. Simpson (cr); A. Cole (dr), Interest a/c (cr).

10.5 Journal total £2,597; P.D.B. total £402·60; S.D.B. £469·70; R.I.B. £33; Cash Book: Cash £5, Bank £484·75; Trial Balance £3,698·45.

10.6 (2) Personal a/cs: (*a*) Sales ledger (dr), (*b*) Bought ledger (cr), (*c*) Sales ledger (cr), (*d*) Sales ledger (cr)—Petty Cash Book credited.
(3) Debit sales a/c £10 and credit suspense a/c £10 (if one has been opened). Through journal debit Postage a/c and credit Sundry Expenses a/c with £1·50.

11.1 P.D.B. Total £193·82: VAT £17·62, Golf £61·20, Tennis £46·00, Winter Sports £69·00, Purchases a/c (debit) Total £176·20 (Golf £61·20, Tennis £46·00, Winter Sports £69·00).

11.2 Journal (opening entries) total £8,630, Trial Balance (17th January) £13,352·00.

11.3 Trial Balance (22nd January) £16,510·72.

11.4 Gross Profit Dept A £2,730 Dept B £260 (Dept C Gross loss £860). Net Profit Dept A £2,647·26 Dept B £164·92 (Dept C Net loss £909·96). Balance sheet total (conventional pattern) £12,072·22.

11.5 See text.

11.6 Gross Profit Dept A £4,500, Dept B £1,600.
Net Profit Dept A £2,622, Dept B £348.
Balance Sheet total (conventional) £15,570.

11.7 Ledger balances: Sales a/c (dr) £288; R.I. a/c (dr) £144; Purchases a/c (dr) £519; R.O. a/c (cr) £120; R.B. £158·40 (dr); E.M. & Co. Ltd £264·00 (cr); R.M. & Co. Ltd (cr) £174·90; VAT a/c £25·50 (dr).

11.8 See text.

11.9 Gross Profit Dept A £916, Dept B £4,328; Dept A 17·3%, Dept B 49·2%; Business as a whole 37·2%.

11.10 Purchase Book Totals: Goods for resale £1,240·60, Carriage £8·00, Heating & Lighting £69·60, Capital Expenditure £614·80 (advertising £5·25, Repairs £4·60, Stationery £12·30—total £22·15, under other revenue expenditure).

12.1 New Cash Book balance £612.
Reconcilation: Bank Statement balance £527+Warner £216 = £743 less Gas Board £22, Murray £109 = £612.

12.2 (1) See text; (2) Debit Bad Debts a/c, Credit J. Williams; Debit W. Fraser, Credit Bank Account; Debit Bank Interest a/c, Credit Bank Account; (3) see text.

12.3 New Cash Book Balance £394·30. Reconcilation: Bank St. Bal. £409·51, add £85·36, Deduct £16·39 and £84·18 = £394·30.

12.4 (Ball) Bank a/c balance £50·22.
Reconcilation: Bank St. Balance (debit) £22·27, add cheque £148·00 = £125·73, less £75·51 = £50·22.

12.5

Balance as for Bank St.	£230
Add premium (S.O.)	25
	255
Deduct div.	15
	240
Deduct:	211
	£29

N.B. (When entries in respect of premium and dividend have been entered in Cash Book the balance will be £19).

12.6

Balance per Bank a/c as amended	£5,550·00
Add cheques not debited	250·00
	5,800·00
Deduct remittances not credited	325·00
Balance as per bank statement	£5,475·00

13.1 Provision for D.D. balance (cr) £640; Prov. for Discounts on Debtors (cr) £304.

13.2

Debit P & L a/c credit Provision for D.D.		£742
In Balance Sheet—Sundry Debtors	£6,000	
less Provision for D. Debts	742 =	£5,258.

13.3 Debit Provision for D. Debts a/c and credit P & L a/c £200 on *credit* side of P & L a/c:

old Provision	£1,000	
less new Provision	800 =	£200.
Balance Sheet: Sundry Debtors	£12,780	
less Provision	800 =	£11,980.

13.4 Debit P & L a/c £149, credit Provision a/c £149.
Balance Sheet Sundry Debtors £16,380 *less* Provision £819 = £15,561.

13.5 Debit P & L a/c £800 credit (1) Provision for Bad Debts a/c £500, (2) Provision for Discounts Allowed £300.
Balance Sheet Sundry Debtors £12,500 *less* Provisions Bad Debts £500 and Discounts £300 = £11,700.

13.6 Debit Provisions for Discounts on Creditors £250 and credit P & L a/c £250. Balance Sheet Sundry Creditors £10,000 *less* Provision £250 = £9,750.

14.1 *Freehold Premises a/c* debit £100,000.
Leasehold Premises a/c debit balance £18,000, closed by transfer to Leasehold Realization a/c.
Leasehold Redemption Fund a/c credit balance £5,100, closed by transfer to Leasehold Realization a/c.
Leasehold Redemptions Fund Investment a/c—debit side: Balance £5,100 & Profit on sale of investments £1,400—credit side: Bank £6,500.
Leasehold Realization a/c debits: Leasehold Premises a/c £18,000, Bank £1,890 (costs).
Profit on sale of leasehold property £8,210. Credits: Bank £23,000, Leasehold Redemption Fund £5,100.
£1,400 profit on sale of investments, and £3,110 being excess of selling price of leasehold premises over cost less expenses (£23,000—£18,000—costs £1,890) should be placed to capital reserve.

14.2 Gross Profit £473, Net Profit £128.
Balance Sheet (vertical form) Net current assets £515, Totals £1,278.

14.3 Trial Balance total £11,716. Gross Profit £1,729, Net loss £78.
Balance Sheet (vertical form) net current assets £495. Totals £3,340.

15.1 Insurance a/c debit balance £25: Rent a/c credit balance £120.

15.2 Operating profit £3,750, Net profit £2,438.
Balance Sheet. Current liabilities exceed current assets by £542.
Totals of Balance sheet in conventional form £11,408.

15.3 Gross profit £4,111·00, Net loss £695·40.
Totals of Balance sheet in conventional form £25,683·60.
Totals in vertical form £17,178·60. Net current assets £11,008·00.

15.4 (*a*) Trial Balance totals £17,280·00.
(*b*) (i) Credit in excess of debit by £32·00.
(ii) Credit in excess of debit by £0·95.
(iii) No effect.
(iv) Debit in excess of credit by £90·00.

16.1 Appropriation a/c debit side: Int. on capital Fowler £600.
Fox £360; Bonus—Fox £941.
Profits £1,882 each: credit side £5,665.
Capital a/cs: Fowler £10,000, Fox £6,000.
Current a/cs: Fowler £170 (cr), Fox £107 (cr).

16.2 Net Trading profit £3,230; Exton £1,372; Wain £1,858.

16.3 Reader's current account balance £240 (cr), Storey's current account balance £40 (dr).

16.4 Balance sheet totals (conventional form) £23,360.
As no new agreement was made, profits and losses will be shared equally.

16.5 Journal (opening entries) £5,000.

16.6 Balance sheet in vertical form: net current assets £2,000, totals £9,000.
Profits and losses shared in ratio M 5/9, N 4/9.

16.7 (1) AB's current account £270 (cr), XY's current account £255 (cr).
AB's capital account £7,000, XY's capital account £5,500.
(2) Equally, in accordance with the Partnership Act, 1890.

16.8 Balance Sheet in vertical form: £16,167 (totals), net current assets £6,505. (Show A's current account as a deduction from B's current account.) Balance sheet totals in conventional form £19,162.

16.9 Groom's current account £1,240 (cr) Tarrant's current account £1,480 (cr).

16.10 (1) Balance Sheet vertical form totals £19,830 net current assets £7,830.
(2) 13·4%.
(3) 5·7%; Balance Sheet totals (conventional form) £30,390.

16.11 Debit Freehold Premises a/c £3,000, Credit Capital a/c (M) £3,000.
Debit Drawings a/c (N) £30, credit Purchases a/c £30.
Debit Current a/c (N) £50, credit current a/c (M) £50.

16.12 Hare's Current a/c £50 (cr); Hound's Current a/c £203 (cr).

16.13 Totals of Realization Account £14,865, Deficiency shared by X & Y in proportion to their capitals £270, £180 respectively, in accordance with the rule in Garner *v.* Murray.

16.14 A's contribution to C's deficiency £138·89, B's £111·11; A receives £5,611·11 and B £4,388·89 cash.

16.15 Net profit £1,639, Expenses for year £1,568.
Current account balances: X £230 (cr), Y £74 (cr).

16.16 Capital a/cs: James £13,240, John £8,160, Mark £4,000.
The proportion of profits to be received by James & John would be 9/20 and 6/20 respectively.

16.17 Gross profit £5,513, Net profit £1,697, Current a/c balances Knowles £2,098, Langley £1,549.
Totals Balance Sheet (conventional form) £14,777.
Totals Balance Sheet (vertical form) £12,647. Net Current assets £7,247.

17.1 Cr balance £7,430·05.

17.2 Dr balance £5,968.

17.3 Dr balance £10,500.

17.4 (1) Cr balance £4,689, (2) See text, (3) Balance on control a/c £4,689 should equal the total of the separate balances in the Purchases Ledger: this balance represents the total sum owing to suppliers.

17.5 See text.

17.6 Gross profit £26,000, Net profit £7,061.
Balance Sheet totals (1) conventional form £29,402 (2) vertical form £21,941, net current assets £20,483.

17.7 (1) Sales Ledger (A–D) control account debit balance £5,136. Purchases Ledger (M–Z) control account debit balance £29, credit balance £6,929.
(2) *Sales Ledger (I–L)*
(*a*) Debit Sales Ledger (I–L) Control account with £594—new balance £5,412 (credit Sales Account with £594).
(*c*) Control a/c unaffected.

Purchases Ledger (A–L)

(*b*) Purchase Ledger (A–L) control a/c must be credited with £10 (Returns outwards debited with £10)—
new control a/c balance will then be £6,308.

(*d*) & (*e*) Only creditors' balances are affected by these errors. £17 from £6,226 = £6,209. T. Little's a/c must be credited with £99 and a similar sum added to creditors' balances, making these agree with Control a/c balance of £6,308.

17.8 Sales Ledger Control a/c balances Dr £3,483, Cr £78.

17.9 Debtors' control a/c balances Dr £560, Credit sales £876, Gross profit £796, Net profit £526.

18.1 (1) (*a*) Debit side of Trial Balance would be £37·05 in excess of credit side.
(2) (*a*) Credit side would be £31·12 in excess of debit side.
(3) (*a*) Credit side would be £20·50 in excess of debit side.
(4) (*a*) Trial Balance would be unaffected.

18.2 Suspense a/c totals £1,088. Rent a/c itself is unaffected. The Trial Balance is unaffected by the errors in (3) and (6).

18.3 (*a*) Gross profit overstated by £80 plus £374·40, (*b*) net profit overstated by £86, (*c*) gross profit understated by £156, (*d*) gross profit understated by £84—net profit overstated by £16, (*e*) gross profit overstated by £191.
Corrected gross profit £8,555·60, net profit £3,054·60.

19.1 Cost of goods manufactured £20,010, Cost of goods sold £19,950.
Gross profit £9,830.

19.2 Total works cost £43,798, Gross profit £12,852.
Ratio of gross profit to turnover 22·5%

19.3 (1) Cost of goods sold £143,080, (2) Total general and administrative expenses £17,210, (3) Total selling charges £22,760, (4) Fixed assets £25,040, Current assets £39,943.
Gross profit £52,920, net profit £12,950.
Balance sheet (vertical form) totals £47,950, net current assets £22,910.

19.4 Total works cost £61,331, Gross profit £41,677.

19.5 Cost of materials used £130,000, prime costs £171,340, Factory cost of goods completed £199,055, Cost of goods sold £198,855, Gross Profit £48,145, Net profit £46,570.

19.6 Factory Cost 'Super' £25,718, 'Standard' £49,086. Gross profits 'Super' £7,500, 'Standard' £12,500, Net profit £11,694. Current a/cs: Wynne £3,327, Pickford £2,883.
Balance Sheet totals (vertical form) £38,210, net current assets £17,374.

19.7 Raw materials consumed £42,000, Factory cost £64,000, Cost of goods sold £65,500. Gross profit £18,770, Net profit £770.

20.1 Bank account overdrawn by the amount of £869.
Amount owing to travellers in respect of commission earned and not yet paid £86.
Rent paid in advance.
£35 collected on behalf of the Inland Revenue and not yet paid.

21.1 Profits: Stationery £60, School meals £35, Tuck Shop £76. Net profit £2,106.

21.2 Profit on bar £543. Balance to Accumulated Fund £34.
Balance sheet totals £1,064, Cash book balances (dr) cash £25, bank £218.

21.3 See text.

21.4 Profit on restaurant and bar £1,890. Excess of income to accumulated fund £460. Balance sheet totals £10,198 (conventional form).

21.5 (1) Estimated gross profit £1,787: sales at cost £10,213, closing stock £1,687, (2) £1,187.

21.6 Profit on refreshments £499. Excess of income over expenditure £19.

21.7 Balances at 1st Jan. 1962: Machinery a/c £4,514·80, Lease a/c £6,870·00.

21.8 Profit on Bar £200. Excess of income over expenditure to Accumulated Fund £24. Totals of Balance Sheet (conventional form) £909.

21.9 Trial Balance totals £2,754. General Fund a/c (credit balance) £352.

22.1 Balance Sheet totals 1st January, 1957 £2,000, 31st December, 1957 £2,770. Net profit for year £541.

22.2 Total statement of affairs £4,948, Profit £568.

22.3 Balance Sheet totals 1st April, 1958 £2,500, 31st March, 1959 £3,580. Net profit for year £1,315.

22.4 Credit Balances on all Capital accounts £8,000. Allen withdraws £500 cash and Newry introduces £1,500 cash.

22.5 Gross Profit £1,696, Net Profit £884.

22.6 Gross Profit £4,938, Net Profit £1,900.
Capital Account balance £12,160 (cr).

23.1 Cash remitted to B £2,851·15, Commission a/c balance £68·85 (cr).

23.2 To P & L a/c Commission £675, Profit £780 (total £1,455); (Norton's share of profit £390).

23.3 To P & L a/c 10% of net profit £100 plus share of profit £450 (Knight's share of profit £450).

23.4 Balance on Consignment to R.T. a/c April 1st, 1964 £684 (dr), Profit to P & L a/c £380, Balance on R.T.'s a/c £526 (dr).

23.5 Balance on Exporters Ltd a/c £1,176 (cr).
Balance on Bills payable a/c £2,500 (cr).

23.6 Profit: Short $\frac{1}{2}$ share £48; Tall $\frac{1}{2}$ share £48.

24.1 See text.

24.2 Fixed assets £69,750, Net current assets £55,250 = £125,000, Represented by: Issued and paid up capital £95,000, Revenue reserves £30,000.

25.1 Stock at 31st May, 1960 £5,200.

25.2 Gross profit as % of turnover Year 1 33%, Year 2 30%; Net profit as % of turnover Year 1 12%, Year 2 12·5%. Although the gross profit per £100 worth of sales was smaller in Year 2 than in Year 1, the net profit was nevertheless larger, £12·50 per £100 worth of sales as against £12 in Year 1.

It would seem that to obtain a larger turnover a smaller profit margin had to be accepted; considerable economies in administrative expenses etc., must have been made in Year 2.

25.3 (1) Turnover increased in Year 2, and out of every £100 worth of sales £35 was gross profit as compared with £34 the year before. Either the trader was able to raise prices during the year and thereby obtain a better margin of profit or suppliers reduced their prices.
As the net profit, as a percentage of turnover, has declined despite the increase in gross profit, there must have been rises in administrative and overhead expenses greater than could be explained by the rise in turnover.
(2) (*a*) Revenue expenditure: an expense in servicing the bank overdraft and chargeable against profits.
(*b*) Capital expenditure: the acquisition of an asset which will be retained in the business to assist in making profits.
(*c*) Revenue expenditure: expenditure incurred in the course of making profits.

25.4 Return on average capital employed 37·3%.

25.5 Returns on average capital employed:
Company A 9.1%, Company B 12·0%, Company C 33·0%.

25.6 Current ratios: Company X 116%, Company Y 229%.
Liquid ratios: Company X 89%, Company Y 145%.

25.7 Gross profit 27% of turnover but net profit on sales only 4%, which suggests that Gale's operating expenses are excessive.
Current liabilities = £970, Current assets = £730. A has withdrawn capital during the year and his liquid resources are insufficient to meet the demands of his creditors.

25.8

	Actual figures for 6 months ended 30th Sept, 1962	*Estimated figures for 6 months ended 31st Mar, 1963*	*Actual figures for 6 months ended 31st Mar, 1963*
Turnover	£540,000	£600,000	£620,000
Gross Profit	£135,000	£150,000	£161,200
Margin of Gross Profit	25%	25%	26%
Fixed Expenses	£24,000	£24,000	£24,000
Variable Expenses	£51,000	£54,000	£64,660
Percentage Increase in Variable Expenses	—	5·9%	27%
Net Profit	£60,000	£72,000	£72,540

Despite an increase of £20,000 in turnover above the estimate for the six months ended 31st March, 1963 and a 1% increase in the margin of gross profit, net profit was only £540 above the estimated net profit on the smaller expected turnover of £600,000. At some point beyond a turnover of £540,000 variable costs begin to rise steeply.

25.9 (i) Cost of goods sold £32,400.
(ii) Rate per cent of gross profit on turnover 20%.
(iii) Rate of turnover of stock 8 times.
(iv) Rate per cent of net profit on turnover 8%.